THE END of
IRISH
CATHOLICISM?

D1245952

D. VINCENT TWOMEY, SVD

VERITAS

Published 2003 by
Veritas Publications
7/8 Lower Abbey Street
Dublin 1
Email publications@veritas.ie
Website www.veritas.ie

ISBN 1 85390 683 2

A catalogue record for this book is available from the British Library.

Cover design by Pierce Design
Typesetting and layout by Veritas Publications
Printed in the Republic of Ireland by Betaprint Ltd, Dublin

Veritas books are printed on paper made from the wood pulp of managed forests.
For every tree felled, at least one tree is planted, thereby renewing natural resources.

In memory of my parents

Do not ask why earlier days were better than these,
for that is not a question prompted by wisdom.
ECCLES 7:10

Halt at the cross-roads, look well, and ask yourselves
which path it was that stood you in good stead long ago.
That path follow, and you shall find rest for your souls.
JER 6:16

Word without verve,
The imperiousness of years.
Their grey film
Fell on my thoughts...

Finbarr and the saints
Are years in the earth;
Enthusiasm's no more
Than frantic illusion.

I'm sick to heart
Of words gone vapid.
Illusion or demon –
Let them distract me.
SEÁN Ó RÍORDÁIN, *EIREABAILL SPIDEOIGE* (TRANS. ROBERT WELCH)

CONTENTS

INTRODUCTION

'...but it was Ireland he thought about, the husk of the old, the seed of the new. And often he wondered what that new would be.'
WILLIAM TREVOR[1]

This is a book I did not intentionally set out to write. An invitation to speak to a seminar in the US on the state of the contemporary Irish Church sparked off a train of reflections, which, almost with an inner logic of their own, organically grew into the six chapters of the present book. From the start, it must be admitted that the end product is somewhat dangerously wide-ranging, going at times from analyses of the past to strategies for the future, and at other times from the apparently trivial (altar linen) to the obviously heavy-duty items (Church-State relations). But then faith touches on all aspects of life. While preparing the manuscript for publication, it struck me, further, that the wide-ranging nature of the book could easily create the false impression that the author presumes to have a solution for all the problems facing the Church in Ireland. This would clearly be, well, a slight exaggeration. Quite obviously, no one – not even a theologian! – has all the answers. Moreover, it is perilously easy to misunderstand the questions raised by 'the Irish Catholic experience'.[2] In fact, the actual subject matter is limited to certain parameters. The following reflections

are mostly restricted to Catholic culture and customs rather than
Catholic doctrine and morals (though the latter are always in the
background – in the wings, as it were – and occasionally come on
stage). In addition, I have tried to highlight areas of practice and
structures that, it seems to me, urgently need to be debated as
widely as possible if the Catholic Church in Ireland is to face and
surmount the challenges presented by the new historical situation
of our country, as she did so impressively in the past. These
different subjects are all interrelated and so cannot be even vaguely
adequately treated in isolation.

I am convinced that the time has come to take a look at the life
of the Catholic Church in Ireland as a whole, not just aspects of it
taken piecemeal. This broad enquiry must be undertaken in such
a way that the major areas of concern can be examined in the light
of the immediate past and against that broader vision which
theology is meant to provide. It is time, in other words, to take a
long, hard, and above all, critical look at where we are, how we got
there, and how we might face the future. This justifies the wide
canvas of this book. I am also convinced that we must be as frank,
fair, and objective as possible about the ambiguities of that past,
the positive achievements of the present ('Modern Ireland'), as
well as the inadequacies of the contemporary Church's response
to more recent cultural developments. If at times I may sound a
bit too certain of my position, I beg the reader's indulgence. My
own excuse is that it is a by-product of my passionate love both for
that religious tradition which endowed me with the inestimable
gift of divine faith – the faith of our fathers – and for that Irish
cultural and political heritage of which I am fiercely proud,
whatever its weaknesses. If what I say, or how I say it, rouses the
reader's passion, then a constructive debate can begin. But such a
debate is not to be presumed.

Irrespective of our natural love of conversation and informal
discussion, the Irish Church has been singularly reticent about
entering into the only kind of public debate that matters, namely
one that leads to a resolution in terms of a change of heart and

mind, or a change of the status quo (structures), brought about by means of reasoned argument. My main concern throughout the book is to illustrate how this lack of intellectual ferment came about, how impoverishing such a lack can be, and hopefully thereby contribute a little to overcoming that deficiency. The book could perhaps best be described as an exercise in *pastoral theology*, namely that branch of theology whose object is to analyse the contemporary experience of a local Church in the light of a clear theological vision with a view to articulating strategies for pastoral practice.

As already indicated, the following essays are the result of reflections sparked off by an invitation to contribute a paper to a seminar organised by the Institute of Irish Studies in Fordham University, New York, on 13 March 2001. The topic of the seminar was 'The Irish Catholic Church Today'. These essays are the product of a lifetime's experience as an Irish Catholic, first as a layman, later as a priest and theologian. Writing this book gave me the opportunity to test my reflections on the 'traditional Irish Catholic heritage' that formed the basis of my faith against the findings of those historians and thinkers, ecclesiastical and secular, who have written extensively on the Church in Ireland. But above all, I am concerned with the state of the contemporary Church and her future mission in a greatly changed Ireland. On sabbatical in Boston, I had both the necessary leisure from my duties as a lecturer and the required distance from home to reflect on the rather dramatic situation of the contemporary Irish Church in a way that would not have been possible in Ireland itself.

Being in America, I became conscious again of the quasi-identity of Irish and Catholic that is still a feature of public discourse in the United States, and so I begin my reflections by looking again at the historical origins of this fusion, which seem to be at least as much theological as sociological (chapter 1). Given this quasi-identity of Irish and Catholic, one may well ask: how Catholic was 'traditional Irish Catholicism'? To reiterate what I said at the outset, the term 'Catholic' is used here to describe a *cultural* phenomenon rather than in its strictly doctrinal sense, though both are interrelated. Traditional Irish Catholic culture, I will argue, carried within it the seeds of its own decay despite its apparent power and splendour in days of yore. Those seeds were primarily of an intellectual, more specifically, of a theological nature, and their fruit is what amounts to a crisis of faith today (chapter 2).

The Church on earth is by its very nature a Church lurching from one crisis to another: it is after all, in more traditional parlance, the 'Church militant', the mystical Body at war with the evil within and without the Christian community. Christians are always a threatened species, and the Church is in every era confronted by what seem to be insurmountable difficulties. But it has always emerged renewed by the struggle. Today's crisis, I am convinced, will in time yield a new flowering of Church life in a new environment, that of modern Ireland, though not without considerable effort and, even more, help from above. That help is assured. Less assured is our indispensable contribution. The limited task of the second part of the book is to explore what human initiatives might be undertaken to enable the Church to respond appropriately to the modern world by – among other things – tapping into the more ancient traditions of the Catholic Church, both local and universal (chapter 3). This in turn demands that we examine in all frankness the viability of the present shape of the 'institutional Church' in Ireland and of any possible structural changes needed to release the real potential within the body of the Church. Humanly speaking, I shall argue that this potential, in the past as at present, has largely lain dormant and is still untapped (chapter 4).

In contemporary Ireland, within and outside the Church, many forces seek to separate what previous generations thought history had indissolubly united. These forces are not exclusive to Ireland and have their parallels in other countries undergoing similar radical cultural changes. They come from the same root: modernity. The (ambiguous) phenomenon of modernity, a theme that runs through all these reflections, has had an enormous impact on Irish society – and we are still far from that collective self-consciousness which is critical of modernity, otherwise described as post-modernity.[3] The question of Church-State relations, therefore, must be seen in this wider context. And so in the final essay, I take a brief look at the relationship between Church and State in Ireland, but doing so in such a way that we can learn some important lessons from the recent so-called Church-State controversies (on amendments to the Irish Constitution) in order to go beyond them and forge a new, constructive relationship between the two. An essential aspect of that relationship will be the development of a new pastoral strategy based on the *cities* rather than the countryside (chapter 5).

The effectiveness of any new pastoral strategy will depend, in the final analysis, on two interrelated factors. In the first place, there must be sufficient priests, religious, and committed laity whose vibrant faith and professional training will enable them to respond creatively to the spiritual and pastoral needs of modern Ireland. Numbers are a secondary consideration; quality alone is what counts. Secondly, there must be a shared theological vision that is at once local and universal. The so-called crisis of vocations is at root but another manifestation of the contemporary crisis of faith, this time primarily among clerics and religious, the recognition of which might be the first step towards overcoming it – and the first step towards the formation of a new kind of Catholicism suited to the twenty-first century. The second step, I argue, will involve a renewal of the theological roots of our tradition (chapter 6).

Professor Corish once warned that 'theologians even more than other academics must be conscious of the fact that it is not their vocation to save the world'.[4] Neither, of course, can they remain silent. One of their tasks is to ask how the Church as a human-divine community, at once local and universal, might fulfil her mission. That mission *is* intrinsically bound up with the salvation of the world. There is a spiritual richness within Irish society, a pearl of great price, today as yesterday, hidden in the lives of many Irish people in all walks of life. The task of the Catholic Church here as elsewhere, I shall argue throughout, is to enable that divine seed to flourish anew within the great Christian vision opened up by the Second Vatican Council. This book is offered, then, as yet another contribution to an on-going debate.[5]

Despite the footnotes – more precisely, endnotes – this is not an academic study. The endnotes indicate the sources for information I draw on to try to clarify my own life-long experience of, and reflections on, Irish Catholicism. Though by no means exhaustive, the endnotes also point to more scholarly studies, enabling the interested reader to pursue a particular topic at a deeper level than is possible in a book of this nature, a book intended for the general reader. More precisely, the following essays are intended to provoke public debate on fundamental questions affecting all our lives. Should they also provoke scholarly disputes – in particular with regard to the chapter on Church-State relations, which is also the most expressly theological – this would be considered a bonus. But in the first instance, it is aimed at those interested in thinking about the future of Irish society and the Church's role within it.

The following reflections are primarily (though not exclusively) concerned with the Catholic Church in the Republic of Ireland. This self-limitation simply acknowledges the fact that the cultural and social situation of the Church in the 'North' differs considerably from, and is in many ways even more complex than, the Church in the 'South', despite so much that we share in common. I should also point out that I am not immediately concerned with trying to assess the situation at 'the grass-roots' but rather with what might be called the public mood and, above all, the public voice of the Catholic Church in Ireland today. That public voice is somewhat muted, it seems to me, because the general framework of assumptions needed to speak and act decisively in the public forum has been weakened. That framework is itself an amalgam of historical, cultural, sociological, and economic elements. But, in the final analysis, it is theological in nature. That is my main thesis.

I wish to acknowledge my debt to Professor McCarthy, Fordham University, New York, whose initial invitation to contribute to the seminar mentioned above forced me to put on paper ideas I had been thinking about for years, and led eventually to the writing of this book. I also would like to thank the countless friends, colleagues, and library staffs who assisted me in various ways with this book in its gestation. My special thanks are due to the Divine Word Missionary Community, Beacon Street, Boston, for providing me with the perfect ambience for the study and reflection during my sabbatical, which issued in this book. Perhaps I may be pardoned in mentioning two people in particular, whose frank criticisms of the penultimate draft did much to improve the text, namely Br Paul Hurley, SVD, and Professor Emeritus Thomas Canon Finan who also suggested further literature, which I have tried to incorporate into the text. My thanks are also due to Br Paul and Lisa Tierney for their invaluable help at the proof-reading stage. All the imperfections in the text are, evidently, my own. And finally, a special word of thanks to Mr Toner Quinn, Editor of Veritas Publications, and his staff, for their patience and professionalism.

D. Vincent Twomey SVD
Royal Catholic College of Maynooth
Feast of St Brigid, 2003

I

THE IRISH CATHOLIC
IDENTITY

*'The Irish probably brought with them something of their own
conviction that Irish Catholicism was in some sense the archetype. The
great missionary Columban had said so long ago...'*
PATRICK J. CORISH[1]

It is a measure of the cultural sea change in Ireland that, whereas
half a century ago to call oneself an 'Irish Catholic' was a badge of
honour proudly worn for all the world to see and admire, today in
the upwardly mobile, modern Ireland south of the border, it is
more often than not an embarrassment to be reluctantly admitted.
It was not too long ago that a close relative, returning to Cork after
a visit to London, told me that someone had enquired of her if she
were a Roman Catholic. To which she had replied, quite
indignantly: 'Not at all. I'm an Irish Catholic.' Her reply was
revealing not only of her self-confidence as an Irish Catholic,
which was shared by most, at least up to the early 1960s, but in the
identification of Catholic with Irish, despite the apparent rejection
of what is specifically Catholic – the Roman connection, as it
were.

But even when she made her boast, in the early seventies, both
terms, 'Irish' and 'Catholic', were in trouble. Considerable public
discussion at the time focused on our 'identity' as Irish, and this in

turn both reflected and helped provoke the incipient crisis in the Church. The questioning of our Irish identity and the slow-motion implosion of the public face of the Church developed in tandem with the increasing prosperity of the South and with the growing intensity of the so-called 'Troubles' in the North. The latter gave rise to an increasing public unease about what was seen as the equivalent of a confessional State in the South.[2] This unease was used to their advantage by various lobby groups who wished the State to ratify practices that were contrary to Catholic moral teaching. Historians began to question the mega-narrative that up to then had justified our collective Irish, nationalist, Catholic identity, while the media began its enlightenment project of bringing Ireland into a modern, 'pluralist' democracy based on secular values. Catholic morality now became identified with an earlier repressive era symbolised by Eamon de Valera and, above all, Archbishop John Charles McQuaid. The new 'values' were presented – and eventually accepted by the public at large – as indispensable, modern, and progressive alternatives.

Few adverted to the fact that more radical but basically similar 'values' were being introduced (again in the teeth of various forms of opposition) in most European and North American countries, each nation playing different variations on the same theme. Chief Rabbi Jonathan Sacks describes these themes as basically 'libertarian', not simply 'liberal', in nature.[3] By libertarianism he means radical individualism rooted in almost unlimited freedom of choice, as distinct from the broader, political liberalism of former generations that, based on a common moral consensus helped mould modern pluralist democracy. That moral consensus no longer exists either in Ireland or indeed elsewhere in the Western world.

The past two decades have witnessed several major controversies usually described in terms of 'Church-State' confrontations (over contraception, divorce, and abortion), with the Church apparently the loser. In many ways, those losses are seen by some commentators as the price paid for what proved to be the pyrrhic victory of the Mother and Child controversy (1951),[4] an incident often cited as the beginning of the end of the Church's prominence in Irish life. But that prominence was itself based on rather shaky foundations, namely the identity of Irish with Catholic.

Here I am not interested in the question of Irish identity as such, except to say that, all appearances to the contrary, the factual identification of Irish and Catholic still lurks at the back of our collective consciousness, even in modern, self-consciously secular Ireland. This identification, which has deep historical roots,[5] is admittedly fading. It should become even more problematical with the changing demographic face of Ireland caused by the new phenomenon of immigration, as well as the more active role of the various Protestant Churches in public life, not to mention the growing number of self-confessed atheists and adherents of non-Christian religions. (Particularly striking in recent years is the disproportionate influence of the vocal few who, born Catholic, are now of no religious persuasion and tend often to be virulently anti-Catholic.) Finally, and most significantly, the long-term implications of the new political situation produced by the Good Friday Agreement cannot be foreseen at the present.

In the meantime, not least due to the stunning success of the Irish economy, the triumph of the so-called liberal agenda, and the presidency of Mrs Mary Robinson, a new Irish identity of sorts has emerged. It is that of 'modern secular Ireland', superficially perhaps the most secular society in Europe, along with the Czech Republic, and almost indistinguishable from either the British or American way of life, apart from Irish traditional music, pubs and 'craic', all eminently exportable commodities, including much of what passes for 'Celtic spirituality'.[6] There is, of course, much to be proud of in the achievements that are summed up in the term 'Celtic tiger'. The recent spectacular performance of our artists, writers, business people, and sportspeople on the international field has contributed to the emergence of a more self-confident, modern Ireland. But there is still considerable truth in the

observation of such critical commentators as Seán de Fréine and
Desmond Fennell that underlying it all is a basic provincialism that
tends to take its lead in the areas of politics, economics, and social
policy, from the former capital, London, and more recently, New
York, though London is closer to hand and so exercises more
immediate cultural influence.[7] The influence of Brussels is more
of an economic nature and, like 'Europe' in general, is culturally
distant and linguistically alien, despite the many who have
emigrated there in recent decades. It is interesting that, in the
debates surrounding the various referenda to ratify EU treaties,
the debates tended to focus on the economic arguments in favour
of the proposed changes, while notional assent is given to such
sacred cows as neutrality and, playing on a residual inferiority
complex that characterises provincialism, threats are made of
being 'out of step' with the rest of Europe, if we do not conform.
Cultural questions rarely surface, for example, with regard to the
need to foster the common Christian heritage that is at the root of
what we call 'Europe'. Our own most important contribution to
European culture – that of the early Irish monks – is rarely
mentioned today. Modern Ireland with its Celtic-tiger economy
would seem to have little in common with the earlier Catholic
Ireland. Ironically, the country's phenomenal economic success
story, it could be argued, was in large part made possible by both
the values and the education system originally created by the
Catholic Church. However that may be, at present to be Irish is no
longer identified with being Catholic as well. And that is not
necessarily a source of regret.

'One of the greatest imperialistic coups of the nineteenth
century was affected not by the British navy but by Ireland's
Catholic politicians: they captured the term "Irish" for themselves
and their co-religionists.'[8] Whatever one may say of this
assessment, the identification of Irish and Catholic is also
theologically questionable. The recent, apparent collapse of the
once all-powerful and omnipresent Catholic Church in Ireland, it
seems to me, owes much to this false identification. The future of

the Church in Ireland, on the other hand, will to a great extent be determined by the Church's ability to recover her true Catholicity, as once expressed in the literature and practices of the ancient and mediaeval Irish Church (Gaelic *and* Norman), and to find new forms of life and language appropriate to a changed, modern Ireland. To the extent that she succeeds, modern Ireland itself will no longer be seen as an obstacle to the Church but as an opportunity for a new and vibrant Catholic Christianity that is life affirming and inspirational. And modern Ireland will find deeper roots for its self-confidence as a nation than the economic boom that of necessity is fragile and ever threatened by external forces and the world markets. But first, we must look more closely at the nature of the identity of Irish and Catholic.

Historical roots
Is there more to the traditional Irish and Catholic identity than the political developments that marked the rise of modern nationalism, in particular the historical conditions of nineteenth-century Ireland? In fact, there seem to be compelling reasons for seeking the origins of this identity possibly in the immediate post-Reformation era, when the modern concept of the nation emerged from the debris of a united 'Christendom'.[9] The Tudors and the Stuarts united Ireland for the first time into a more or less effective administrative unit. But, with the monarch an Anglican and the great majority of subjects made up of different ethnic groups (Old Irish, Normans and Old English) united only by their common Catholic faith, the situation was anomalous for an era which witnessed the emergence of the confessional Nation-State in Europe.[10] If Ireland were to be seen as a Catholic nation, some other criteria would have to be found, other than the religion adopted by the monarch. To have found such was probably in large part the achievement of Irish priests exiled on the Continent at the dawn of the seventeenth century, a century 'so disastrous physically, materially and politically' that it has been described as 'the most important in the whole literary history of Ireland'.[11]

Like much of what formed our present collective consciousness, the identity of Irish and Catholic was the product of exiles far from their native shores. Thomas O'Connor recently published some findings from his research into the writings of Irish émigré priests living in Paris at the beginning of the seventeenth century. These he credits with 'the invention of the Irish *Natio* according to the criteria of seventeenth-century Catholic *ancien régimes*'.[12] One of them, Fr Thomas Messingham, composed a *Florilegium* (1624) of the lives of Irish saints, which apart from being a work of edification and apologetics, also 'entailed the presentation of Ireland to a European audience as a distinct historical and political entity whose Christian identity could be traced back to apostolic times'. And he adds, 'The central defining characteristic of the Irish *Natio*, as Messingham conceives it, is Catholicism.'[13] Catholicism here is understood *not as a body of doctrines* but as the faith exhibited by the heroic, miracle-working saints of old. These saints, it is claimed, 'display the natural aptness of Catholicism for the Irish'. Indeed, Messingham seems to have defined Irish rather narrowly in terms of 'solicitude for the faith', which cancelled out 'differences of geographical and racial origin', while, conversely, 'solicitude for the *Natio*' was seen as more important than personal conviction.[14] Indeed, in his scheme of things, the Irish *Natio* was even assured of its own place in the heavenly hierarchy.[15] These are all rather disturbing traits, since they define Catholic not in terms of belief but of race, and they give primacy not to personal conviction but collective or national identity. These traits, it could be argued, have marked, and marred, more recent Irish Catholicism.

A more sophisticated, indeed more acceptable, version of this theory is to be found in David Rothe's *Analectio sacra et mira* (1616). Rothe 'developed the conviction that Ireland was not only a *natio* but a very particular type of *natio*, a model for its European neighbours of how Catholicism is creative of civility even in confessionally divided jurisdictions'.[16] His work was, among other things, a plea for tolerance. But that is not the issue here. What is of note is his understanding of the Irish *Natio*, which is described by O'Connor as 'the community of individuals who have been specially elected by God to remain faithful to Rome and thereby demonstrate that, in the modern world, loyalty to King is compatible with loyalty to the Pope'.[17] Though couched in other terms, this protest of loyalty would later become the sometimes desperate plea of Catholic leaders, lay and clerical, in Ireland from the middle of the eighteenth to the end of the nineteenth century. Again, that is not the main point.

The most significant aspect here is the notion of election, not simply the election or predestination of individuals to grace, but the collective election of the Irish nation to be the special instrument of God on earth. This is a sentiment that might well have roots in a more primordial native experience. As one writer put it, 'To the poetic Celt the love of country tends to become almost a religion.'[18] This seems to have left its mark on the early Irish Church, as the scholar-monks re-created the prehistory of their country in the light of salvation history. It seems that Patrick's late seventh-century biographer, Muirchú, was the first Irish writer to think about Ireland and its inhabitants as a nation,[19] and who portrayed the Irish not only as a *gens* (a nation in the sense of Mt 28:19) but even as 'a chosen race' (using the Old Testament text referring to Israel that 1 Pet 2:9 applies to the Christian community, the Church).[20] Kim McCone comments: 'Early medieval Ireland's monastic men of learning could hardly make the unbiblical claim that their gentile race had enjoyed a covenant with God before the coming of Christianity, although ... they eventually developed ambitious doctrines that came perilously close to this position.'[21] So the émigré clerics were but expressing and further developing an ancient and deep-seated self-consciousness of being an elect race.

Moreover, in the seventeenth century, it was not the only nation making such a claim, though the way it couched its claims was unique. A similar claim is made for the English nation in Foxe's *Book of Martyrs*, 'which vigorously expressed the dynamic myth

that the English were the Elect Nation, a notion that informed the
early Puritans and has left its mark on much of American history
since then.'[22] And the English and Scottish settlers in the north of
Ireland, as is well known, shared (and share) a similar self-
consciousness, which is of Calvinist origin. That is another topic.
(However, it confirms, yet again, Akenson's thesis that Irish
Catholics and Irish Protestants are more similar to each other than
they wish to admit, though at times the similarities are more like
mirror images.) What is also common to both is a common
Gnostic (or Puritanical) tendency that, among other things, tends
to collapse religion into politics or, visa versa, transforms politics
into a religion, 'the cause' on whose altar men sacrifice both
themselves and the innocent. This inevitably leads to a black and
white approach to political questions, absolutist positions ('No
surrender') that exclude compromise, the life-blood of genuine
politics. But, as I said, that is another topic, one albeit with
enormous implications, which I will touch on in the final chapter.

If, when, and how this notion of being the chosen people was
transmitted down through the following three centuries is
something for historians to examine. But it seems that some vestiges
of it must have been handed on with the faith. It is difficult to
explain how the notion of the election of the Irish Catholic
race/nation could be maintained in the face of its many defeats in
battle, not to mention the Penal Laws and the Great Famine, unless,
that is, such calamities were understood in a somewhat dubious
theological sense as God's punishment for the sins of his chosen
people.[23] The sufferings of Irish Catholics could also be interpreted
in a more profoundly theological sense, namely as putting his
chosen ones to the test, as he had with Abraham, with a view to
their future mission.[24] The long-lasting impact on early mediaeval
Europe by Irish monks, and the remarkable spread of the Irish
Catholics in the nineteenth century to Britain, North America,
Australia, and New Zealand, where they formed the basis of the
local Churches in those lands, could indeed be interpreted as
confirming such an election. As St Paul proclaimed: 'it was to

shame... the strong that God chose the weak of this world; those the world considers common and contemptible God chose, those who are nothing to show up those who are everything' (1 Cor 1:27-8). Compared with other European nations in all their power and glory, the Irish nation was indeed nothing, and yet it had enormous spiritual potential that was channelled into what became known in our day as 'traditional Irish Catholicism'.

Commenting on the remarkable resurgence of the Catholic Church in Ireland in the 1850s and 1860s, the new self-confidence which caught the attention of external observers, Patrick J. Corish notes: 'The fact was that as the Irish lost one identity they found another, and the new identity was Catholicism.'[25] The giant whose shadow falls on the latter half of nineteenth-century Catholic Ireland, Cardinal Cullen, was acutely aware of this identity, though it 'was not just Paul Cullen who felt that the Irish race could be equated with the Catholic Faith, in Ireland and far beyond it'.[26] Commenting on the identification of 'Irish' and 'Catholic' that was axiomatic for Cullen, Corish outlined the archbishop's political vision as follows: 'Catholics would convert the world-empire of Protestant England to the true Catholic faith. It did not seem altogether impossible, given the new mood of confidence he had done so much to develop in Catholic Ireland.'[27] The Maynooth Mission to India c. 1840 and the foundation of All Hallows College in 1842 to provide Irish priests for the English-speaking world marked the beginning of the renewed missionary dimension of the Irish Church.[28] At the turn of the century, Cullen's vision was being realised, not only through the millions of Irish Catholic emigrants gathered in communities throughout the empire on which the sun never set, but also through the new missionary expansion into the new British colonies in Asia and Africa. This missionary phenomenon also enabled the Church at home to overcome in part her growing insularity and provincialism – and so helped preserve one dimension of the Church's catholicity among the faithful at large, despite a growing alienation between the missionary and the diocesan clergy.

All this reached a climax with the notion, popular up to fifty years ago, of Ireland being the centre not of a worldly empire, as in the case of Britain, but of a spiritual empire spread throughout the world.[29] Ireland was, and is still, the only predominantly Catholic nation in the English-speaking world. Irish people could not help either conceiving their own collective identity in terms of their imperial neighbour or seeing their unique position as in some sense providential (which, it could indeed be argued, was in fact the case). After the civil war ended in April 1923, 'Nationalist Ireland was never in greater need of an identity; it had to be either the Irish language or the Catholic Church, and for most people it was in fact the Church.'[30] In 1945, one Monsignor James H. Cotter could boast: 'Ireland, standing majestically among the wrecks of earth ... is still a brilliant apostle among the nations.'[31] An apostle is one who is specially chosen and sent. A decade later, Alexis Fitzgerald, distinguished adviser to two Taoisigh and brilliant lecturer in political philosophy at University College Dublin, could affirm, as though it were self-evident, that: 'If the historical operation of emigration has been providential, Providence may in the future have a similar vocation for the nation.'[32]

However that may be, growing up in the Ireland of the 1940s and 1950s, I was certainly aware that part of our self-identity as Irish Catholics was to see ourselves as 'Christian Jews', God's chosen people, materially weak but spiritually strong, spread diaspora-like throughout the world,[33] ever loyal to the faith of our fathers.[34] And indeed, as some authors have pointed out,[35] there was a remarkable resemblance between the Jews and Irish Catholics, especially in their approach to dietary and similar laws. Also common to both was the identification of race and faith. You were born a Catholic as you were born a Jew. According to Seán de Fréine, one of the secondary consequences of the loss of the Irish language was a distortion of history, resulting among other things in the paradoxical need for 'the Irish' to be seen as 'a race apart'.[36] As was the case with the Jews, the common daily and family-based rituals together with the detailed laws on fasting and abstinence, for example, which were minutely observed and hotly debated, assured Irish Catholics of their identity no matter where they were. This, of course, is not something negative per se. Such practices accounted in no small measure for the preservation of the Irish Catholic identity from Boston to Brisbane,[37] at least up to the Second Vatican Council. In addition, as Catholics, there was the not always humble consciousness of belonging to the one, true Church, which set us apart from the majority population in the Anglo-Saxon world, who often responded with anti-Catholic bigotry, especially in Britain and America.

Theological critique

The notion of being the chosen people is not particularly unique to Ireland as we saw. But wherever it is found, it is of dubious theological value. It is a highly charged notion of even more dangerous political value, as the Boers or Afrikaners in South Africa have demonstrated in recent times, not to mention our own Unionists in the North. There is, of course, but one Chosen People, the Hebrew people. The New Israel is not any particular race but is made up of both Jews and Gentiles, that is, people from all races and nations now united in one faith, one baptism, and one Church. There is probably some justification in Scripture for attributing some kind of significance, though not without reservation, to each nation as defined by their linguistic and cultural differences. In fact, the consciousness of being the Chosen People posed problems for both Israel and the early Church. According to the story of Babel, the multiplicity of nations defined by their own language is the effect of the Fall, which, according to the later prophetic promises, would be reversed by the nations streaming to worship on Mount Sion. These promises were fulfilled at Pentecost. What marked the early Christian experience was the trans-national character of the Church, its catholicity. One early text (written in the second or third century) well illustrates this: '[Christians] dwell in their own countries, but only as sojourners; they bear their share in all things as citizens, and they endure all hardships as strangers. Every foreign country is a fatherland to them, and every fatherland is foreign.'[38] That changed in the fourth century with Constantine and the effective adoption of Christianity as the State religion.

The ambiguity in assessing the theological status of the nations is highlighted by the development, first in the later Jewish tradition and then in the early Church, of the teaching regarding the guardian angels of the nations.[39] According to one Patristic scholar, these were the personification of that which binds a people together, what today we would call nationalism. Nationalism was seen as something negative and was characterised in the Jewish and early Christian tradition as, among other things, a tendency to draw people away from God by making the nation an end in itself, or the tendency of empires to claim divine status for one's own nation.[40] They were, in other words, fallen spirits sometimes identified with the gods worshipped by the nations. However with the so-called conversion of Constantine a new attitude emerged reflecting the new positive relationship between Church and State. The fourth-century court-theologian, Eusebius of Caesarea, the Father of Church History, saw the Roman Empire as part of God's providential plan for the redemption of humanity,[41] a notion that left its mark on eastern Christianity.[42] The development in Western Europe was more complex. Under the influence of St Augustine's theology, which separated the transcendent City of God from the terrestrial city of man, and with the growth of the papacy as a representative symbol for the unity of the Church that transcended boundaries of race and language,[43] nationalism was kept in check by the consciousness among the various peoples or nations of belonging to Christendom. With the Reformation, the fragile unity of 'Christendom' collapsed. As the Western European nations grew ever more 'sovereign' (absolute), mutually exclusive, and antagonistic, they too became ends in themselves and developed into empires spanning the world. It took two World Wars and the horrors of Stalin's ethnic cleansing in the name of ideology to produce a more sombre assessment of the significance of nations (itself now threatened by the phenomenon of globalisation).

That new evaluation is summed up by Solzhenitsyn, speaking out of the darkness of the Soviet Union that tried to wipe out all differences between peoples: 'Nations are [part of] the wealth of mankind, its collective personalities; the very least of them wears its own special colours and bears within itself a special aspect of divine intention.'[44] This seems to fit with the more positive thrust of Christian tradition. Each culture, each people has its own contribution to make to the history of salvation and human flourishing in general.[45] The diversity of cultures is mutually enriching and is part of the common good of humanity. Christianity enriches – and is enriched by – the various cultures, but it ultimately transcends culture. And so, the Church, though it only exists as local communities, is not a national entity but Catholic or universal.[46] 'All the nations are as nothing in his presence' (Is 40:17; cf. Job 12:23). In sum, no one 'Christian' nation has been signalled out. Alas, not even the Irish!

A corollary to the above is the fact that nations belong to this world that passes away. The growth and decay of nations is part of the dynamic of history. The Lord 'makes nations great, then destroys them, he enlarges nations, then leads them away' (Job 12:23). At this juncture in our history as an independent State, we are witnessing quite a different and disquieting development. The very concept of nation, not to mention nationality, seems to have vanished from public discourse, not least due to the 'Troubles' in the North – we now refer rather disparagingly to 'this island'. In addition, national identity is difficult to reconcile with the vague cosmopolitanism of our new mid-Atlantic identity. Perhaps the imperative of our time might well be to recover the importance of a shared national identity as the basic communal condition for human flourishing. It should be added that the nation, which is a cultural phenomenon (incorporating both Catholic and Protestant traditions), is an entity distinct from the State, which is a political structure to represent and administer the nation. It is, unfortunately, a tendency of governments to want to control all aspects of our lives and thus collapse the nation into the State. This, basically totalitarian, tendency of any bureaucratically dominated democracy could be exacerbated in our own country by unrealistic expectations of an essentially passive public that spontaneously turns to the Government to solve all its problems. But that is another subject.

To return to our analysis of the notion of being a chosen people, what, then, are the dangers inherent in the self-understanding of any one race or nation appropriating to itself a claim that is exclusive to the Jewish race? The most obvious one is the danger of presumption, as the Prophets warned the real Chosen People of old, who so often took God's choice of them for granted and did not do what they should but what they wanted to do, provided they kept up the empty rituals. The gap between religious practice and upright moral living, between being a regular Mass-goer in the morning and a thorough scoundrel for the rest of the day, is not simply the product of some novelist's imagination. To say that someone was a 'good Catholic' often meant little more than saying that, despite whatever people may say about the person's behaviour, he or she never missed Mass and fulfilled his or her other 'duties' as a Catholic. By way of contrast, Irish Protestants, apart from being more prosperous and less ritualised, were generally respected as being more honest and decent.

The consciousness of belonging to the Chosen People inevitably fosters collective pride and arrogance, of feeling oneself superior to all other races. Many an English Catholic in the not-too-distant past patiently endured the unflattering comparison made from the pulpit by their Irish parish priest between 'pagan England', as it was often described, and holy (mostly rural) Ireland. Further, Irish Catholics, especially their pastors, were not likely to entertain the notion that other Catholic Churches in, say Germany or France, could have anything to teach the Irish Church. (In the nineteenth century, Canon Sheehan of Doneraile seems to have been the exception that proves the rule.) In the 1950s, those poor benighted Catholics on the Continent seemed to be in dire straits, mired in all kinds of theological disputes (unknown to ever-loyal Ireland), struggling with falling numbers, alienated from the working classes, and so on. This was the time when the Irish Church basked in the self-satisfied glow of almost total attendance at Sunday Mass, sufficient vocations to supply most of the English-speaking world – and no theological doubts. Someone once described the theologians of the time as swaggering about with the ludicrous pomposity of self-appointed kings in a doll's house!

Implications for Irish theology

A less obvious, but more far-reaching, danger of being God's chosen people, is the way it undermines the need for personal conviction, as noted above. It fosters instead a collectivist consciousness, 'what everyone thinks' or, to put it more simply, unthinking conformity to accepted mores and opinions.[47] As the chosen people, the Irish might suffer physically and economically, but they would always hold fast to the faith, unthinkingly more often than not. This is not necessarily something negative, as illustrated in the following story I once heard.

A woman, living in a thatched cottage under the shadow of the high wall protecting the local estate of the 'Ascendancy', once extended simple hospitality to an English tourist seeking shelter from the inevitable Irish rain. Over a cup of tea by the open fire, the English visitor, charmed by her warm and witty personality, mentioned the owner of the Big House up the road, presumably occupying the land of the woman's ancestors. Was she not hurt, he asked, by the evident injustice of it all? 'Ah, sure no,' she replied with a smile, wiping her hands on the apron ingeniously made from a flour-bag, 'sure who would envy him that bit of comfort and consolation, and him not of the faith.'

The Irish Catholic tradition did nourish a profound faith, a joy that overcame great adversity, and a genuine spirituality forged in the crucible of life. Faith was an anchor in the rough seas of life, and simple devotions, such as the Rosary, the Stations of the Cross, and visits to ancient holy sites (mostly ruins), nurtured a deep spirituality that enabled ordinary people heroically triumph over the vicissitudes of daily life, poverty, and oppression – and retain their cheerfulness and humour.[48] The centrality of the Cross in this spirituality enabled them to preserve an inner detachment from worldly success and personal tragedy. At the root of that spirituality was the cultivation of an attitude of mind that 'offered up' whatever misfortune should befall one, and by so doing excising the roots of bitterness and resentment to achieve that 'perfect acceptance in grief', which is the pinnacle of wisdom and serenity sought by all the great religions of the world.[49] The depth of this authentic spirituality is best illustrated by a story told by one of a number of distinguished French scholars who visited Ireland in the nineteenth century.

> A man of eighty and his wife of seventy-four had been evicted in Partry [Co. Mayo]. As they were being turned out she said to her husband: 'Here I am, at seventy-four, without a shelter in the world; I who never wronged anybody, and often opened my door to the poor and the unfortunate; what have I done to deserve this?' He replied: 'Peace, my dear, peace; the passion and death of Christ were more than this.'[50]

Leaving aside for the moment the notion of the chosen people, let us take a brief look at the distinct but related notion of the identification of Irish and Catholic. It could be argued that the gradual identification of Irish and Catholic in the course of the nineteenth century and the effective (though not formal) recognition of the Catholic Church as a quasi-established Church[51] of the newly independent Irish Free State, could in the long run only undermine such a faith-inspired tradition and spirituality. By becoming, not in law but in effect, the established religion, the

Catholic faith was thereby effectively transformed into a civil
theology and made subservient to the political entity. As a civil
religion, transcendent faith tends to become immanent, the bond
that binds the nation together (as implied by one etymology of the
term 'religion' itself), and so the Church serves the nation rather
than transcending it. Nationalism, even with a 'Catholic' face, runs
the risk of become the 'angel of the nation' ('the cause') who sets
himself up against God. More seriously, faith loses its essential
'other-worldly' edge, its transcendental or prophetic dimension.
The emotional bonding of Church and Nation/State breeds
conformism and fear, not only of 'unhealthy outside or foreign
influences', but also of the challenge of any independent thinker
in its midst. It resulted in the suffocating censorship of 1940s and
1950s, that 'muting of the critical intellectual voice', which the
writers of the day argued, was 'shortsighted, unhealthy, and
damaging'.[52] It also called for the exercise of the virtue of fortitude
(moral courage) to an heroic degree, which seems not to have
been fostered[53] and few seemed to have achieved. There is a lot of
soul-searching going on at present about the revelations of serious
misdeeds, possibly even criminal behaviour, in the State's
industrial schools run by some religious congregations up to the
sixties, another manifestation of the symbiosis of Church and
State. One of the questions raised is: why did no one do anything
about these horror stories? Why did everyone keep silent? Why
did so many conform? Why was there such a singular lack of
moral courage? Perhaps it was the heavy price paid for becoming
in effect the established Church of a fledgling and impoverished
State.

What was the ultimate cause of the implosion of the public
face of the Church over the past thirty years? Could it be that
unquestioning faith which marked Irish Catholicism? The figure
cut by the contemporary Catholic Church in the public forum – a
pale shadow of its former self, insecurely facing a predominantly
hostile domain – and her apparent inability to respond
convincingly to the challenges of today might well be part of the

price she is paying for that unquestioning faith. A young and gifted theologian said to me some twenty years ago in a city parish, where he was a curate, that talking theology there was like bringing coals to Newcastle. How wrong he was. His people, the faithful, were indeed asking questions, radical questions, but did not address them to him or to his fellow-clergy. People were hungry to hear reasons for the faith they held. They still are. More often than not, their questions were, and are still, not even being heard. But his answer also reveals a rather impoverished understanding of faith, since, as St Anselm at the dawn of the High Middle Ages recognised: faith seeks understanding. A living faith is a questioning faith, searching to comprehend the incomprehensible, God, our goal in life, and His love towards the world revealed in Jesus Christ.

Brian Fallon's aptly titled book *An Age of Innocence* attempts, among other things, to arrive at a balanced judgement on the state of the Catholic Church between 1930 and 1960. Contrary to the prevailing opinion today, the Church at the time was not anti-intellectual, as Fallon perceptively points out. After all, it established and serviced a greater part of the entire school system. Neither were the priests, nuns, and brothers entirely devoid of artistic or other cultural appreciation; they generally tended to respect scholarship and were often patrons of the arts. All this notwithstanding, Fallon's overall judgment on the clergy is quite devastating. 'Intellectually they were often naïve – an admiration for G.K. Chesterton, for instance, was equated with mental sophistication, and the bulk of them regarded modern thought, literature and art as predominantly "pagan" (a favourite word of the period), dangerous, and subversive, part of the corrosive modernism which was eating away at the foundation of the whole Christian world.'[54] This rather sweeping judgement can be debated. But what seems to be beyond doubt is that the self-sufficiency of the Irish Catholic tradition, which had survived dungeon, fire, and sword, was such that its clerics had no questions themselves, at least questions they could voice, and so were unable to listen to the questions raised by these thinkers or indeed make any attempt to address them.

Consequences for the Church today

The Swiss theologian, Hans Urs von Balthasar, once warned the Church of his day with its appearance of an impregnable fortress, that unless it faced up to the demands unleashed by the modern world and reformed itself from within, God himself would raze the bastions of the earthly city of God, and tear down what had become nothing but an empty edifice.[55] Whatever about the Church in other countries, the Second Vatican Council had that effect on the Irish Church, though it took several decades for the impact to become evident to all.

An American sociologist, commenting on the situation of the Church in the US, itself heavily influenced by Irish Catholicism, once wrote that the day the Friday fast and abstinence was abolished, it was only a matter of time before a priest and nun would walk down the aisle as man and wife. In other words, when one thread in the tightly woven fabric was pulled, the whole thing unravelled. However that might be, the fact is that the changes introduced by the Second Vatican Council radically upset the security and the sense of superiority of what was known as traditional Irish Catholicism. Before the Council, there was little public discussion about reform of the liturgy, little exposure to new ideas about the nature of the Church or ecumenism, not to mention the challenge posed by atheism or the question of the relationship of the non-Christian religions to Christianity.

Unthinking to the end, a provincial and submissive Church simply and obediently carried out the instructions coming from Rome that unintentionally but effectively dismantled their own, deeply cherished version of Catholicism. There were no public controversies of note in Ireland after the Council, such as those which raged elsewhere about the abolition of Latin in the Mass, communion in the hand, turning the altar around to face the people, etc. There was simple, uncomprehending obedience to the letter of the law. Later, there were some unseemly public disputes about alterations to church buildings, in particular the removal of the altar rails or the destruction of many an original, highly decorated altar. Very often, altar rails, indeed the altar itself, had been paid for by benefactors whose descendents still lived in the parish. They were understandably upset by this desecration of their family's pride and piety. The zealous reforming clerics resorted to a rather traditional form of clericalism: they called on the authority of the Council (the liturgical reform ordered by Vatican II) to justify what often amounted to vandalism.

Generally speaking, a somewhat traumatised Church loyally and obediently implemented the letter of the new laws mostly without demur. The main exceptions were to be found among women religious, members of missionary orders, young seminarians, and a handful of educated laity (many of them ex-seminarians), who generally welcomed the changes enthusiastically. But for most priests and people, their heart did not seem to be in it, as the various attempts at ecumenical dialogue would seem to indicate, though here the fault might not all be on the side of the Catholics. (Indeed, the theological situation in the various Protestant Churches may not have been much better.) Short and popular courses in theology to update clergy and interested laity were organised around the country by younger, more up-to-date theologians, but they could not remedy a chronic situation. Indeed, they may have exacerbated it. Much of the theology was (necessarily) superficial, with the result that, whatever standing theology previously had in the eyes of sceptical clerics, it was undermined by the half-baked ideas that were presented to them as the new theology or the spirit of the Council. One of the most impressive attempts to introduce modern theology to the Irish Church was that undertaken by the Maynooth Summer Schools, which began before the Council. Internationally renowned theologians, mostly from the continent, attracted huge crowds of clerics after the Council. By the mid-1970s, they faded out, I gather, for lack of support. One Irish cleric, asked why he no longer attended, is reported to have replied in effect that he was fed up of listening to theology in a foreign language. Listening to lectures not delivered in the mother-tongue can indeed be tiring. But is it possible to detect a more significant criticism? The theological discourse itself was and is foreign, marked, as it necessarily must be, by the particular cultural context of the European Churches out of which it emerged. The concerns of continental theologians, their traditional theological discourse itself, though not entirely alien, is still not that of the Irish Church or, indeed, that of the English-speaking world, which is our dominant cultural matrix.

In addition, such 'critical' theology itself raised questions, which the theologians themselves could not answer.[56] I remember as a seminarian attending the National Mission Congress at the headquarters of the Columban Fathers, Dalgan Park, in June 1968, attended by hundreds of Irish missionaries (mostly on home leave) to discuss the new theology of mission in the light of Vatican II. One could observe how the Council was 'received' by the most whole-hearted supporters of reform, namely Irish missionaries abroad. The week began with enthusiasm and a sense of liberation. It ended with more than a touch of existential angst. The whole gathering was left pondering one simple question: Why mission? None of the experts, many of whom were frequently on the circuit of Ireland bringing the clergy 'up-to-date', could provide a convincing theological foundation for mission. By the end of the week, the optimism of the opening days had evaporated with the gradual awareness that, if 'anonymous Christianity' is true (as originally proposed by Karl Rahner and accepted by most theologians at the time), then what is the point of our life-long commitment to the missions? Was our toil under the tropical sun all in vain? The question has not yet been answered. Future historians might well date the end of the modern Irish missionary movement to that week in 1968. It is no comfort to me to say that I witnessed it with my own eyes and ears. But other cracks were appearing in the walls protecting traditional Irish Catholicism.

The strongest branch of Irish theology before the Council was moral theology. Like moral theology anywhere at the time, it was excessively legalistic.[57] But in Irish Catholicism, it perfectly matched, and nurtured, the obsession with rules and regulations that is typical of a religion marked by a strong ethos of social conformity. (As I hope to indicate, there were probably more deeply-seated reasons for this obsession.) Newly ordained clerics left the seminary with the supreme confidence that comes from thinking that they knew all the answers to every moral dilemma. Such moral dilemmas dealt with obligations like the Eucharistic fast, restitution for stolen goods, and matters pertaining to the Sixth and Ninth Commandments. Apart from some unresolved questions concerning the Sunday obligation, there seemed to be nothing to add to the intricate, minutely worked-out scheme of morality.

But the Council singled out moral theology in particular as in need of radical renewal. In addition, the assembled bishops promulgated a vision of sexuality in *Gaudium et spes* that did not quite seem to tally with what most clerics had learnt in the seminary. The finely tuned laws and rubrics surrounding all things sacramental, any single transgression of which, it would seem, merited mortal sin on all occasions, were suddenly obsolete. Things were permitted, like attending services in a Protestant church, which up to then had been strictly forbidden under all kinds of dire penalties. This is all well known and its effect on the faithful has been noted. But few have pondered the effect it must have had on the majority of priests, many of whom, up to relatively recently, controlled all the strings. The ground had been taken from under them. Most pastors contented themselves with what they always did best, helping the poor and afflicted, visiting the sick, consoling the bereaved, managing schools, keeping the fabric in good shape, using published sermon notes – and generally withdrawing from the fray. But their deepest assumptions had been questioned not by any hostile critic, but by the Church's highest authority.

Then came *Humanae vitae*. Some prominent post-conciliar theologians had been preparing the clergy for a change in the teaching. But there was 'no change', though in fact the matter was more complex than that rather simple statement at the press conference in Dublin to announce the encyclical (see Appendix II). Neither was there any significant public discussion within the Irish Church. One priest voiced his dissent, was dismissed from his post, and went to Africa as a missionary. The others literally took to the hills, kept their mouths shut – and held on to their chairs in the various faculties. A few theologians experienced a *metanoia*, a change of mind. The complications created by this anomalous situation added to the confusion, and created a potentially explosive situation, one that has not yet been resolved. It may well account for much of the demoralisation to be found among the clergy today. Despite complaints to the contrary (presumably by those who no longer regularly attend Mass), few priests today speak about the Sixth and Ninth commandments – or indeed any other of the Ten Commandments – in their homilies. The various public controversies involving the legalisation of contraception, divorce and abortion were marked by the general silence of the clergy and by very mixed signals from the theologians, not to mention the bishops.[58] The final blow to the old order came with the more recent clerical scandals. Coping with these would have been difficult in any circumstances, but in Ireland the requisite resources – thinkers who could articulate, debate, and propose solutions from the perspective of the faith – were and still are rather thin on the ground.

Today, clerics and laity alike cite a lack of leadership for their demoralised state. Many speak of a lack of vision, a rather dangerous concept itself. But there can be no genuine vision, whatever that is, or leadership without hard thinking – and moral courage. These, it could be argued, had been weakened by traditional Irish Catholicism. Likewise a case could be made that more recent developments in moral theology might have undermined both. But there were other factors, the most important being the whole phenomenon of secularisation, a phenomenon that has haunted continental Europe for the past two centuries at least. European theologians and philosophers (Catholic and Protestant) had wrestled with such issues for over a century and a half. But the Irish Church was suddenly confronted by all these questions and found itself unprepared, with few thinkers within the fold who, while grappling with these issues, had the ear of those who exercised responsibility for the welfare of the Church. The latter were content to condemn the few thinkers from afar.

The unspoken questions that rise in the hearts of all, cleric and lay, are concerned with issues deeper than clerical scandals or new moral dilemmas created by the sexual revolution and the related revolution in biotechnology, significant indeed though these are. When the winds of change after Vatican II had blown down the thin barriers erected around it by 'traditional' Irish Catholicism, the Catholic Church was exposed to the raw winds of modernity and post-modernity, though if churchmen had been attentive, they might have noticed that modernity was not simply a matter of 'foreign' influence alone. Karl Marx described Ireland as the crucible of modernity.[59] Joyce and Beckett express the soul of modernity, and they do so by drawing on their experience of Dublin at the beginning of the last century. But the Church was blind to that experience – or was it, unwittingly, one of its causes? This will form the subject of the next chapter.

It is clear that inspired leadership presupposes people, lay or clerical, who have the confidence and the competence to be able to address the deeper issues of the day. The lack of a rich tradition of systematic (self-)questioning and searching, which is what theological scholarship is, coupled with the way whatever little writing on the subject to appear in Ireland has been effectively ignored, may well be the price we are paying for the assumption that, since we were a chosen nation, we would never lose the faith; we did not have to think things through. We did not accept, to use Augustine's words, quoted recently by Pope John Paul II, that 'To believe is nothing other than to think with assent ... Believers are also thinkers: in believing, they think and in thinking, they believe ... If faith does not think, it is nothing.'[60] In its infancy, Christianity presented itself to the learned world of late Hellenism as the ultimate philosophy needed to heal the intellectual sickness of humanity, the source of all its ills.[61] In time, this tradition gave rise to the very idea of a university during the High Middle Ages, and has continued through the centuries to be central to the Church's mission down to our own day. Theology is not an optional extra for the Church, but is at the heart of the Church founded on incarnate Reason, the *Logos* become Man. Thus Newman could affirm: 'I say, then, theology is the fundamental and regulating principle of the whole Church system.'[62] But not in Ireland.

2

HOW CATHOLIC IS IRISH CATHOLICISM?

Our order broken, they who were our brood,
Knew not themselves the heirs of noted masters,
Of Columbanus and Eriugena.

We strove to no high reach of speculation,
Towards no delivery of gestated dogma,
No resolution of age-long disputes.
PADRAIC COLUM

It is wrong to judge Irish culture by the flotsam from the wreck of the
past which chance has deposited on the shore of the twentieth century.
SEÁN DE FRÉINE[1]

On the completion of my studies in Donamon and Maynooth, I was sent as a newly ordained priest to Germany for postgraduate studies, first to Münster, Westphalia, and then to Regensburg, Bavaria. Both *Länder* (States) are Catholic. Though very different in character and culture, both were at the time unselfconsciously, indeed unabashedly, Catholic – but Catholic in a way I had not experienced up to then. The contrast with my own Catholic upbringing in Ireland was illuminating in several ways. Limiting my remarks to the time I spent in Regensburg, I will try to evoke some of the flavour and characteristics of that very different Catholic experience.

Another Catholic culture

In the first place, I gained a new insight into the meaning of what is meant by cultural tradition, Catholic style. The river Danube rises in the Black Forest, flows northwest to Regensburg (named after the tributary, the river Regen), and then southeast to enter the Black Sea. At this strategic location, the Celts founded a settlement (Ratisbona) some 2,300 years ago, which in AD 179 under Emperor Marcus Aurelius became a garrison town (*Castra Regina*) on the *limes*, the border between the Roman Empire and the barbarians to the north. Already at the end of the third century and the beginning of the fourth, a Christian community had been formed there, the origins of the Diocese of Regensburg. The present Cathedral parish church, built after 1152 and still in use, occupies the site of the earliest known bishop's church (*Niedermünsterkirche*), under which archeologists have uncovered the remains of three earlier churches among the layers of a thousand years of history going back to the walls of the Roman garrison. The earliest church on the site was built around AD 700 to house the tombs of Bishop St Erhard, and his friend Blessed Albert, Archbishop of Cashel.[2] As far as I know, there are no relics of any of the early Irish saints in Ireland preserved *in situ*, as it were, where they were originally interred and venerated.[3]

Regensburg became one of the great mediaeval cities of central Europe (now the best preserved), where the *Diet* or parliament of the Holy Roman Empire regularly assembled. During my stay there, the choir of its magnificent Gothic cathedral, the famous *Domspatzen* (i.e. cathedral sparrows), celebrated the thousandth anniversary of its foundation. The choir regularly sang at what was still called the High Mass on Sundays and Feast Days in the great Gothic cathedral. In 1983, the Dominican contemplative nuns in Regensburg celebrated seven hundred and fifty years of uninterrupted study, prayer, and praise of God in their monastery. Around every corner are to be found magnificent churches of all architectural styles, from the sombre Romanesque through the sublime Gothic to the sensuous Baroque and flamboyant Rococo. One of the most beautiful sacral buildings of all is the almost perfectly preserved *Schottenkirche* (Church of the Irish), originally attached to the Irish Benedictine monastery of St James (founded 1090), the centre of the last wave of Irish monks to the European mainland, whose monasteries stretched from Kiev to Vienna.[4] The Irish monks came from priories at Cashel and Rosscarbery. Now it is the main church of the diocesan seminary, where I lived for two years completing my doctoral studies. Each morning, I celebrated Mass in the Romanesque chapel,[5] under the old high altar of which rested the relics of St Muredach, the original Irish hermit who came to Regensburg with two companions in 1072. As already indicated, it was not the only connection with the early Irish Church and early Christian culture in the city, but it was the most striking.

The exposure to this rich Catholic cultural tradition hewn in stone, expressed in art and music, and alive in the parishes and diocesan institutions, brought home to me how impoverished we are in Ireland with regard to the still intact public monuments reflecting our former Christian cultural greatness, living memorials to the rich stream of holiness and beauty that the encounter between the Christian faith and native Irish traditions once produced. Why this is the case, is open to debate.[6] What is beyond doubt is that without such memorials it is easy to become 'unremembering hearts and heads', as W.B. Yeats put it. Today, that earlier architectural tradition has practically vanished from public view[7] and thus from our collective consciousness. One can hardly overestimate the cultural damage done by the abolition of the monasteries in Ireland – ever the main sources of culture in any Christian country – and the destruction of the mediaeval rituals and life-forms, such as the public sacral times and spaces, the great cathedrals, the pilgrimages, the public feast days, which were also fair days, and so on. The rich sacral music, art, and architecture of Catholic Europe continue to inspire even the atheist European thinker and artist, just as the art of the Renaissance in the Catholic churches of Tuscany inspired Hughie O'Donoghue's magnificent cycle of painting and etchings of the Crucified One.[8]

In Ireland, it was our proud boast that we had preserved the faith down through the centuries despite persecution and deprivation without any such props. It is not an empty boast. But today it, too, tends to be forgotten. Apart from the shrine to St Oliver Plunkett in Drogheda and a number of recently restored abbeys now functioning as religious houses or parish churches, what living tradition is there to remind us of them, or to inspire the present generation? So estranged from our tradition have we become, that when a significant number of Irish martyrs were beatified recently, that event found little resonance among the public in general or even among the clergy and religious. Likewise, the beatification of Edmund Ignatius Rice, founder of the Christian Brothers, gave rise to little enthusiasm and less public cult. (Here, of course, the scandals about the industrial schools did not help.) There is little popular devotion either to the beatified martyrs or the rest of the 259 men and women who gave their lives for the faith in the sixteenth and seventeenth centuries at those places associated with their lives and their heroic deaths. There are few visible memorials to recall the long period of the persecutions, apart from the Mass-rocks and holy wells, which today are often neglected. While impressive monuments to the Great Famine now grace the public spaces of our cities, there is nothing comparable to recall the heroic Christian witness of the Irish martyrs.

With the exception of the cathedrals and churches still used by the Anglicans, all that is left of the earlier (Gaelic) and mediaeval (Norman and Old English) Catholic Church are ruins, now visited by European tourists who first discovered their cultural significance.[9] These ruins are presently being marketed for the tourist industry and suffering the final desecration by the installation of modern, mostly secular, interpretative centres in the vicinity of the sacred sites. Again, this is symbolic of the underlying utilitarianism and commercialism of the dominant Irish culture. It is not unrelated to Ireland's puritan tradition.

Important aspects of the mediaeval Christian culture, its cathedrals and music, were preserved by what was the established State Church, the Anglican Church of Ireland. Those vestiges of the past are the source of much of the vitality of the Church of Ireland today in the cities. When the Catholic Church emerged from the underground in the late eighteenth and early nineteenth centuries, it required a new architecture, much of it quite magnificent and a true source of pride.[10] One thinks immediately of the still impressive Armagh, Thurles, Enniscorthy, and Cobh cathedrals, not to mention the other masterpieces by Pugin, such as SS Peter and Paul's parish church in Cork, or those by the great J. J. McCarthy, such as Maynooth College Chapel and St Saviour's, Dominic Street, Dublin. Newman's little gem, the University Church on St Stephen's Green, deserves special mention. All in all, it was an impressive achievement and perhaps we have not fully appreciated how impressive it was, considering the political and economic situation. But that architecture was derived: neo-Gothic, neo-Romanesque, neo-Classical, even neo-Byzantine, and reflected the growing cultural dependence of Ireland on what was happening abroad, especially in Britain. They were not 'of the soil', and so the pragmatic clerics of our own day, most of them apparently devoid of any aesthetic sense, who were intent on introducing the new liturgical reforms did not hesitate to demolish and rebuild the interiors.

Celebration – Catholic style

In Bavaria, secondly, I learned what is meant by feast days, the public celebration of religious events. What in Ireland are called Holy Days *of Obligation*, are, for example, in Austria, Switzerland, Germany, Poland, Italy, and elsewhere, State-recognised public holidays, occasions for leisure, celebration, feasting, singing, something which, it is said, the Spanish do best. Even secular France celebrates the Assumption of Our Lady as a public holiday. According to Patrick Kavanagh, the Assumption 'was a great Feast in our part of Ireland, greater even than St Patrick's Day'. (In the Southeast, it found a fitting secular expression in the Tramore Races.) The General Assembly of the Catholic Confederation of Ireland, meeting at Loughrea on the vigil of the Feast in 1650, decreed the Virgin Mother of God to be the Patroness of Ireland under the title of the Immaculate Conception and that this feast be solemnly observed in Ireland to the end of time. It is ironic that, when the Republic of Ireland was forced by the EU to introduce an additional number of public holidays – revealingly called Bank Holidays in Ireland, as in England – to bring us in line with public celebrations of Catholic Holy Days in other parts of Europe, to the best of my knowledge, no one at the time dared to suggest that one or other of the new public holidays could be recognised as a Catholic Feast Day.[11]

While in Europe, I learned how the rest of the Catholic world celebrates Advent, for example, namely as a true preparation for, not an anticipation of, Christmas.[12] There I experienced Christmas as a Christian feast that was not just a one-day affair, but a full Twelve Days that lasted to Epiphany (also a public holiday in central Euorpe). And in the predominantly Catholic cities, such as Cologne and Mainz, the austerity of Lent was introduced by the noisy and gaudy celebrations of *Fashing*, Carnival.[13] I could go on. The point of all this is that, while in Regensburg, I began to suspect that Irish Catholic culture might not be quite so authentically Catholic after all. It looked more and more like a Protestant culture decked out with some second-hand Catholic garments made of various neo-something-or-other art and architecture, French or Italianate devotions, and plaster saints. To be more specific, 'traditional Irish Catholicism', to an alarming degree, seemed to be, if not Jansenistic, at least puritanical both in the original, historical sense of the word (as being iconoclastic, dualist, and militant) and in the narrow sense of disdain, not to say, hatred for the pleasures of the body in a mistaken notion of Christian piety.[14]

Theology as a way of life and a public activity

Finally, at Regensburg, I learned what theology was. I studied at the newly opened State University, the core faculty of which was, in the tradition of the German universities, the faculty of Catholic theology.[15] There was also an independent chair of Lutheran theology. What a contrast with the situation in Ireland! The Bavarian government automatically bore the cost of my tutorial fees, something that is still unthinkable in the Republic. (It is ironic that the tutorial fees of seminarians from Northern Ireland studying in Maynooth have long been paid for by the British government.) More significant is the simple fact of the public recognition of theology as an academic discipline by the German State, and a straightforwardly confessional theology at that. Theology, as I will mention later, is by its very nature denominational.

The centuries-old tradition of *denominational* theology on the university made German theology one of the most formidable influences on the modern Church. This can be seen in the way it helped shape the Second Vatican Council. But what struck me so forcibly in Germany was the realisation that theology *mattered*. For most Irish seminarians, theology was a hurdle to be overcome before ordination. For their teachers, it was a means of providing professional training needed by future pastors. But it seemed to have little value in itself, as a scholarly discipline, and had less impact on public discourse. My own impression when I first went to Maynooth was that few teachers or students seemed to be even remotely aware of the void opening up behind the Catholic mask of Irish society or aware of developments in society that would in time lead to the present impasse. It was probably not a fair assessment but neither was it entirely off the mark. It made me a rebel!

But in Münster and Regensburg, I discovered that theology mattered both to those who studied it and to the public at large.

Theologians such as Rahner, Küng, and Ratzinger, were evidently engaged in a public debate with the most significant currents in modern thought that were shaping society. Their scholarly achievement gave theology public recognition, while this public recognition of theology in turn heightened the scholarly rigour. The findings of theologians were discussed in the public media, and the quality of the contributions made to public debate by bishops, theologians, and philosophers, lay and clerical, was and continues to be impressive, which is not the same as saying that it was always effective. Much the same can be said about France and Austria, for example. Impressive too was the critical, yet respectful attitude of the media to theologians who defended viewpoints at variance with the established liberal consensus.[16] The contrast with the situation in Ireland could not be more crass. If an Irish theologian does not come out in support of the position advocated by the media in a controversy involving Church-related matters, he will find himself in a very hostile environment indeed, facing ridicule, at times barely disguised disdain. Blame for the hostile atmosphere in the media cannot simply be attributed to the dominance there of the new establishment ('Dublin 4'), since the media in most Western countries has adopted a similar agenda (that of libertarianism) and yet is generally devoid of the bitterness and disrespect found in Ireland. What then is the cause of this hostility?

Is perhaps the Church herself to blame? Did she raise expectations that she failed to meet herself? Has she produced credible public representatives, whose firm grasp of the issues and whose debating skills could earn the respect of the public at large, even of the media? The answer to the latter question, unfortunately, is in the negative. Such is the price the Church (and, indirectly but more painfully, society at large) is paying for the absence of any serious theological reflection on the human condition in Ireland for over a century or more – though there were sufficient intellectuals at the time critically examining the direction society was taking and the currents moulding contemporary culture. Canon Sheehan should be mentioned in this context. His novels expressed a gentle, humorous but penetrating criticism of society, and of the Church, in imaginative form.

According to Brian Fallon, it is obvious that there could be few areas in common between the clergy and the typical Irish intellectual from 1930 to 1960. 'The clergy wanted the people to believe, to "keep the faith" first and last; in contrast, the intellectuals wanted them to think and to question things rather than swallow them unconditionally.'[17] Irish intellectuals such as Liam O'Flaherty, Frank O'Connor, or Seán Ó Faoláin, often depicted as anti-clerical (which seemed to have been considered almost on a level with apostasy), might appeal to Newman, Pascal or Mauriac, Fallon recalls, but in vain. The leading clergy did not want 'a new generation of independent-minded, highly educated and literate Catholic laymen quoting Pascal or Mauriac, who might ask awkward questions and undermine the people's unquestioning belief in their priests'.[18] What is interesting is that such intellectuals could nonetheless hold individual priests and religious in unalloyed affection and respect, as can be seen in a collection of short stories by Frank O'Connor.[19] In her introduction, his widow noted that O'Connor 'had little time for the institutional Church's pedantic and legalistic moralizing.... But towards the actual men set apart by the collar... he had an attitude compounded of amusement, respect, curiosity and, above all, compassion.'[20] This was not untypical: a degree of alienation from the institution coupled with affection for the local priest. And it is still the case, to judge from the results of the sociological survey conducted by Fr Andrew Greely and Fr Conor Ward and published at the end of 2000.[21]

However, the real issue here is the question of why theology did not, and still does not, really *matter* in Ireland. Why, to use Brian Fallon's words, was there 'no Irish Catholic philosopher of European stature in the modern epoch, no thinker/theologian of the calibre of Barth or Tillich or the [German] Karl Rahner...' or, one could add, the French Henri de Lubac, the Swiss Hans Urs von Balthasar, the American John Courtney Murray, or the Polish Karol Wojtyla? Why was there 'an overriding conformity and mediocrity, a decision to go almost always for the "safe man" and the orthodox mentality, for which the Church is paying in Peter's Pence today'?[22]

Origins of 'traditional Irish Catholicism' as a cultural phenomenon
Perhaps part of the answer is to be found in the experience of the Irish Church in the nineteenth century. By abandoning the Irish language, the nation's last and most significant hold on the rich traditions of a truly Irish Christianity, much of the Gaelic-Christian worldview that alone sustained Irish Catholics for generations through difficult times was also lost. An intriguing analysis of this development is to be found in a series of articles published by Desmond Fennell in *Doctrine and Life* during the first half of 1966, to commemorate the fiftieth anniversary of the 1916 Rising. His main preoccupation is with the intellectual movement that created the Irish Revolution and what he sees as the (as yet) unfulfilled promise of that rebirth of the Irish nation.[23] But his analysis is also of relevance to our present topic.

His basic concern is to define freedom and the conditions of freedom. More than simple choice or absence of constraint, freedom means living according to some insight into one's being, and to be in communion with other people who are also free. Fed from sources within ourselves, freedom implies participation in a free self-defining, self-reliant nation, fashioning its own communal way of life from its own spiritual, intellectual, artistic and material resources, in interaction with other truly independent nations engaged in the same exhilarating task. Modern Irish nationalism, he claims, with its vision of genuine liberation was essentially humanistic in inspiration.[24]

The essence of freedom, it is claimed, is to be able to affirm the goodness of life as it is, this life in the body, in this particular time and place, and to celebrate it in art and music, in song and dance, *because* one sees one's own life as being truly worthwhile, as being affirmed. To be free is to be able to praise, to worship, to echo God's Yes in the continuous act of creation, to lift up one's head and one's heart, *sursum corda*. Yes, it is good to be here, good to be, and to be who we are, what we are, embodied and rooted in this world and in this particular community with its distinct history and traditions, yet open to the rest of the world – and to eternity. Full freedom is impossible, ultimately, apart from Christ. But modernity, in claiming mere liberty of choice has produced slavery, the serf mentality of the un-free and so has again reduced individuals and nations to dependency status, as it were, provincial-minded in the sense described by Patrick Kavanagh: 'The provincial has no mind of his own. He does not trust what his eye sees until he has heard what the metropolis – towards which his eyes are turned – has to say on the subject.'[25]

According to Fennell, this provincial mentality is the dominant feature of politics wherever modernity has taken hold, but it has been particularly evident in Ireland. For the first time in its history, Ireland became provincial-minded in the nineteenth century, both technically – no longer a distinct Kingdom of Ireland but since 1800 part of the 'United Kingdom of Great Britain and Ireland' – and, in a more important sense, culturally. The latter was achieved not simply by the loss of the Irish language. The adoption of the English language by the majority and the influence of a late-Tridentine form of Catholic life and theology were, according to Fennell, also significant factors. As Heidegger says: 'Language is the house of being. In this house man dwells.' The result of the adoption of the English language (and the decline of Irish) by a largely impoverished nation[26] was to make Irishmen and women in effect culturally rootless, exiles in their own country.[27] In a similar vein, Joseph Lee ponders: 'It may be that there is an Irish emotional reality which is silenced in English. It may be too that many Irish no longer experience that emotional reality, that it has been parched out of them, that a particular stream of Irish consciousness has dried up with the decay of the language.'[28] But it meant more than that.

'Our greatest misfortune', Fennell says, 'was not... that we abandoned Irish. That was a tragedy; but far more grievous was the fact that we adopted a provincial version of nineteenth-century English and a clerical language [which he later calls Latinoid] in exchange. Irish gave the Christian man, priest or pauper, a unitary world view, at once natural and supernatural, which had not suffered from the reducing influences of Puritanism, rationalism or cultural insularity à l'anglaise'.[29] This was because '[t]he language of Victorian England was, in its predominant form and tendency, that of a people whose character John Stuart Mill saw as "chiefly shaped... since the days of the Stuarts" by two influences: "commercial money-getting business and religious Puritanism". That, he [Mill] believed, was the reason why they were incapable of taking art seriously. But how much more than art is man! How much more again is God-in-man.'[30]

According to Corish, the adoption of English as the lingua franca had already begun in the previous century in the cities and then spread to the rural areas in the following century. In the cities, the merchant classes together with an incipient middle class were endeavouring to accommodate themselves to a new situation marked by commercial and other opportunities opened up by the relaxing of the Penal Laws, the new prosperity, and, it is claimed,[31] the collapse of any hope of a restoration of the old Gaelic order in the wake of Culloden (1746). The English-speaking towns were, not surprisingly, the first to adopt the 'more personal devotion..., more markedly Italian in general tone, genuinely more human but not without some danger of sentimentality'[32] that spread after the Famine into what was Gaelic-speaking Ireland.[33] 'It was at this stage that English won over Irish even in the concerns of the soul.'[34] The English-speaking spirituality which would leave its mark in Irish Catholicism developed an 'anxious severity' that was not strictly speaking Jansenistic but 'must rather be traced to the devotional reading available in English'[35] such as that written by Richard Challoner (1691-1781).[36] The sadder note in his writings reflecting his experiences as a bishop in penal-day London evidently appealed to Irish Catholics.[37]

The social pressure exerted on the 'upwardly mobile' Irish, especially in the cities, to conform to the prevailing norms of 'Christian behaviour' as determined by the Protestant ruling class must also have been considerable.[38] Christian life at the time was defined by one overriding concern: 'respectability'. It became the distinguishing mark especially of the Victorian era.[39] Irish Catholics ambitious for a higher social standing would have had to prove to a sceptical and self-satisfied Protestant middle-class that they too were 'Christian' in the sense defined by that same class – namely, measured in terms of conformity to the accepted social behaviour. Such a mentality can already be discerned in the *Address of the Roman Catholick Noblemen and Gentlemen of the Counties of Meath and Westmeath*, which appeared in the *London Gazette* on 3 February 1761.[40] This mentality would have been reinforced by a narrow, legalistic (casuistic), approach to moral theology that dominated Catholic theology[41] at the time, and lasted right up to the Second Vatican Council. However, this was ameliorated somewhat by such popular devotions as that to the Sacred Heart, the pre-eminent symbol of divine mercy. In addition, a predominantly rural, post-Famine Ireland preoccupied with inheritance patterns developed a technique of birth control (late and few marriages) that 'required rigorous sexual self-control from the disinherited, and indeed from the inheritors until they belatedly came to their legacy.'[42] As Lee comments: 'The obsessive equation of sin with sex was much less pronounced in popular, pre-Famine Irish traditions. It was partly imported from Victorian England, where it flourished for somewhat different reasons.'[43] But the end result of these mutually supportive developments was the kind of suffocating, often dehumanising, 'Catholic morality' which was identified with 'traditional Irish Catholicism' and in turn gave rise to the moral revolution in Ireland in more recent decades.

Fennell highlights a more profound defect in the new language adopted by the majority as their lingua franca. There was 'no place in that tight language for urgent, reflective discourse on the human situation in face of the seeming "death" or "absence" of

God or of "the sacred", no place for existential "dread" … Plato's "we discussed the true, the beautiful, and the good" could be translated by a scholar as "we discussed mental and moral problems" (nothing exciting gentlemen, nothing exciting at all!).'[44] He has a point. The language we adopted, the English that had been spiritually dehydrated under the influence of Hobbes and was consequently incapable of metaphysical discourse, was blind to the mystery of man, opaque to the mystery of God, and so incapable of theology.[45] In reaction to the Puritans, Hobbes had effectively banished religious discourse from the public realm.[46] The result, it seems, was the hegemony of rationalism and utilitarianism, and a nation of shopkeepers, the national religion of which, according to Newman, was notional not real, what he calls 'Bible Religion', a religion 'of sacred scenes and pious sentiments'.[47]

Again, this must be seen against the broader European background: '… in the nineteenth century, Western Man moved across a rubicon which, if as unseen as the 38th Parallel, seems to have been as definitive as the Styx'.[48] In the early part of the last century, David Jones and his circle of friends in Britain christened it 'The Break'. It 'had reference to something which was affecting the entire world of sacrament and sign'. Jones continues: 'We were not however speculating on, or in any way questioning dogma concerning "The Sacraments". … Our speculations under this head were upon how increasingly isolated such dogma had become, owing to the turn civilization had taken, affecting signs in general and the whole notion and concept of sign.'[49] It would take us too far away from our topic to explore this, more profound, dimension, but I mention it at this stage as an reminder that the transformation of Irish Catholicism in the past century and a half was, and still is, part of a larger and more far reaching transformation in Western culture. But it also may help to explain, at least in part, Fennell's dilemma, namely why, having adopted in place of Irish the *koinê* (lingua franca) of the new civilised world, we failed to fashion it into a new *koinê* as a suitable vehicle for probing the depths of the human condition and expressing the mysteries of our faith.[50] But there were also other factors at work in the Irish Church to hinder such a philosophical and theological project.

Apart altogether from the language question, the nineteenth-century Church adopted a form of late-Tridentine, Catholic tradition that was, according to Fennell, other-worldly to the point of angelism, a tradition moreover that denied the goodness of the here and now. Life here below was to be held in contempt in favour of life hereafter. As Nietzsche (so influential on Joyce) might have said, it fostered the slave-mentality, encouraging the denial of one's own nobility; it could not offer the freedom implied in the affirmation: Yes, it is good simply to be. This view of Fennell's was the standard view in the late sixties, when Trent was unfashionable and Vatican II was 'in'. But perhaps it is a view that has to be modified.

My own experience of the Counter-Reformation Baroque in Bavaria, Austria, and Italy, brought home to me the impoverished nature of the Irish variant of the so-called late-Tridentine (or, to use Corish's term, neo-Tridentine) tradition. This tradition was characterised by a legalistic moral theology, a highly centralised, authoritarian institution, and a sentimental spirituality; it dominated the Irish Catholic experience up to the Second Vatican Council. By way of comparison, the art historian, Kenneth Clarke,[51] described the baroque art and music of Counter-Reformation Rome as the natural reaction of Catholics to the world-negating and body-denying spirituality of the Reformation. Whereas the intellectual life developed more fully in the north, Clarke admits (somewhat patronisingly): 'The great achievements of the Catholic Church lay in harmonising, humanising, civilising the deepest impulses of ordinary, ignorant people.'[52] One such human impulse was the importance of the 'female principle' that found expression in the cult of the Virgin.[53] Another was the impulse to confess, another the need to make tangible contact with the holy, as fulfilled in the veneration of relics.[54] But above all, another strength of the sixteenth-century Catholic Church was that 'it was not afraid of the human body'.[55] In the work of Rubens and Bernini 'the conflict between flesh and spirit is gloriously resolved'.[56] That artistic achievement was made possible by the enlightened, not to say breathtakingly risky, patronage of popes and cardinals.

The Baroque captures the spirit of the Counter-Reformation more than any abstract theology or organisational structures. The genuine, life-affirming spirit of Trent (as well as its underlying spirit of triumphalism) is reflected in the design and execution of such churches as the Baroque *Karlskirche* in Vienna, the flamboyant Asam churches of Bavaria, like the oval monastery church of Weltenburg,[57] or the Jesuit Baroque masterpiece, the *Gesù*, in Rome. There are countless others dotted around southern and central Europe, many (like Weltenburg) with an 'Irish connection'.[58] They, and the rich baroque liturgy expressed in sublime sacred music, for which they provided an almost theatrical setting, kept the more austere ascetical and moral strictures of the post-Tridentine Church in balance. Even the ascetic St Charles Borromeo, one of those entrusted with the task of purifying the music of St Peter's, 'doesn't seem to have objected to the sensuous beauty of Palestrina's sound'.[59]

The nineteenth-century interpretation of Trent known to us in Ireland may well have had more to do with the peculiar socio-economic conditions in Ireland and the puritan ethos of the United Kingdom at the time, of which kingdom we were part, than with the actual decrees and canons of that reform council. Many of the decrees of Trent were applied in Ireland some two hundred years after they were passed. Moreover, they were rigorously applied to a situation which the council could hardly have envisaged – a country where the predominantly Catholic majority had, after an heroic struggle (Catholic Emancipation), just achieved limited political representation and were eager to achieve some cultural standing in the public realm dominated by a highly developed, sophisticated, but predominantly alien, culture. It had not only been deprived of a substantial public Catholic

culture for over a century and a half, but its public culture was
dominated by a desiccated English Protestant cultural tradition.
Applying the strictures of Trent to the situation of the nineteenth-
century Irish Church was a little like prescribing a diet for a
malnourished patient. In any case, whatever its cause, Irish
Catholicism at the time tended, indeed, not to be particularly life-
affirming. 'Traditional Irish Catholicism' was perhaps
otherworldly in a negative sense. But it may not be fair to place all
the blame on Trent or indeed its nineteenth-century interpreters.

Be that as it may, Fennell argues more convincingly that: 'The
first three commandments of the law of God cannot be obeyed if
language is inadequate. They tell us how men must do him
honour. But we cannot be men if our linguistic dwelling cramps
our manhood…'[60] We create false gods, which cannot sate our
craving for ultimate meaning and freedom. If the experience of
'nothingness', a term that is almost meaningless in English but not
in French or German, is the modern experience par excellence,
then, Fennell claims, Dublin was the most modern city in Europe
at the turn of the twentieth century, as captured above all in the
writings of Joyce, who rebelled against it. For the quintessential
Dubliner, men and women had been reduced to empty shadows
wandering aimlessly around a gray, meaningless city, unable to see
the sacrament of the apparently trivial. They were 'outcasts from
life's feast'.[61] Beckett too depicts the emptiness of language
divorced from being and the consequent aimlessness of waiting
for nothing to happen. Devoid of familiar access in everyday life to
metaphysical realities[62] – the true, the good and the beautiful –
what is left is a void at the heart of ourselves and society, a black
hole that sucks us down into oblivion, unless we find some
escape.[63] Somewhat later, Francis Bacon gave supreme, artistic
expression to such metaphysical horror at times evoked by images
associated with the Catholic tradition,[64] though he himself, like
Samuel Becket, had a Protestant upbringing in Dublin.

Much of the sociological history of Irish Catholicism during
the last century and a half, as Fennell and others have noted, has

been marked by the search for an escape from a country in which the majority of its inhabitants were effectively exiles. Irish Catholics, he claims, lived in a countryside that no longer spoke to them of the invisible, in the long shadow of ruins that had forgotten a glorious past, or in colourless towns and cities populated by the living dead. As a result:

> Apathy and lifelessness take over. Resigned to unfreedom in respect of the here and now (it is *not* good to be here), intellectually stagnant, blind to self, land or money could suddenly come to seem an overriding goal – not for any particular purpose, but merely for security's sake, for power's sake, for some sort of hold... As sadness turns to sourness, the urge to praise is suppressed utterly; a carping, begrudging spirit takes over...[65]

This in turn gives rise to the need to escape, to emigrate and loose oneself in the anonymous crowds of the big cities in England and the US. But Fennell also suggests that the quite phenomenal rise in vocations to the priesthood and especially the religious life may have been a form of escape for the strong willed, who opted for a quasi-angelic form of existence. Otherwise, 'According to opportunity and with due regard for taboos or prohibitions, a list of very dreary, very ancient outlets to illusory non-existence or transcendence can be chosen from: suicide, alcohol, physical violence, hypnotic or ecstatic religious devotions, routine, danger, sex, speed, regular overtime, feverish activity, delirious dancing, the various angelic or purer-than-thou illusions of radicalism, *soi-disant* enlightenment, or pride. With critical reason suspended, salvation myths and magical healing methods are in vogue again.'[66] It all sounds a bit familiar, not just in Ireland, and not just a few generations ago.

This assessment is perhaps somewhat 'overblown'. Historians are likely to demonstrate that the situation was somewhat more complex and nuanced than that described here. But, nonetheless, it seems to me that Fennell has put his finger on what might well be the ultimate reason why theology does not really matter in Ireland. Namely, we have not yet fashioned our adopted mother-tongue (as did the great converts in England)[67] into 'a receptacle for God's presence among us *which* [receptacle, like the chalice] *he allows us to make'*.[68] The result is the most radical experience of alienation of all, the feeling of being abandoned by God. John Waters writes of the contemporary situation: 'One way of describing the nature of the collapse of spiritual values in Ireland would be to say that the Irish people did not so much stop believing in God as that they came to believe God no longer believed in them ... The reason for the level of addiction in Modern Ireland is the need to temporarily fill in the yawning chasm in the national soul while we are waiting for God's faith in us to be restored.'[69]

The significance of the Second Vatican Council

The challenge that faces the Catholic Church in modern Ireland is nothing less than to replace that yawning chasm with the Real Presence,[70] to reveal and articulate anew God's faith in us. It is against this background that the significance of the Second Vatican Council must be seen. The council undertook the most extensive overhaul of the Church for some 400 years. In the first place, it called for a renewal of the liturgy, a renewal that was carried out in Ireland according to the letter but, I venture to say, has on the whole not yet been carried out according to the spirit. Until such time as the liturgy has been renewed in harmony with the letter *and* the spirit of the Council, the Catholic Church faces a rather bleak future. Here the inspiration of a profound theology of liturgy[71] must precede any changes in ritual. The nature of sacred ritual – which belongs to the common human experience found in all religions despite its specific Judeo-Christian form and so cannot be concocted on *an ad* hoc basis by experts or a committee – needs to be rediscovered:[72] the nature and shape of that sacred space and time, sacred movement, music, and art, which is specifically Christian.[73] It is precisely the sacral nature of the liturgy that needs to be recovered, as indicated by the Second Vatican Council:

> [E]very liturgical celebration, because it is an action of Christ the Priest and of his Body, which is the Church, is *a sacred action surpassing all others*. No other action of the Church can equal its efficacy by the same title and to the same degree.
>
> In the earthly liturgy we take part in *a foretaste of that heavenly liturgy* which is celebrated in the Holy City of Jerusalem toward which we journey as pilgrims, where Christ is sitting at the right hand of God, minister of the holies and of the true tabernacle.[74]

By allowing the vernacular to be used as the language of the liturgy, the Council challenged each culture to make its own language capable of expressing the divine mysteries. In the absence of a general recovery of Irish as our common mother tongue, we in Ireland have yet to forge the mother-tongue of the majority into a theological idiom. The need for this is nowhere more obvious than in the banal, at times theologically questionable translations of the new Missal.[75] We have yet to find our divine voice.

Secondly, the Council renewed the Church's own self-understanding as the sacrament of salvation for the whole world. It also clarified the relationship between the Church and the other world-religions, seeing how all relate to the Body of Christ.[76] This doctrinal development, it seems to me, has enormous significance for the role of the Catholic Church in modern Ireland. The Catholic Church now has a clearly worked-out, inclusive vision of her relationship to all Christian Churches and ecclesial communities, as well as to the non-Christian religions and those who have no religion; the significance of each is fully recognised and respected, without abandoning the essential claims of the

Catholic Church, which had been hidden under an exclusivist, not to say distorted interpretation of these claims. The simplistic claim of earlier generations to be the one, true Church, to the exclusion of every other Christian tradition, was not unconnected with the dominant culture, that puritanical mindset, which tended to see everything in black or white. One writer described it as the 'sacred-profane disjuncture' that was common to both Catholic and Protestant cultures.[77] The ecumenical thrust of the Council, together with the *Declaration on Religious Liberty* (the right of all people to worship according to their conscience) established the basis for a more nuanced approach that should promote greater tolerance and respect between various religious traditions, without forcing either to abandon their own integrity or encouraging indifference.[78]

Finally, in *Gaudium et spes*, the Council re-examined the relationship between the Church and the world. It is the latter that most concerns us in this context, since it firmly rejected any form of angelism, any attempt to make the faith something entirely other-worldly and treat the concerns of this world with little more than contempt. This is neatly summed up in article 38. After acknowledging the ambiguity of human progress due to the prevalence of sin in human activity, the document reminds us that God, on becoming man, 'entered human history, taking that history into himself and recapitulating it'. He taught the law of love, not as an impossible ideal, but as a real possibility for the here and now. Working in the hearts of all by his Spirit, 'not only does [Christ] arouse in them a desire for the world to come but He quickens, purifies and strengthens the generous aspirations of mankind to make life more humane and conquer the earth for this purpose.' The programmatic nature of this teaching has yet to be translated into a spirituality, namely a way of life for Christian living characterised by the struggle to improve the socio-economic and cultural conditions of living in this world without abandoning the primacy of the transcendent, namely prayer and contemplation.

3

WHICH PATH
TO FOLLOW?

*[T]he priest and the writer ought to be fighting side by side, if for
nothing else than the rebuttal of the vulgarity that is pouring daily into
the vacuum left in the popular mind by the dying out of the old
traditional life.*
SEÁN Ó FAOLÁIN[1]

*Ich am of Irlaunde
Ant of the holy londe of irlonde
Gode sir pray ich ye for saynte charite,
come ant daunce wyt me
in irlaunde.*
(HIBERNO-NORMAN, CA 1300/1350)

My own, probably selective, memories of growing up in Cork in
the 1940s and 50s are shot through with light and sunshine. It was
a mildly prosperous, slightly self-satisfied, port-city that was yet
essentially outward looking, even somewhat cosmopolitan. I still
remember the excitement of discovering music, drama, art and
world-literature (alas, only in translation). I basked in the pride of
being the son of a newly independent nation, and tended to look
down on the Scots and Welsh for their failure to cast off the
shackles of English domination. But above all, I remember the

regular experience of the awesome mystery of the Mass, the inspiring annual liturgy of Holy Week as conducted by the Dominicans in St Mary's, Pope's Quay. In short, I grew up in a world that was Catholic in every sense, that is, upper and lower case 'c', and where, in Newman's words, religion was real, not notional.[2]

Alice Taylor's *To School through the Fields* depicts rural life at that time, full of gentle humour and humanity, faith and common sense, which account so resonated with people that, it seems, it sold the most copies of any book ever published in Ireland.[3] The atmosphere of the 1950s has been immortalised by Heinrich Böll in his *Irish Journal*.[4] For all its alleged weaknesses and failures in the early part of the last century, the Catholic Church in Ireland produced many 'life-affirming' people, such as the missionaries in the mould of Bishop Joseph Shanahan, Fr Blowick, and Mother Mary Martin, who sowed the seed of the Gospel and more (education, health-care, etc.) in Africa and Asia. Despite everything, the living faith that inspired our ancestors was indeed passed on in the home, school, and chapel, despite, or even thanks to, the devotions and plaster saints from Italy and the Infant of Prague. As Brian Fallon observes: 'Under all the sentimental popular religiosity, and the dogmatism and myopia of unimaginative clerics, there was a pure underground stream of something which can only be called "soul".'[5] It is still there.

And it is not so easily extinguished. The author of a recent book on the Irish Americans, now greatly assimilated into 'White Anglo-Saxon Protestant' society, highlights the almost non-eradicable nature of the best of Irish Catholic spirituality, its sense of the transience of this world, the fleeting nature of fortune, the inevitability of tragedy, the centrality of humility, and the importance of loyalty to family and friends. 'In the secular trinity of Irish-American values, loyalty and humour are father and son. Self-deprecation is the spirit that works in mysterious ways'.[6]

The motley garments of another culture have been stripped away from us, and the once self-confident 'institutional' Church has in many senses imploded. Despite all that, the latest sociological survey[7] claims that Ireland still has the highest rate of practice in the world, that the majority of those questioned still believe in the core tenets of the Catholic Church, that trust in the priest as a person is still strong, and that the lower age-bracket held more or less the same values as the higher. Trust at the level of personal relationship between priest and people has always been the real strength of Irish Catholicism.[8] The survey confirms that even the recent scandals could not shake it, and this despite a significant level of those who expressed disappointment with the appointed leaders of the Church. Yet, the Church continues to mediate Christ. The Church is, after all, the sacrament of God's presence on earth, a sacrament that is efficacious, *ex opere operato*, that is, irrespective of the moral or other human qualities of those who administer the sacrament, namely the clergy. It is an aspect of the Church's teaching that needs to be kept in mind in these inauspicious times for Irish Catholicism. 'We are no better than earthen vessels to hold this treasure ...'(2 Cor 4:7). It is the bedrock of hope for the so-called 'institutional' Church.

On the other hand, the void at the heart of society has, if anything, spread over the past thirty years, as evidenced by the increase of suicide, crime, of recourse to various forms of escapism offered by the booming Celtic-tiger economy, and of 'atheism' as a fad. In this context, it is worth noting the comments of a contemporary American theologian. 'John Henry Newman', he wrote, 'once likened unbelief to an epidemic –"wonderfully catching," he put it – not because of secularizing reason, as so many others had diagnosed, but because of the allure of imagination. Newman took his jaundiced view because he knew that imagination has a clever way of initially presenting a "possible, plausible view of things which first *haunts* and at length *overcomes* the mind." It is not "reason that is against us," he said, "but imagination".'[9] Conversely, our response must, in the first instance, take place at the level of the imagination. The Church must once again catch the imagination of people at large, appealing first to the heart. What is needed is pre-evangelisation. Discourse comes later.

What all this amounts to is the need for a new, more imaginative look at Catholic public culture, above all the liturgy and the shape of our Feast Days.[10] Art and architecture, music and ritual, need to be developed that will enable us to raise up our hearts to God, truly celebrate our liberation in Christ, and forge communal bonds through public celebration. Dostoyevski perceived that, when truth is hidden by public lies, and goodness hidden from public view, then beauty – art, music, literature, and I would add liturgy, which is, or ought to be, art at its most sublime – will save the world.[11] Admittedly, beauty is constantly in danger of descending into something superficial and ephemeral, indeed narcissistic, that is, the aesthetic as an end in itself. It needs, to quote Joyce out of place, to be 'strengthened in the school of old Aquinas', subjected to the rigorous intellectual self-questioning that marks genuine theology. Beauty enjoys a certain existential primacy, but it must always be subject to the demands of truth and goodness.

The recovery of the Church's public face and voice

Since the Second Vatican Council, there has been a gradual but radical erosion of the Church's public face and voice. The public face of the Church is, in part, made up of her public institutions, many of which, like the convents and seminaries, have been closed down and sold to developers. This has happened not without a certain amount of scandal to the public at large. More seriously, many schools and hospitals have been emptied of the public witness of the nuns and brothers who founded them.[12] The greatest loss in contemporary Ireland is not the closure of convent buildings and monasteries, but the decline in numbers of believers, lay or religious, who are willing to commit themselves publicly to a life-long service of others, especially those most in need of help, and who do so out of love of God. To be a teacher or nurse was once seen primarily as a vocation; today they are increasingly seen as careers.

This development is intrinsically linked to a crisis of confidence in what we believe. Faith is a vision of life that places God at the centre, and so sees things in the perspective of eternity. It gives meaning to life, engenders hope, and expresses itself in love for others. To be able to articulate one's faith is to have achieved maturity in one's faith.[13] It gives one the confidence to enter into public debate as a citizen, a politician, or civil servant, and to seek for solutions to contemporary questions that are in harmony with one's deepest convictions as a Catholic. This is the secular voice of the Church, a subject to which I will return. But the crisis of confidence is more serious for those believers who officially represent the Church, namely priests and bishops.

Much (though not all) of the blame for the silencing of the Church's public voice has been attributed to the media, and so we must take a brief look at this charge. According to Tom Inglis, commenting on what he saw as the Irish Church's former moral monopoly, 'The media have driven a stake into the heart of the institutional Church from which it will recover, but never fully.'[14] One may contest this, but it reflects a commonly held view, even among clerics. However, it attributes an influence to the media that, it seems to me at least, seems somewhat exaggerated. The media did not so much drive a stake into the heart of the Church as give a succession of heaves to help bring down the rather porous walls of the bastion that would in time have collapsed in any case. What is incontestable is that, from the point of view of the Catholic Church, the Irish media can be described as the most hostile media in the developed world. Colleagues from abroad have commented on it. From my own limited experience of participation in public debate, it can best be compared with playing a game with the dice loaded against you. To be interviewed by an Irish journalist is more an interrogation by the thought-police, and any slip-up can be fatal. On the other hand, my experience of being interviewed by foreign journalists has been invariably positive. You are treated with respect, no matter how penetrating the questioning may be. Taking part in a discussion on, say BBC Northern Ireland, can be genuinely stimulating, not to mention civilised.

The general coverage of religious affairs in Irish newspapers is negative, at times downright nasty. Whereas national newspapers tend to engage qualified scientists or recognised literary experts to cover science and literature, they rarely employ recognised theologians to cover religious affairs. In addition, there is little interest in fairness or objectivity, above all, when issues of law and morality are at the centre of public debate. An editor of one of the national papers once admitted in a letter to me that his paper had its own clearly worked out position on what are called euphemistically 'social issues'. As a result, the best 'quality' newspapers in Ireland compare poorly with the more objective and competent coverage of ecclesiastical and theological issues in such national papers as the London *Times, Le Monde*, the *Frankfurter Allgemeine Zeitung*, or the *New York Times*. These newspapers are not particularly sympathetic to the Church,[15] but they employ theologically literate journalists and feel themselves evidently bound by codes of civility that ameliorate their own secular sympathies.

Modernity tends to be reductionist, that is, it reduces the complexity, indeed the tragedy of life, to simplistic solutions and attempts to apply these solutions to heal society's ills by various forms of social engineering. This was the case not only in the former communist countries in Eastern Europe but applies in various degrees to Western Europe.[16] This is the phenomenon one encounters in the Irish media. It has dominated Irish politics in recent debates on divorce, contraception, and abortion, and has been used to good effect by well-financed lobby groups such as the Irish branch of the International Family Planning Association with their well-worked out (amoral) strategy to promote their aims.

In response, the Church may be tempted to adopt the public-relations tactics developed by the spin-doctors. This temptation, I suggest, must be resisted. As the Second Vatican Council reminded us: 'If anyone wishes to devote himself to the ministry of God's word, let him use the ways and means proper to the Gospel, which differ in many respects from those obtaining in the earthly city' (*Gaudium et spes*, §76). What are these ways? In the first place, it is well to remember that we have at our disposal the most effective medium of all to persuade, convince, and enlighten, namely the pulpit.[17] Secondly, there are the old-fashioned ways of contrition and forgiveness. We must ask ourselves to what extent does the Church bear some responsibility for the present hostility in the media, namely in its failure to produce a theologically literate laity? Finally, we are called to repay hostility not with hostility but with forgiveness, even gentleness – though without forgetting the need to keep on the alert and be shrewd (cf. Mt 10:16). Clerics cannot withdraw from public debate, or be intimidated into silence, but those who do enter should know what to expect, and not be surprised at the fact that fairness may not be meted out to them. Did not somebody once warn his followers that they were being sent out as sheep among wolves? But one should not underestimate the hope and encouragement to others by taking an honest stand on a controversial issue, a stand that many agree with but rarely hear articulated in public. Honesty is the key. Clerics cannot be seen to be just toeing the party line. If they do not in all honesty hold something to be true, then they should say nothing, even if they are bishops. Others may only be able to say that they accept a particular ruling and will abide by it in humble obedience. That too is honest. But for anyone to engage in public debate is to be ready to take it on the chin, provided that one has used the proper means.

The primary means proper to the Gospel is, of course, to speak the truth in love, in season as well as out of season, that is, irrespective of the sound and the fury kicked up by a media whose cherished values and assumptions are thereby questioned, as questioned they must be. One of the inherited weaknesses of being a Church of the people, i.e. one with mass appeal, as was the case in Ireland up to the recent past and still is to a considerable extent, is that priests and bishops might be tempted to behave

somewhat like politicians who are always testing the waters of
public opinion before they speak.[18] Politicians fear unpopularity,
priests should not (or at least not for the wrong reasons). Such fear
is, in any case, often unfounded, as far as clerics are concerned,
since those who are most offended are not the faithful themselves
but the promoters of various brands of political correctness. In
any case, the faithful in the pews, who despite recent trials and
scandals have mostly remained just that, loyal and faithful, are
more frequently bewildered than offended, not by the way
statements by some prominent bishop or other are taken out of
context and blown up into a 'controversy', but at the silence of
clerics in general. People feel let down. By fearing unpopularity,
we make ourselves seem irrelevant.

Faith can, of course, be reduced to a sterile 'orthodoxy',
namely the repetition of pat answers or quotations from Church
documents, important, indeed crucial though such documents
may be. Or faith can be re-cycled to suit passing fashions. In either
case, faith fails to be what it should be: critical of all easy solutions
to the complexity of the human condition. More dangerous than
either of these is the tendency of popular religion – particularly
evident in the past and a constant temptation now as ever – to
become exclusively sentimental. Sentiment is, of course, essential
to religious experience. But the powerful emotions that religion
generates – sometimes to the extent of fanaticism – should not be
underestimated. And it is here, above all, that theology has its
central and indispensable role. To quote Newman, 'in religion the
imagination and affections should always be under the control of
reason', and again 'religion cannot maintain its ground at all
without theology'.[19]

The recovery of the Church's public voice means that
believers, lay and clerical, have something to say to the modern
world that only they can articulate. And this means recovering the
true meaning of catholicity, its doctrinal claims, above all the
recognition that the truths of our faith throw indispensable divine
light on the human condition, that they are truly salvific, that is,

they are healing truths. The doctrines of the Church do not put shackles on the adult mind, but rather open it up to the meaning of existence and the secrets of the human heart. The teaching of the Church is a stimulus to search for understanding, for truth. A renewal of theology is the *conditio sine qua non* for the recovery of the Church's public voice. And for that voice to be authentically Irish, it must return to the sources, including the 'holy wells' of Irish Catholic experience,[20] and be articulated in dialogue with the most significant contemporary thinkers. This is part of the personal quest for what Newman called 'complex assent', the assent of the mature Christian who can give reasons for his faith, someone who has achieved 'luminous certitude'.[21] Such a person is also able to stand on his or her own two feet – and take on the world. It means being able truly to act according to one's conscience.

The recovery of the Church's secular voice

By secular voice, I mean the quiet but firm conviction of the average Catholic, especially when engaged in public affairs, either as a citizen, a businessman, or as a public official, who is able to stand up and be counted. It has often been remarked that as a people we tend to be good fighters, soldiers, and sportsmen, physically courageous, and often full of bravado – but weak in moral courage.[22] This is nowhere more evident at present than in the political sphere, where politicians of all parties toe the party line even in measures that are difficult to reconcile with their own conscience. It is quite extraordinary that, in all the recent debates on various referenda relating to 'social issues', the number of politicians who challenged their respective party's line could be numbered on the fingers of one hand. The consensus among the parties is itself questionable, and even more questionable is the imposition of the party whip in the first instance on substantial matters affecting life and death that should be left to the individual conscience. In either case, what we have is institutionalised conformity, which is the death of genuine discussion, and which in

time robs democracy of its life-blood. In the final chapter, I will
return to this topic.

There are evident sociological or historical reasons to account
for a huge tendency in Ireland to conform. In rural areas, for
example, the very nature of small tight-knit communities induces
a certain conformity, while, in addition, lack of opportunities can
lead to dependency on whoever has power or influence (such as
the priest in earlier times) thus increasing the need to conform. In
the urban areas, the dominant moral code of middle-class
respectability created a different but no less effective atmosphere
of conformity. Finally, there was the tendency, already mentioned
above, to present the faith as something to be accepted
unquestioningly, something to which we simply had to conform.
If priests themselves are not questioning, seeking understanding
of what are in the final analysis divine mysteries revealed for the
salvation of all humanity, or if they are not engaged in debate with
the ideas that are shaping our world, then there is little incentive
for the faithful to do likewise. But there is another reason.

The validity of traditional mores has been radically questioned
in recent decades, and here the Irish Church was largely
unprepared. As already indicated above, the Irish Church was to a
great extent characterised by a spirituality shaped by such factors
as an anxious severity, the dominant Victorian Puritanism, an
enforced celibacy for much of the population – and the narrow
legalism of the prevailing form of Catholic moral theology. That
theology, which was in effect functioning as a branch of Canon
Law, had transformed moral principles into a system of legal
obligations and (often unreal) moral dilemmas.

What Christopher Dawson said at the dawn of the sexual
revolution in the 1930s in England, applies *a fortiori* to the more
recent experience of the average citizen and politician in our day.
He claimed that most citizens, though not in favour of the new
morality advocated at the time (by writers such as Havelock Ellis
and Bertrand Russell), were unable to articulate their objections
even to themselves, and so the more articulate proponents of the

new morality won the day.[23] It is however a hopeful sign that the most vocal and articulate opposition to the many proposed changes in 'social' legislation in Ireland today comes from a handful of well-educated laymen and women such as William Binchy, Patricia Casey, and Joseph McCarroll. Their power to convince and hold their own in public debate, even in the face of great hostility, rested on solid foundations: within the sphere of his or her own professional competence, each one had worked out their positions intellectually.

With regard to social issues in the wider sense, there are many other questions of a moral nature affecting modern society in Ireland beyond the range of topics that have preoccupied public debate. In the past three decades, enormous effort has been invested in creating a new Ireland of economic expansion, rocketing house prices, and a 'quality of life', measured almost exclusively in goods and services, almost unrivalled in the world today. The Celtic Tiger, despite its drawbacks and the inequality in the distribution of its benefits, is in many ways to be welcomed and affirmed as basically good; however, it is essentially fragile and not without its inherent ambiguity, such as the increasing gap between the rich and the poor, not to mention the phenomenon of consumerism, and the underlying insecurity, a feeling of dread about the possibility of the economy crashing. On the other hand, it must be admitted that, apart from the spectacular increase in the quality of the material conditions of life, our economic performance has also contributed greatly to a restoration of our sense of self-worth as a nation. Young people, in particular, display a refreshing sense of self-confidence, which they did not have some decades ago.

Other trends are less admirable. There is a growing dearth of volunteers among the voluntary societies caring for the less well off.[24] Further, the common friendly courtesies, which according to St Thomas Aquinas[25] make living together in society bearable, are vanishing from public intercourse, from our streets and public places, to be replaced by a certain aggressiveness. The sense of any real obligation to society or commitment to improve it (such as active involvement in local and national politics) has weakened. And there is little sense of direction to society, a weakened sense of purpose or common goal, that is particularly evident among politicians, who seem to be led by what the media (or the latest survey) determines is 'public opinion'.

Even the value of our membership of the European Union seems to be exclusively utilitarian. There is little commitment to, not even the vaguest interest in, the vision of a new Europe based on a common Christian culture which inspired the founding fathers of the Union, mostly Catholic, after the Second World War.[26] The result is a society drifting rudderless into an uncertain future. The dramatic increase in drunkenness, drug abuse, crime, suicide, violence even against the old and infirm in the countryside, are symptoms of a deep malaise in Irish society. After describing the escalating night-time violence on Dublin streets, youngsters travelling in hordes, the girls as violent as the boys, drunkenness and misbehaviour that would not be tolerated elsewhere, one journalist asked: Is this a wider symptom of the endemic changes in Irish society? 'Consumerism is in the process of replacing Christianity as the shaping influence on all our lives... There is a sense out there that the whole business is out of control... There is no longer any national consensus about what we want as a society, merely a bunch of politicians making it up as they go along.'[27]

The Irish Church will recover her secular voice only when we begin, clerics and laity together, to address publicly the aimless drift of modern Ireland. Rejecting the provincial mentality mentioned above, it is time unashamedly to search for genuinely Irish solutions for Irish problems (I deliberately use this much abused phrase). We have no reason to be shy about looking to our Catholic heritage for inspiration, or indeed about seeking inspiration abroad. When we look to other countries, we will find that they, too, are grappling with similar problems and so we can enter into dialogue with them and search together. But we need not slavishly imitate what others are doing, or underestimate our own ability to tackle these questions and give the lead to others. At the political level, there are obvious structural problems to be addressed, such as the creation of genuine local, participatory democratic structures perhaps along the lines formerly advocated by Tom Barrington, which have been tried and tested in other countries. But new structures alone will not solve any problems on their own.

The recovery of virtue is the sole means of eliminating some of the worst features of personal alienation that is at the root of the aimlessness that finds temporary resolution in drugs, drink and sex. Virtue appeals to people's innate dignity, challenging us to become men and women of character, valuing moral integrity and courage above all else. At the core of virtue is reverence combined with moral courage. Virtue in turn only makes sense if there is a transcendent goal in life, if God is our ultimate goal.

The recovery of the Church's divine voice

There can be no real liberation, we saw, without insight into who we are, into our dignity, and the resulting assumption of creative responsibility for ourselves and our community. Behind this, Fennell's basic affirmation, is the voice of Nietzsche, who, like Joyce, rejected the slave-mentality, which he blamed on Christianity. If the main characteristic of Irish Catholicism at the beginning of the twentieth century was angelism, namely a disdain for this world in favour of the next, then Catholics in Ireland could not feel at home in the here and how; neither could they celebrate life in the present. The result was a void at the heart of society, an inability to say: it is good to be here. It is undeniable that there is enough evidence to indicate that Irish Catholic life was not quite as bleak as that depicted by Fennell – one immediately thinks of the pattern days or the 'wakes', with their age-old, somewhat ambiguous, traditions of affirming life in the very experience of death, and the dancing, music, fun and games that marked the 'pattern' days. And yet, it seems undeniable that there was a marked change of atmosphere between the beginning and the end of the nineteenth century, in particular in urban areas.

It is well to recall in this context that, in the early part of the nineteenth century, the liturgy of the Catholic Church in Ireland, apart from the inherent beauty of the rich, dense rituals of the Roman Missal,[28] was neither totally devoid of music, nor incapable of celebrating its sacred festivals with due solemnity. Such can be gleaned from the letter (dated 14 January 1822) written by Bartholomew Keegan, a schoolmaster at Rathangan in the barony of Bargy, Co. Wexford, to a Franciscan in Rome, a fellow-Wexfordman. Keegan describes how he made the 'science of music' his chief study, conducted two choirs in the parish, and played the bassoon and 'clarionet' at Mass. He noted:

> We do have great work here on festivals. On Corpus Christi we have a procession of the Blessed Sacrament, on Palm Sunday a great procession of palm, on 15 August, our patron day, a grand solemn Mass and procession of candles. Every Sunday in Lent we sing round the Stations, and on other festivals we have a Benediction of the Blessed Sacrament, all which serve very much to excite devotion in the people.[29]

Mention should also be made of the extraordinary tradition of the singing of Christmas carols on the twelve days of Christmas in the Parish Church of Kilmore, Co. Wexford, for over three hundred years. The extant Wexford Carols, as they are known, were composed by Luke Waddinge, Bishop of Ferns, and first published in Ghent in 1684, and by Fr William Devereux, c. 1730, but the tradition itself probably predates the Reformation. 'Manuscript copies of these carols... are still being transcribed in Kilmore, a parish that has kept up the singing of the carols in Devereux's *Garland* to the present day. Formerly they were sung in Piercestown, Ballymore, Mayglass, Lady's Island, Tacumshane and Rathangan, but they died out in these parishes due to the neglect of priests who preferred the formality, the chiasmi and the dogmatism of hymnody. The religion of the heart has lost out to what Yeats called the dead hand of decorum.'[30]

After the 'language cataclysm' (de Fréine) of the nineteenth century, as we saw, Irish Catholics, especially in the urban areas, tended to become more and more smothered by 'decorum' and alienated from the here and now. But things have changed utterly. The end of the twentieth century witnessed a massive reversal of the former trend. Indeed, modern Ireland has scant regard for decorum and is almost frantically caught up in the celebration of the here and how, with little thought for the hereafter. Apart from the booming glitzy modern/traditional lounge bars and discos filled to the brim, the crowded restaurants and wine bars, there has also been a remarkable renaissance in the arts, music, poetry, literature, and dance – though faith rarely seems to have been a direct source of inspiration in any of these art forms.[31] Following the example of Joyce in literature and Francis Bacon in art, the Irish Catholic experience of the past is often quarried as a source of negative inspiration. On the other hand, secular feasts of every kind have proliferated,[32] including street festivals, summer schools, *fleadhanna ceoil*, and parties of all kinds. These have certainly added colour to everyday life and provided a certain amount of communal cohesion. But, welcome though they are, they are not the answer; they provide no real liberation, only a substitute, and in many cases only provide entertainment as a form of escapism. Often, the one common denominator in them all is drink. When the alcoholic and other substance-induced haze lifts, the void is still there.

Nietzsche once said that in order to celebrate one has to be able to say Yes to all that is, one must be able to affirm the world as it is, namely oneself and one's place in the world. Since there is much in the world and in ourselves that cannot simply be affirmed unconditionally, we need to experience that which restores the goodness of being. This is the mystery of God's redemptive presence in word and sacrament, as in hearing the words 'The

Body of Christ', or 'I absolve you'. The restoration of goodness is a ritual sharing in the sacrifice of the Lamb who takes away the sins of the world and makes communion with God and with each other possible at the deepest level imaginable. The Sunday Mass is the weekly ritual of re-creation, of being able to say, Yes, it is good to be here. And so its liturgical expression, its embodiment in ritual, music and art, must express something of that joy, which is an anticipation of the future joy of paradise.[33]

The Church's divine voice finds its primary expression in joyful worship and communal celebration. 'The very purpose of the Church is to give us the experience of festivity.'[34] In the first place, such celebration must be the expression of what might be called a conscious or adult faith, one that has been theologically and spiritually nourished. This demands a systematic instruction in the theological meaning of the sacraments, including the Mass, and this is part of the new 'evangelisation' called for by the Pope. Over and above this catechesis, special attention needs to be given to the beauty of every celebration of the sacraments, a celebration that, as already mentioned, is not confined to within the walls of the church. But within those walls, genuine liturgical celebration calls for a huge investment in music, art, and architecture, so that something beautiful for God can lift up the hearts of all. It calls above all for a resolute rejection of all utilitarianism when it comes to church buildings and the surrounding space. There are, indeed, encouraging signs that this renewal is already under way, especially in the field of Irish sacred music. The object of any liturgical renewal was articulated by St Paul when the Church was still in its infancy. Your communal worship must be such, he wrote to the Corinthians, that when the unbeliever enters, the secrets of his heart will be disclosed 'and that person will bow down before God and worship him, declaring, "God is really among you"' (1 Cor 14:25).

The reform of the liturgy after the Council was carried out according to the letter but not always according to the spirit. It is imperative that we recover the spirit, including a rich theology of liturgy.[35] But there is also a need to become aware again of the importance of ritual (rubrics), namely the regular performance of predetermined small gestures and words of infinite significance, and the rhythm of ritual movement, which is not dependent on the whim of the celebrant. The new, reformed liturgy reduced rubrics to a minimum, in order to recover the dense meaning of each gesture. In many ways, this has been an enrichment, and where the celebrant is aware of such meaning, the result can be a profound spiritual experience. But the reduction of the rubrics was never intended to remain a bare skeleton. The minimalist legalistic mentality, which, it seems to me, dominated and still dominates liturgical celebration in Ireland, has even dispensed with many of the rubrics as not being absolutely essential or strictly 'obligatory', for example the position of hands, blessings, kneeling, pause, the use of vestments of a certain kind and colour, and so on. Indeed, ritual movement has been effectively reduced to standing at the ambo or altar or sitting on a chair. To make up for the present sterility of so much liturgical celebration, all kinds of secondary elements have been introduced as substitutes. These include extended offertory processions (often bearing the most ridiculous 'offerings'), transforming the sanctuary into a garden, children's Masses of a purely didactic character, replete with movement of a non-ritual nature, posters made by the children, and even dance, etc. These, it could be said, are commendable to the extent that they are attempts to overcome the banality of the present 'ritual' and bring a certain colour into the churches, now more often shorn of their original beauty and integrity. But we have to ask whether or not they are perhaps more a distraction from the solemnity and real beauty of the liturgy – even in the case of children's Masses?[36] Do they simply entertain, or do they promote a true sense of the *sursum corda*?

Liturgy is where we encounter God, the source of our joy, who takes the initiative to come to us and transform us, both personally and communally, in the encounter. It is the place where we experience the Church transcending herself, the place 'where the

Lord himself enters and makes the Church his house and thereby makes us his siblings'.[37] Liturgy is not our doing, something we make ourselves, but is something given – it is of God, of apostolic origin, having grown in the course of time in the faith.[38] Awareness of this can only elicit an attitude of profound reverence and awe on the part of everyone who participates in the liturgy, but above all the priest and those who serve at the altar, who are neither talk-show hosts or drama producers but 'stewards entrusted with the mysteries of God' (1 Cor 4:1).

The recovery of the Irish spirit of celebration

The ritual of the Mass is not confined to what happens within the walls of the church. It incorporates both the preparation before Mass and the overflow into everyday life after Mass. The spiritual tradition of the Irish Church, even during times of persecution and economic hardship, bears witness to this truth. It produced prayers of exceptional beauty and theological depth to help the faithful prepare for Mass and enable the grace of the Mass to overflow into the details of everyday life.[39] The stress on fulfilling one's obligation – something positive in itself, as it attests to a basic conviction and seriousness – can however lead to what seems to be little more than a dashing in and out of church. Again, most pastors tend not to judge this apparently perfunctory attendance too harshly. They know it is as much as many a harried mother or father may on occasion be able to achieve. But generally, the Sunday Mass should be something special, especially for the young family, while the day itself should be a time to leave aside the sphere of the profane, what is dominated by utility, a time simply 'to be', a time for genuine leisure, which is the re-creation of the soul. And this includes sport.

Remote preparation – as called for by the much reduced eucharistic fast – is a way of preparing ourselves exteriorly and interiorly for the most sublime of all events, our encounter with Christ in the Sacrament. While visiting the Church in China a few years ago, many of us were struck by the way the faithful prepared for Mass by coming to the Church about thirty minutes before the Mass, each one praying out loud.[40] 'Dressing up in one's Sunday best' used to be an Irish tradition, as it still is in other countries (for example Switzerland, the Philippines or the Caribbean, to take widely different cultures). 'To dress up in one's Sunday best' is, of course, an echo of a primal ritual gesture found in all cultures and religions. The general experience of the Mass itself should be that of having a heartfelt sense of gratitude for all that has been, all that is, and all that will be. It should, on occasion at least, be a taste of the sublime beauty of God. But even devoid of rich music or art, the sober simplicity of the new Roman rite has its own inherent beauty – when liberated from the arbitrariness of the celebrant who wants to experiment with the sacred liturgical text. However, it needs to be said in the humble spirit of Ps 118 (119): 'Accept, Lord, the homage of my lips.' The very simplicity of the spoken word reveres the incomprehensible mystery it effects.[41]

It may seem superfluous to mention such apparently trivial things as the need for clean altar linen, chalices of artistic merit, as well as missals, lectionaries, and sacred vestments that are truly worthy of the divine service. In recent times, these sacred instruments and cloths tend to be made of cheap materials, and are often in poor condition, torn, unwashed. In a word, they are not exactly edifying. While the modern world is rediscovering the magic of candles, the Irish Church has reduced them to a minimum (usually of inferior quality, even imitation candles or a flickering electric light instead of a sanctuary lamp). The liturgy is about great events taking place by means of small gestures, where everything used takes on infinite significance. Careful attention to the details (linen, candles, vestments, etc.) expresses the celebrant's awareness of the great mysteries for which he is responsible and conveys to others present something of the awesome presence in the Sacrament. Despite his poverty and his care for the poor (such as the orphanage he ran), the Curé d'Ars procured the richest of vestments and most elaborate sacred vessels he could find in the city of Lyons for his humble, rural parish church.

Above all, more care and attention needs to be given to the distinct – and audible – articulation of the words of the ritual, in particular, but not only, the Word of God and the Canon of the Mass, while respecting the instructions regarding certain prayers (usually for the priest himself) which ought to be inaudible, and those moments when compete silence is called for, as after Communion.

The recovery of the emotional and bodily dimensions of religion
Part of the dissatisfaction with the new liturgy may be due to the fact that the reform also coincided with (or caused) the effective undermining of the whole network of devotions that catered for a greater part of people's religious affective needs – the confraternities, sodalities, May devotions, Solemn Benediction, novenas, parish missions, etc. Some of these were in many ways imported pieties, second-hand garments with which a culturally impoverished Church (deprived of its mediaeval art and the language of its ancient spirituality), but newly emerged from the underground, decked herself, especially in the cities. They also tended to be sentimental, verging towards the effeminate, although some could be aggressive enough, like the men's parish missions and the confraternity in Limerick. But they did cater for genuine religious emotional and social needs.

However we may judge them now, in their day the imported devotions fulfilled a number of important roles, not all of them religious. Thus, for example, they provided many a single person, especially single women, otherwise isolated from much of the social life that was dominated by marriage and the family, with a means of forging an independent identity, achieving a broader socialisation, and providing some form of celebration. Above all, they provided a sense of direction in life. Isolated devotional practices have survived, such as novenas, and indeed some still attract large followings on occasion. But they are no longer universal. The parish mission seems to have lost its 'edge' and its sense of purpose. Today, there are prayer groups and Bible study groups in almost every parish. These may, in time, form the basis for new popular devotions, though at present they exist, as it were, in the underground, as small 'house churches'; and perhaps that is as it should be. Indeed, some have already borne fruit in terms of vocations and in terms of new lay movements still in their infancy.[42] Nonetheless, there is an urgent need to create new forms of public devotions of a more universal nature – especially those geared to young men in particular, where they could experience the Church addressing their specific questions, offering them new challenges, and restoring their sense of direction and hope. The liturgical renewal opened up the possibility of creating para-liturgies for special occasions, that is, services outside the strict liturgical celebration of the sacrament, made up of music, symbolic movement, and a liturgy of the Word, such as a ceremony of light on the evening of All Souls Day to commemorate parishioners who died the previous year (each family lighting a candle for their departed loved ones), or a ceremony of welcome around the feast of the Epiphany for the newcomers to the parish who had newly taken up residence. These are two I happen to know about; no doubt there are many more. This is an area rich with promise. It might help cater for some of the deeply human and emotional needs that can only be addressed by collective ritual. And there is an urgent need, as Newman insists, for a theological underpinning of all such devotions and celebrations. People's hearts *and minds* need to be touched.

For men, especially in rural areas, the more sentimental tendencies of traditional Irish Catholicism were probably to a great extent offset by the revival of Gaelic games in the latter half of the nineteenth century, which so profoundly influenced Irish culture and politics.[43] The Church's parish system provided, and still provides, the basic structure of the Gaelic Athletic Association (GAA), so that, whatever reservations the clergy might initially have had about Fenian nationalist influence on the incipient athletic movement,[44] it evidently did not adversely affect the close identity that grew up between the GAA and the Catholic Church. Since sport, which in many ways is a modern substitute for the ancient initiation rites into masculinity, can easily become a religion,[45] it was therefore also fortuitous that the GAA was incorporated into parish life, with the result that (probably without any conscious reflection) the powerful, quasi-religious practice that is sport was (once again) 'christianised'. It is thus not surprising that from its ranks came its finest priests,[46] to such an extent that it was no exaggeration to say that, in rural areas at least, the Irish Catholic Church was the GAA at prayer. One of its greatest trophies is, significantly, a replica of the Ardagh Chalice.

Celebrating feasts – recovery of the spirit of the Pattern days
Catholic celebration is not limited to the chapel, but overflows into the everyday world of the market-place and the fairground, both of which were situated immediately in the square outside the doors of the cathedral and parish churches in mediaeval times, as can be seen in most continental cities to this day. The theological basis for parish celebrations of a non-liturgical kind is to be found in the imperative arising from the New Testament notion of Christian brotherhood as the most basic meaning of our new life in Christ and so of the Church. Commenting on the practice of the early Church to combine the Eucharist with an 'agape-meal' that gave concrete form to Christian brotherhood, one scripture scholar pointed out that, since such cannot be replicated in present circumstances, 'the need still remains for parishes to develop appropriate forms of community life outside the liturgy in order to supplement the liturgical gathering and make possible direct brotherly contact.'[47] Evidently these forms will vary according to circumstances, but one general point remains valid, Cardinal Ratzinger says,

> ...inasmuch as brotherhood in the parish is, as it were, divided up among different societies or organizations, it is necessary to keep bringing people together in larger groups in order to

emphasise their relationship to the greater unity of the parish. The individual organization is justified only insofar as it serves the brotherhood of the whole community. This aim of making the parish community a true brotherhood ought to be taken very seriously. Today a trade union or a [political Party] can exist as a live and fraternal community, and so the actual experience of brotherhood for all the Christian members of a parish community can and, therefore, should become a primary goal. It would be a universal experience which transcended all barriers, of course, for in every parish there are men of different professions and often of different languages and nationalities. It is this universality which gives the parish a superior position to an organization based on any other community of interests.[48]

Any such effort at parish gatherings or celebrations will demand both time (in preparation) and the availability of the appropriate space. Leaving aside the question of a suitable parish hall for the moment, more reflection may be needed on the way the space around the cathedral or parish church is designed and used. One peculiarity of Irish churches (Catholic and Protestant) is the way they are usually surrounded by high walls and iron gates. With regard to Catholic churches, this may be due to the historical fact of their origin as (non-conformist) chapels barely tolerated by the Establishment, and so essentially 'private' prayer halls, while the walls around the Protestant churches may have expressed their factual alienation from the majority of the public despite their legal status as the State Church. Be that as it may, such churches tend thereby to be reduced to private buildings, to the detriment of their character as public buildings. By way of contrast, the great cathedrals and churches of Europe are usually the main public buildings in the cities and towns – very often in competition with the city or town hall for prestige and representational significance. And they simply stand there rising up majestically in the square, often the market place, pointing to the beyond and drawing the public's attention to God's presence in their daily lives of business and pleasure.

Though some will argue that the high walls and gates are still needed in our increasingly lawless society, perhaps the time has come to remove them altogether and give some consideration to a more appropriate design for whatever space is left around the church. Many churches have space for the creation of a plaza in front of the main entrance, possibly a tree-lined square decorated with gardens and seats, where, at least in summer, people are invited to linger and enjoy each other's company – not simply large car parks, as is the case today.[49] Such a space would also be the ideal location for those 'overflow' celebrations which are so essential to building up the community spirit, including the tradition of harvest thanksgiving[50] still celebrated in rural areas in Catholic Europe at the end of the harvest but which in Ireland and Britain are associated exclusively with our Protestant brethren. (As mentioned earlier, the Church of Ireland in particular, has preserved a considerable amount of the pre-Reformation Catholic culture, including parish fêtes, and we should have the humility to learn from them.) Such 'overflow' celebrations could on occasion be developed into full-scale festivals to celebrate the great feasts, like Easter and Christmas, or the feast-day of the local church or patron (Pattern Day), occasions such as First Communion and Confirmation, and, in particular, weddings, ordinations or First Mass.[51] And it is here that music and dance could find their place as part of the 'overflow' liturgy. Sport too should regain the central role in Church-holiday celebrations it once had in Ireland.[52]

Which brings us to the parish hall, maybe the only realistic location for such parish gatherings, given the Irish weather, unless, that is, a parish can afford marquees. Unfortunately many parish halls tend to be dismally functional and unattractive, even perhaps situated in some communal no-man's-land – and very much out of touch with modern Ireland's new sense of design and colour. Greater care needs to be given to their architectural design and interior décor, as well as their location in an attractive landscape that may include some space for playing fields. Such factors, it seems to me, need to be taken into consideration, in particular, in designing churches and parish halls in new residential estates.

The preparation for parish or cathedral festivals would demand a considerable amount of planning and creative involvement on the part of the local community, including the schools. Even preparation itself helps to create community.

Pilgrimage, Irish style

One ancient practice that was revived with astonishing success during the Great Jubilee was the pilgrimage on foot to some local shrine or holy well. These traditions are not simply Celtic but Catholic, that is, universal, and are more honoured in continental Europe and Latin America than here at home. At many of the ancient places of pilgrimage associated with a local saint, the 'Pattern Days' were celebrated in former times. They had their origins in the mediaeval celebrations of the local patron saint on their feast-day, as still found today in most Catholic countries throughout the world. By the seventeenth century, it is claimed, superstitions had strongly marked the 'patterns'.[53] 'The Church authorities had finally set their face against them in the 1780s; the priests ceased to attend, and in many cases the religious element was altogether forgotten.'[54] Further, they tended to degenerate into rowdy social occasions marked by drunkenness, debauchery, and fights, which the Catholic bishops vigorously opposed during the following centuries, until they went into decline by the end of the nineteenth century,[55] though they never completely died out. According to Seán de Fréine, the decline of the Irish language and the simultaneous suppression of the many social occasions, such as pilgrimages, fairs, gatherings and traditional customs, were important factors in the creation of a new spirit of materialism that has left is mark on nineteenth- and twentieth-century Ireland. 'Life became narrower, more calculating.'[56] He has a point.

The unexpectedly high participation in the pilgrimages to the traditional holy places during the Jubilee Year 2000 – in particular on the national day of pilgrimage – astonished everyone, not least the clergy. It was a reminder of how deeply embedded these holy places are in the Irish folk memory.[57] One might also ask: to what extent is the negative image of the patterns justified, which image, as we just saw, tends to be confirmed by historians? There is no doubt that these practices had become tainted by excess revelry and superstition, but then, as the late Donal Kerr pointed out, similar problems are faced by the Church in Latin America with the local *fiesta*,[58] but which, to the best of my knowledge, did not produce any attempt to forbid them outright. The excesses associated with the Pattern Days, and condemned by clergy in the eighteenth and nineteenth centuries, might well be attributed to the social conditions of the day in the less developed parts of rural Ireland: poverty and deprivation, lack of education, and the absence of other opportunities to socialise. The Pattern Days were their only vent, as it were. Lack of instruction coupled with the quasi-underground existence of the Church during the Penal times would in any case have inevitably led to the re-emergence in their original state of the more pagan elements that may indeed, in some instances at least, have been the original source of such practices,[59] which since the dawn of salvation history had been disciplined and transformed by the experience of faith.[60]

The fact is that the Catholic Church in the nineteenth century was under pressure from the 'New Reformation' types like the Reverend Caesar Otway.[61] Otway persuaded the novelist William Carleton to hold up 'to the light the superstitions of the people as he had seen them: the superstitions of pilgrimage and priesthood and prophecies, ... voteens and holy wells'.[62] Under the influence of Otway, Carleton saw superstition where he had previously seen austere beauty and even more austere piety among a motley band of pilgrims who would delight a Catholic Chaucer but not a self-righteous puritan.[63] The clergy, anxious to disprove the 'Roman' Church's supposed laxity towards superstition, could hardly condone what had on occasion deteriorated without doubt into superstition.[64] But it is more likely that the rigorous moral, not to say puritan, streak in Irish Catholicism of that time was primarily responsible for the opposition of the clergy to the celebration of 'pattern days' or similar local feasts – and, unwittingly, responsible for the suppression of what was good in them?[65]

Not all patterns were debauched. This can be gleaned from the way, at the time of the Great Famine, a Kerry woman consoled herself on the death of her twin boys by the thought that in heaven they would talk about the excitement of the regatta at the Pattern.[66] It must have been innocent fun. After the nightly vigil at St Brigid's Well between Liscannor and the Cliffs of Moher, Co. Clare, '[m]ost of the congregation then repaired to the beach at Lahinch three miles away for a day of races and other sports on the strand, ending with dancing, music and merriment'.[67] Patrick Kavanagh's description of a pilgrimage to Lady Well he once made as a boy on the Feast of the Assumption is instructive. The Pattern, as he describes it, is not without its superstitious element, but it is above all marked by unaffected piety mixed with humour, good spirits, wit, and a bit of 'divilment'.[68] He notes:

> There were no priests or monks or any official religious there. The priests didn't like the Well and tried to discourage the pilgrimages. They said it was a pagan well from which the old Fianians drank in the savage heroic days. The peasant folk didn't mind the priests. They believed that Saint Brigid washed her feet in it, and not Finn Mac Coole.[69]

Just as confession issues in the joy of absolution, penance, which is of the essence of pilgrimage, necessarily issues in joyful celebration, as in the feast given by the Father on the return of the Prodigal Son.[70] Music and dance are essential components of such feasts (see Lk 15:25!), as can still be found in such Catholic countries as Poland and Slovakia with their colourful folk-dancing on celebratory occasions. This too was part of the more ancient Irish tradition, it seems.[71] Carleton observed how the 'preternaturally-looking' penitent countenances of worshippers at their midnight celebrations[72] were transformed into loud laughter and gabble; the penitents on bare knees would rise up to dance 'with ecstatic vehemence to the music of the bagpipe or the fiddle'.[73] And well they might.

The recovery of the contemplative dimension of Irish Christianity

Finally, the recovery of the Church's divine voice will only be complete with the reform and restoration of religious life or, to give it its more apt description, consecrated life in all its fullness. The Second Vatican Council, in a text already mentioned (*Gaudium et spes*, 38), recalls that the Spirit calls everyone 'to dedicate themselves to the earthly service of men and in this way to prepare for the kingdom of heaven'. That is the vocation of all the faithful. But before this statement, it affirmed that 'some [people] testify to mankind's yearning for its heavenly home and keep the awareness of it vividly before men's minds'. This is the primary purpose of the consecrated life.

In Ireland over the past two centuries, most religious orders were engaged in some form of apostolic work, or, as they are called today, active ministries, such as teaching, nursing, or missionary activities abroad. There was always a core of strict contemplatives, men and women, and indeed most active orders (especially of women) had, before the Council, evolved into semi-contemplative orders with strict enclosure. The initial implementation of the decrees of the Council by the active congregations resulted in the gradual removal of the contemplative dimension almost entirely. Greater emphasis was given to the active or 'pastoral' dimension. Members of religious congregations became more politically active in the world, taking up various causes. Many moved out of their large convents and 'inserted' themselves as small communities into deprived neighbourhoods as an expression of their 'option for the poor'. What used to be the Conference of Major Religious Superiors is now primarily renowned for the public statements issued by its

Justice and Peace Desk before and after the Budget. But, as we saw above, vocations have almost dried up. Good and necessary though these social concerns are, one may well ask: should they be the main focus of attention for those consecrated by vows to the religious life? Or should men and women religious perhaps be more concerned with testifying to 'mankind's yearning for its heavenly home', as the Council put it?

Down through the centuries, beginning with St Basil in Cappadocia, Asia Minor, the monasteries were not only the great providers of alms for the poor and agents of social change. They were also and primarily the wellsprings of culture – of the cultivation of the land as well as culture in the sense of art, architecture, and music. And the source of both cultures, spiritual and material, was divine worship, or cult in the strict sense of the term. According to the Council, the primary significance of consecrated life is to keep 'the awareness [of the transcendent dimension of life on earth] vividly before men's minds'. In the monasteries, the Church developed its sacred music and art, the appropriate means needed to sing the divine praises and so experience that *sursum corda* mentioned above that we so desperately need. Ireland's golden age in art is entirely the product of the monasteries. Should the various Orders recover their contemplative dimension, should their magnificent churches in the cities once again become centres of a renewed worship, a liturgy that is truly sublime in every sense, should their houses become once again centres of scholarly theological reflection and research, as well as sacred art and music, then the Church in Ireland will have fully recovered her divine voice. And, indeed, the signs are that this is already under way.[74]

Whatever about its much vaunted (and often exaggerated) weaknesses, Counter-reformation traditional Irish Catholicism did contain a divine spark that was never extinguished, that was hidden to all but a few, that frequently flared up into heroic virtue at home and abroad, that in turn enkindled numerous fires of divine faith, hope, and love in many parts of the world. It is still

there. We are not, as a nation, the Chosen People. But as Irish
Catholics we are part of the new chosen people that is the Church
universal, and as Irish citizens with our own unique history,
culture, and experience, we have at various times in the past
offered something unique to the rest of the Church. We still have
it to offer. The Irish Catholic experience was and remains part of
God's providence for humanity, even though – to quote a
colleague – nature at times seems to have triumphed over grace.

APPENDIX I:
ON PENANCE

Penance and austerity are the specific characteristic of our principal pilgrimages, associated above all with Lough Derg and Croagh Patrick. Both characteristics are probably rooted in pre-Christian religious (and political) practices of fasting.[75] As is well known, Lough Derg became famous throughout Europe,[76] attracting pilgrims from as far as Hungary, and giving rise to fabulous stories and visions, one of which probably served as a source of inspiration for Dante's *Divine Comedy*. What is quite remarkable is that these early mediaeval, Irish Christian practices survived the almost total destruction of the public face of the Catholic Church from the seventeenth to the early nineteenth centuries. And when Knock emerged as a new place of pilgrimage at the end of the nineteenth century, it too took on a strong penitential aspect.

Penance is the means of restoring our at-oneness with God and his creatures. It is also a way of uniting ourselves with Christ: 'Suffering with the gentle Christ who suffered for us is integral to the tradition.'[77] Asceticism hurts. Penance humiliates. It cauterises in order to heal. But it is not the last word. That is peace, born of forgiveness, inner healing, and restored hope. And they too need to be celebrated. Is there sufficient provision in our penitential pilgrimages for such communal celebrations of the joy that arises from forgiveness received?

Whatever the answer to that question, the Irish tradition of penance offers us a quintessentially, though not exclusively, Irish Catholic way to confront the recent scandals that have rocked the Church in Ireland, namely through public penance. Solzhenitsyn has written convincingly of the need for public penance in order to purify a nation, to enable it to face up to the sins of its past and so make a new start to renew its spiritual life.[78] Until public penance is made for clerical sins (and not just sins of a sexual nature) committed in the past – such as an annual penitential rite in every cathedral at the beginning of Lent devoted precisely to this act of communal contrition – the divine voice of the Church cannot but sound hollow.

4

STRUCTURES FOR A NEW MILLENNIUM

Where there is no vision, the people get out of hand.
PROV 29:18 (JB)

If you should consider what [the bishop] is in himself,
he is a human being. But by giving him extra honour,
you, as it were, make up for his shortcomings.[1]
ST AUGUSTINE

The great achievement of the Synod of Kells in 1152 'was the establishment of a diocesan system that with minor changes has lasted to the present day'.[2] Even disregarding the upheaval of the past fifty years, it is an understatement to say that Ireland itself has seen considerable change over the past eight and a half centuries! The persistence of the diocesan system is extraordinary in more than one sense of the term. The system was based on the then existing civil territorial divisions – petty kingdoms or, perhaps more accurately, tribal territories – as first outlined by the Synod of Rathbreasail (1111).[3] The primitive tribal underpinning of the diocesan system should not be underestimated. It is a primal feeling of loyalty to place and to one's own people, with the bishop, as the local *taoiseach* (leader), representing both place and people. However, the present ethos of the actual shape of diocesan system is possibly more recent, the product of the reforms introduced by the Synod of Thurles (1850).

The growing centralisation of the Church in Ireland under Cardinal Cullen,[4] to whom the modern identification of Irish and Catholic was axiomatic, served to strengthen the hand of the bishop within the diocese. The Synod of Thurles deprived parish priests of the right to appoint curates and placed it at the discretion of the bishop. Further, according to Corish, for perfectly valid reasons the Synod permitted the bishop to proceed administratively against delinquent clergy and so bypass the general law of the Church that regulated such matters by way of ecclesiastical tribunals.[5] These alone would have ensured the concentration of power in one man, the local bishop, though at the time it may not have seemed in any way strange. It was, in fact, in line with that movement towards centralised administrative control which is one of the early manifestations of modernity. Its ecclesiastical form was ultramontanism.

In the nineteenth century, ultramontanism was the 'spirit of the times'. It has been described as 'a tendency in the RC Church which favours the centralization of authority and influence in the papal Curia, as opposed to national or diocesan independence'.[6] But this tendency was also reflected in the inner diocesan centralisation focused on the bishop, while the life of the modern priest of the nineteenth century and beyond 'was to centre on his church, the focus of sacramental life'. The priest himself was 'a man apart, marked out by his black or dark dress and Roman collar, prayerful, devoted, carefully nourishing his necessary learning.'[7] The parish priest in turn held all the strings of power within his parish, buttressed by the fact that he also became manager of the National School after the introduction of the system in 1831.

The new structures produced a strong, well-organised Church led mostly by a highly motivated and disciplined clergy under a strong centralised authority structure. Though their numbers increased during the nineteenth century, the role of the regular clergy tended to be auxiliary to the diocesan and parochial structure, with a strong emphasis on the apostolate of the parish mission given by such newcomers as the Vincentians, Jesuits, Passionists, and Redemptorists.[8] Most newly founded Irish congregations of sisters and brothers were dedicated to the educational and health apostolates, and were locally based. The new religious congregations tended to be organised along diocesan lines and so became absorbed into the diocese – under the control of the bishop. It was a most impressive achievement. It produced the extraordinary phenomenon of perhaps the most vibrant local Church within the whole Catholic Church throughout the world in the first half of the twentieth century, whose influence was universal through her emigrants and her missionaries in almost every country.

Analysis

Today the type of Church shaped by Cullen is criticised for its 'excessive institutionalisation'.[9] 'The supreme age of institutionalisation', it is claimed, 'dates roughly from the time of Pope Pius IX to that of Pius XII (*c.* 1850-1950), and that coincides exactly with the modern reorganisation and institutionalisation of the Church in Ireland.'[10] I wonder. Perhaps it would be more accurate to say that it was the great period of *centralisation*, that is, of a particular *kind* of institution characterised by its tendency to centralise all authority in one figure of authority: pope, bishop, parish priest – with a parallel tendency to increased 'infallibility', the lower one's position in the hierarchy! Those not reckoned part of the hierarchy – curates, regular clergy, religious sisters and brothers, and laity (again in a decreasing significance) – had no voice. They still have very little.

The Second Vatican Council tended to give its primary attention to the role of the bishop and the newly recovered diaconate (something the Irish Church has just begun to implement), but gave comparatively little attention to a theology

of the priesthood, despite promulgating a decree on the subject.
The Council, in other words, gave even greater theological
prominence to the role of the bishop than heretofore.

However, the new significance given to episcopal conferences
in the wake of the Council seems to have had the unintended
effect, at least in Ireland, of undermining the role of the individual
bishop in public discussion, at a time when people are suspicious
of any corporate body and search in vain for a human face, a
recognisable voice. The individual bishop now tends to become
absorbed into the collective and to lose his individual public voice.
The need for consensus among such a large body as the Irish
Bishops' Conference tends to produce (at times ambiguous)
statements that are increasingly treated with indifference, if not a
certain scepticism, as are most documents produced by a faceless
bureaucracy. They lack the authority of personal conviction
expressed by a familiar face holding high office – and speaking out
of responsibility for that sacred office, not just to grab the
headlines.

The institutionalisation of religious life
Within religious orders, inner-religious developments over the
past thirty years have been marked by different but related
tendencies. These included the transformation of 'superiors'[11] into
administrators, and the restructuring of the Conference of Major
Religious Superiors, now known as the Conference of Religious
Orders of Ireland,[12] into what seems to be a parallel episcopal
conference, including the setting up of 'desks' to co-ordinate
various tasks, ministries or apostolates. The diocesan structure of
various Irish-founded congregations has tended to be replaced by
a national (and international) structure, with the accompanying
tendency to concentrate authority on a newly established central
authority, a superior-general or provincial and their councils (or
'leadership teams'). There is much to be said in favour of these
developments, which, by the way, are not exclusive to Ireland. But
they also represent an increased institutionalisation of the Church

– which is not to decry them, since in principle no human organisation can operate without some institutional structure. The paradox is that the conscious effort within religious orders (especially of women) to try to abolish all figures of authority, now seen increasingly as one of the last vestiges of patriarchy, is accompanied by even greater institutionalism – and endless meetings. Recent experiments, such as collective responsibility (without any elected or designated superior), soon made it clear that some authoritative figure within the community was needed after all. In response, some religious congregations – more precisely their central 'leadership team' – embarked on another experiment, namely to place the newly appointed 'superior' or 'facilitator' in a house or community other than the one she is supposed to 'lead'! This is called 'remote control' by the more perceptive Sisters who have to endure such experiments.

These developments – many of which were inevitable, some of which are positive, indeed welcome – have nonetheless produced a more 'institutionalised' Church than the so-called 'excessive institutionalism' of the previous century. Bureaucracy has increased, as has the amount of time spent on commissions and committees – and all of this at a time of falling vocations and ageing membership. The impression I get is that the new excessive institutionalism has engendered a serious degree of, if not alienation among religious who are not superiors, then at least indifference towards these great but anonymous bodies to which it is difficult to relate. Communication is often reduced to impersonal newsletters or the like. But who ever reads the numerous newsletters and diverse documents that are produced by various commissions and assemblies, often at considerable cost?

While conceding that all this activity has also brought important benefits, one may ask, if this is what consecrated or religious life is supposed to be about. Is it just another form of activism to hide a deeper crisis of identity? The tradition of religious life within the Church is by its very nature prophetic and, in a sense, 'outside' the establishment. The many religious orders with their diverse traditions, spiritualities, and ministries, are the source of genuine pluralism in the Church. But the new institutionalism tends to make all conform to a common pattern (as in the case of the use of strangers as facilitators to 'guide' the decision-making within congregations).

It is evident that each religious congregation must have its own structure of authority and decision-making. Once (and, to some extent, still) the responsibility was invested in someone known personally to each member, who was elected by the community, and lived within the same community. But now it can happen that decisions affecting communities and the lives of individual religious are made by managerial-type boards (sometimes including total outsiders as experts or advisers). The decisions are those of the quasi-anonymous 'leadership team' – and are often the cause of considerable personal suffering to the individuals affected. Anonymous decision-making, whether within religious congregations or within the bishops' conference, though sometimes necessary, can often be a mask behind which moral weakness and lack of real leadership take refuge. Demoralisation is the result. It is time to change.

Proposed structural changes at the diocesan level

Even those who criticise the so-called 'excessive institutionalisation' of the Church admit that some form of institution is necessary. The question is which? Perhaps we could avoid misunderstanding, if, instead of the term 'institution', we used the term 'structure'. No community, no corporate body, can operate without certain structures to facilitate comprehensive and responsible decision-making. These structures are determined by the nature of the enterprise or the community. They exist, in the first instance, to enable that collective enterprise to achieve its goal, which, in the case of the Church is to carry out the mission entrusted to it by Jesus Christ. Central to that mission is the (human and eternal) flourishing of the Church's members, including those who have dedicated their lives to fostering that mission and the transformation of society in harmony with God's plan for humanity. It must suffice to say that its inner structure is sacramental in nature, one that is set in a complexity of human relations, which in turn calls for secondary structures, such as the diocese, parish, lay associations, and, in their own special place apart, religious orders. But the basic 'secondary structure' is the diocesan one, rooted as it is in the primary (or sacramental structure) of the Church's apostolic nature.

There is something anomalous about a secondary structure that was devised almost a thousand years ago and is still in place, namely the Irish diocesan system based on civil territorial entities that no longer exist – or rather only exist as tribal loyalties felt mostly among the governing Brahmin class, the clerics. The centralisation of the diocesan structure in the nineteenth century increased that sense of diocesan identity. But it was the system of diocesan colleges – boarding schools serving the function of the minor seminaries intended by the Council of Trent – which cemented the individual priest's strong sense of loyalty to his diocese. In addition, most Irish dioceses are tiny by any standard. These factors create their own serious problems for the mission of the Church, namely 'the question of clerical cliques and dynasties within dioceses'[13] that once threatened the reform of the Church championed by Cardinal Cullen in the nineteenth century. His way out of this dilemma was to use his influence in Rome to appoint 'successful administrators, college professors, or members of religious congregations'.[14] This might not be an option today for various reasons, some good, others less so.

The process of consultation among the clergy of the diocese (or at least some of them) before the nomination of a bishop is evidently something to be welcomed, when one considers the central, not to say centralised, role of the bishop in the diocese. However, the way consultation is carried out in practice has not always inspired confidence in the procedure. Blame may not necessarily be laid at the door of those responsible for such a procedure. This may be due to false expectations with regard to what 'consultation' is supposed to mean. Other complications arise from the fact that the smaller the diocese, the fewer are the number of suitable candidates. Growing demoralisation, coupled with the general insecurity among clergy about their role in Irish society, must eventually result in the inordinate influence of diocesan loyalty in the selection of a bishop with the accompanying danger that a man from within their own ranks ('one of our own') may simply not be up to the task. This is understandable, given the enormous amount of authority still vested in the Irish bishop, far greater than any religious superior. And he is appointed until he retires at seventy five, which is as good as for life. His word decides the fate of each priest in the diocese for the best part of their remaining life, and there is, in effect, no recourse to any higher authority, except in the case of some demonstrable legal irregularity. If the bishop is 'one of our own', we can hope that he will understand us, and not dare to ruffle our feathers too much.

It is natural to fear that someone from outside the diocese (especially a religious) might introduce changes, which an insecure clergy are not ready to entertain, though all admit in principle that change is necessary, even desirable. But the precarious nature of the Church in Ireland today makes for an instinctive conservatism even among otherwise 'progressive' or 'liberal' clerics that can be paralysing. Should an 'outsider' be appointed against the wishes of the dominant clique in the diocese, then, unless he is uniquely gifted, it is unlikely that he could administer effectively in the long run. (A similar fate may be in store for him in the bishops' conference, which has a long tradition of effectively co-opting most of its members.) The smaller the diocese, the greater the threat of a silent boycott, the technique of dissent 'made in Ireland'.

In a word, there is a real danger that most Irish dioceses might become almost ungovernable and unwilling to entertain any serious change. Even where there is a readiness to change, the size of the diocese may simply make any proposed change unworkable. In addition, the demands of an increasingly complex pastoral and cultural situation in Ireland calls for a level of expertise and specialisation among its personnel that few dioceses could afford. (In the case of marriage tribunals, this led of necessity to the creation of regional tribunals.) Even if the will were there, the rather narrowly perceived 'needs of the diocese' usually take precedence, namely filling traditional placements in parishes. This itself can be the source of grave injustice, as it can amount in effect to an offence against the demands of distributive justice. The priest in question may not be suited to the task, or may have talents that find no outlet in such a situation, but which would otherwise enrich the diocese or the Church at large, if the requisite structures were in place. If a square peg is forced into a round hole – and the power of the bishop's *fiat* must do what nature never intended – not only does the unfortunate community suffer, not only is the Church deprived of the use of some special talent, but the individual is thwarted in developing his abilities. This is a recipe for bitterness and disappointment. It undermines personal flourishing and the fulfilment that comes out of the opportunity to make the best of one's abilities. What psychic ills it causes can be left to the experts to decide.

Figure 1						
	Catholics	*(% of pop.)*	*Parishes*	*Bishops*[15]	*Priests (dioc)*	*Priests (rel)*
Austria	6,163,000	81.89%	3,058	19	2,752	1,817
Ireland	4,575,000	74.89%	1,365	51	3,393	2,365

There are simply too many dioceses in Ireland, and most of them are too small. Austria, which is slightly smaller in size than Ireland (83,853 and 84,405 sq. km respectively) but with a majority Catholic population of over six million, has 12 dioceses (two of which are metropolitan sees, namely with an archbishop rather than a bishop). Ireland, with a Catholic population of around four and a half million, has 26 dioceses (four of which are metropolitan sees). A comparison of the statistics is quite revealing (see figure 1).[16] For a country that has a Catholic population only three-quarters of that of Austria, Ireland has around three times the number of bishops serving twice as many dioceses as Austria. Further, Ireland has 540 more secular priests serving 1,693 fewer parishes than Austria – not counting the 548 priests, who are members of religious congregations, some of whom are now working in Irish parishes. And yet we moan about the shortage of priests! But that is a side issue here. The main point is that the Church in Ireland is burdened with an excess of bishops – and of dioceses.

More significant is the fact that Irish dioceses no longer coincide with the existing civil territorial divisions. Further, most are too small to produce the 'supra-parochial' structures demanded by a more urbanised Irish society, which would also allow young men of administrative ability take on responsibilities when they have the energy and creativity to do so. In many dioceses, the seniority system, whereby vacancies were filled not on merit but on seniority, is still in place, though there are signs that this is changing.[17] Any fully-fledged diocese needs such supra-parochial structures (specialised ministries and apostolates, academies, conference centres, etc.), which, in turn, provide opportunities for those with special talents (laity as well as clerics) to put their expertise at the service of the entire diocese (the local Church). These structures would give people (clerical, religious *and* lay) the space they need to develop initiatives as well as find fulfilment in their lives, a fulfilment that God desires for each of us. The absence of such outlets for special abilities and the accompanying reduction of the priestly vocation to parish work is also bound to affect the selection process within the seminaries. Only those candidates are deemed suitable for ordination who can be expected to engage in the limited range of activities open to the traditional role of curate or chaplain. Seminarians with rare gifts or intellectual propensities often don't fit the narrow template of the pastoral priest. But without the gifted, though not necessarily 'pastoral', priest – even at the price of somewhat eccentric behaviour sooner or later – the Church would be poorer in many respects, not least in humanity.

For evident historical reasons, the diocesan structure had to be based on the twelfth-century Irish social structure that was predominantly clan-based and rural, rather than based on the city or metropolis,[18] as was and is the case in the rest of the Church since New Testament times. But today, it is simply incongruous in a modern Ireland of an increasingly urban character that, for example, Tuam and Cashel should still be metropolitan sees, while Belfast, Cork, Galway or Limerick are not. The importance of the cities as the focus of the Church's mission from the very start (Antioch, Rome, Corinth, Thessalonica, Alexandria, etc.) needs to be recovered in the Irish Church. The city (above all, the capital) is the place where ideas are discussed and where decisions are made that affect the rest of the country in a short time, a time made ever shorter by the mass media. This is where the Church must concentrate its resources, if it is to achieve its sacred task – and complete that process of urbanisation that began with the Normans and which we have all too frequently resisted.[19] This should become the focus for the secondary structures that make up the institutional Church. To say that a Church institution based on non-existent tribal territories is not suited to our times is an understatement. As Cardinal Ratzinger once said: '...it's precisely the fact that the Church clings to the institutional structure when nothing really stands behind it any longer that brings the Church into disrepute.'[20]

Thinking the unthinkable

In the light of the above reflections, I wish to make a proposal about the restructuring of the Catholic Church in Ireland that may initially seem to many to be bold, if not actually rash. But the situation of the Catholic Church in Ireland is such that somewhat radical measures are indeed called for, though, as I will indicate later, I do not underestimate for one minute the very serious obstacles to these proposed changes. I am convinced, nonetheless, that it is high time to contemplate something like another national synod, comparable to that of Kells in 1152, to redraw the diocesan boundaries and bring them more into line with the contemporary civil realities. With the exception of Dublin, which might be trimmed back to the size of the present County Dublin, the number of dioceses should be reduced to or amalgamated into (at the very most) twelve in all (corresponding as far as possible with present county boundaries or clusters of counties).[21] Armagh/Belfast,[22] Dublin, Cork, and Galway might become metropolitan sees, each with two suffragan sees. Auxiliary bishops should be very much the exception. A smaller bishops' conference should, for various obvious reasons, ensure more active participation by all members as well as greater cohesion and effectiveness as a national body. But it should not take away from the primacy of the individual bishop's voice in the public forum.

Within the enlarged dioceses, episcopal vicars (who would administer the former cathedrals and conduct most confirmations) and deans with some real responsibility would form the second level of administration, and could be given derived but real administrative authority. The Council of Priests and/or the Diocesan Chapter would naturally have a greater input into the decisions affecting the diocese, such as the drawing up of parish boundaries, educational structures, pastoral strategies – and naming possible successors to the bishop. Regular pastoral synods should provide a forum for the various corporate entities in the diocese, including parish councils, religious congregations, and voluntary organisations, to discuss pastoral initiatives and thus give the laity a genuine voice in the Church. However, in general, lay initiatives should be allowed their own 'space' and relative autonomy, with the role of the clergy directed primarily to spiritual direction or chaplaincy, after the model of the Legion of Mary, the St Vincent de Paul Society, and more recently some of the lay and youth movements.

The redrawing of parish boundaries following on the restructuring of the diocese might seem to be less problematic, since present parish structures are less than two hundred years old, but could prove in practice to be even more difficult, as parish loyalties are often stronger than diocesan ones.[23] Still, it is hard to justify a parish made up of only 250 'souls' with its own parish priest, or a parish of 2000 souls ministered to by four priests,[24] to mention two I know personally. Rather than wait for the inevitable amalgamation of neighbouring parishes as the shortage of clergy increases – and the resulting demoralisation at all levels – it is surely better to have some pastoral strategy worked out for the diocese as a whole and so demonstrate that there is some order and *purpose* behind the changes at parish level. A restructuring of parishes might take into consideration such factors as the actual cohesion of existing communities, commitments to schools, new demographic developments (including migration into the cities and urban centres), the fall-off in religious practice, the availability of personnel, and the needs of parish-based sporting and cultural clubs, as well as new approaches to parish ministry. In some dioceses, I gather, there are pilot projects (allowed for, I am informed, by the new Canon Law) involving team ministry where the parish priest is replaced by a 'moderator'. These experiments might pave the way for future parish structures. Full-time lay pastoral workers as well as women religious dedicated to pastoral work, who are at present doing impressive work at parish level, ought to play a more significant role in the parish of the future, as well as at the level of supra-parochial institutions.

The spiritual mission of religious orders

Apart from those congregations that have adopted parish work as their specialised ministry, most other religious congregations, as I mentioned above, are in a sense outside the diocesan structure of the Church, though they have their own internal structures. The older, 'exempt' orders are the original supra-parochial, indeed supra-diocesan institutions and need to retain that status. Each offers a rich and ancient tradition of spirituality (Augustinian, Franciscan, Dominican, Carmelite, etc.); they provide specialised ministries in the cities, such as confession and spiritual direction, care for the homeless, drug addicts and similar social projects. Many post-reformation congregations (Jesuit, Vincentian, Redemptorist, Passionist, etc.) have their own unique contribution to make to the recovery of the transcendent in the modern world by providing a new stimulus to the local church either through their intellectual pursuits, their schools, or parish missions. Others like the Divine Word Missionaries and the Jesuits promote, *inter alia*, the media apostolate and communications. Thus, clerical congregations should not be seen primarily in terms of providing substitutes for the diocesan clergy. Neither should the main contribution of religious orders consist in taking over parishes from the diocese, though evidently semi-retired missionaries will continue to make an important contribution to alleviating the shortage of parish clergy.

The significance of the missionary congregations for the Irish Church is threefold: to keep before the mind of the local Church the world-wide responsibility of all Christians for the evangelising mission of the Church universal, to promote solidarity with the poor and the marginalised throughout the world, and above all to get vocations to continue this mission. In shorthand, the aim of that mission might be described as the full restoration of each human being to his or her original dignity through reconciliation with God in Christ and the continual effort to create an environment worthy of that dignity.

It is worth recalling that in 2001 there were some 2973 Irish missionaries serving in 93 countries overseas.[25] Apart from some spectacular news items, such as the murder of Columban priest, Fr Rufus Haley, in the Philippines (29 August 2001), these Irishmen and Irishwomen rarely feature in the discourse about the state of the Church in Ireland today. Though I am obviously partisan, it cannot be denied that what they have achieved, and are still doing, is extraordinary by any standards. The Irish missionaries are an essential though often forgotten dimension of the contemporary Irish Church.[26]

The revitalisation of the great missionary tradition of the Irish Church is needed in itself, if the Church is to remain true to her apostolic nature. Foreign missionaries keep the mission of the universal Church before the local Church, and so enable it to be not simply nationalistic but Catholic or universal. While keeping the world-wide issues of justice and peace to the fore of the public consciousness, the missionary congregations perhaps need to recover again the urgency of the primacy of evangelisation, including the re-evangelisation of Europe, beginning with our own country. Some missionary congregations also have the expertise to confront a totally new situation for the Irish Catholic Church: the existence of Catholic refugees to our country who need special pastoral care, as well as making contact with those communities constituted by non-Christian religions. Dialogue with the other great religious traditions of the world is demanded by our faith as articulated by the Second Vatican Council. But in addition, since many adherents of these religions will increasingly share our common destiny as a nation (and can be expected to enrich our country in so many ways as former waves of immigrants have done since the dawn of time), we must simply learn to live together and interact as communities.

The recovery of the various traditions of consecrated life, in particular those devoted to teaching and health care, is greatly needed to promote a genuine plurality of spiritualities and ministries within the Church. There is an urgent need for religious sisters and brothers to witness to Christ, to be the human face of the Church in the schools and in the hospital wards. All religious houses should become once again oases of prayer, personal and communal, within the desert of the modern city. The more strictly contemplative orders (male and female Cistericans, Benedictines, as well as the female Dominicans, Poor Clares, Redemptorists, etc.) remain the primary witnesses to the *unum necessarium* because of the radical nature of their enclosed way of life. Such orders have often been the pioneers in the liturgical renewal. From the beginnings of the Church in Ireland, the monastic ideal set the general cultural pattern of Christianity.[27] The renewal of the life of the modern Catholic Church will depend in the final analysis on the extent to which that monastic ideal once again ignites the imagination of the present generation.

Even though by their nature, religious and missionary congregations are 'outside' the diocesan structure, they often play a major role within the various dioceses. Without absorbing them into the diocesan structure, there is perhaps a need for some structural link between the bishops and the religious congregations beyond what is presently practiced (namely occasional meetings between representatives of the episcopal conference and of CORI). Is it possible, for example, for representatives chosen from religious orders and missionary congregations (male and female) to be made permanent observers (for the duration of their office) at the Episcopal Conference? They would have a right to contribute to the discussions, and sit in on various commissions, but not the right to vote. They would, of course, be bound by the same rules of confidentiality as the bishops. Their input into the major decision-making in the Church at the national level should be an enrichment to the whole Church and help overcome the ancient alienation between secular and religious. And again, there is a kind of precedent. When the last reforming synod met at Thurles in 1850, three priests representing their old and infirm bishops had been given votes by a Roman decision, while the Cistercian Abbot of Mount Melleray was given a vote by the decision of the synod.[28]

Obstacles to change

I fear that the above suggestions will be met by the numbing force of 'tradition' Irish-style, namely a dour and silent clinging to the *status quo* in the name of a 'realism' that is often mere pragmatism, and in the name of local loyalties that are parochial in the worst sense of the term.[29] Even if this fear proves unfounded – and I do have reason to believe that many clerics are now open to change in a way that was unthinkable up to recently – other more human factors cannot be ignored. To expect a bishop to agree with changing the boundaries of his own diocese – not to mention any possible amalgamation of his diocese with another or the downgrading from archdiocese to diocese – is perhaps to expect too much of human nature. The same probably applies to the diocesan clergy, especially given the inner-diocesan cohesiveness described above. Thus, the prospect of a synod comparable to that of Rathbrasil or Kells must indeed be remote, unless the situation deteriorates even more drastically. By which time, of course, it may be too late to do anything other than cater for a tiny remnant.

On the other hand, it is instructive to remember that, if such a sweeping transformation of the structures of the Irish Church was once possible in historical circumstances perhaps no less difficult than our own,[30] and in the teeth of considerable opposition, then it should be possible today, though evidently not overnight. Any change would have to be organic and the process would take considerable time. It is also instructive to look more closely at the actual tradition itself. It seems to me that it was not always quite as stable as is claimed, but adjusted to changing historical circumstances. The reforming synods of the twelfth centuries amalgamated smaller pre-existing dioceses into larger ones, as for example in the case of Meath.[31] But even after the Synod of Kells, change was possible. The case of Down and Connor is interesting. The two dioceses were initially administered separately until finally amalgamated in 1453.[32] 'The Dioceses of Cork and Cloyne were united by Papal Decree under Bishop Jordan Purcell in 1432 and remained so united until 1747,'[33] that is, for over three hundred years. The present diocese of Galway, Kilmacduagh and Kilfenora was the result of a complicated process of amalgamation that was only completed in 1883. Cashel and Emly, Waterford and Lismore, Cork and Ross, are further examples of canonical unions, though the latter also illustrates some of the very real human problems that can result. Nonetheless, amalgamating dioceses and creating new ones is not exactly foreign to our tradition.

Is there an alternative to a reform synod? How otherwise can structural changes be put in place to tap the enormous potential that up to now has not been realised in the Irish Catholic Church and so enable a genuine renaissance take place? I do not know. Perhaps help from outside might be needed.[34] But there are severe limits to what, for example, Rome could do. Any change must be preceded by serious debate within the Church, leading hopefully to a general will to undertake such radical alternatives. And the implementation of any generally agreed change must be gradual and organic, preserving local traditions and loyalties as much as possible but incorporating them into larger and more representative entities.

Italy, which has a number of smaller dioceses, is, I gather, in the process of amalgamating some of the smaller ones. Why not here?

5

BEYOND
CHURCH v. STATE

For amongst us it is not a man's station but his
principles that matter.
ST COLUMBANUS TO POPE BONIFACE[1]

The greatest danger to religion is likely to accrue from any serious
attempt on the part of the clergy to deprive the laity of their political
rights, under the pretence that such rights counted as nothing when
weighed against the danger to faith and morals.
WALTER McDONALD[2]

Church-State relations are but one aspect of a much broader relationship between the Church and society as a whole.[3] The broader context is the relationship between the Church and the 'world' that is not 'Church', but within which the Church carries out its divine mission to effect the redemption of humanity. Unfortunately in Ireland, the nature of Church-State relations is generally conceived in the narrowest of terms.

Most recent 'Church-State' controversies were, interestingly, more or less related to sexual matters – contraception, divorce, abortion. In part, these controversies are part of a reaction to the repressive sexual mores that characterised Irish Christianity

(Catholic and Protestant) at least since the mid-nineteenth century. In this, they amount to a replay in Ireland of developments that took place earlier and over a longer stretch of time in other countries, such as Britain and America.[4] The media itself has been a major player in such controversies, not always as neutral reporters of events on the public stage, but enthusiasts of enlightenment. Journalists seem to have their own agenda, which at times seems to amount to a mission to change Ireland irrevocably by liberating the country from its oppressive Catholic past. Most contemporary Irish politicians (with an eye to the next election) give the impression of being very anxious not to be seen as 'conservative' or out of step with 'public opinion' (created by the journalists), whatever their private misgivings, if any. Some are genuinely 'liberal' or rather, to use the term now in favour, 'libertarian'. Together, journalists and politicians constitute the new establishment, whose object might best be described as the imposition of 'fundamentalist individualism' as the new State religion of modern Ireland, where self-interest is the great modern motivating principle[5] – and all in the name of personal liberty and emancipation. In any case, the media has been the principal battleground for this thirty-year-old unbloody civil war that has raged in the Republic of Ireland, distinct from – and yet greatly influenced by – the bloody civil war in the North.

In a word, the so-called Church-State controversies in the Republic were in the main more accurately Church-media tussles that found their closure in some kind of public decision (in legislation or in a referendum).[6] The new 'values' proved to be relatively easy to impose on an otherwise reluctant, mostly Catholic, and generally tolerant, citizenry, who were somewhat over-anxious not to be seen as upholding a confessional State or being out of step with the rest of the modern world. This is a by-product of the dominant provincialism that characterises much public life in Ireland,[7] though by no means exclusive to Ireland.[8] It must also be admitted that the proponents of change sincerely thought that it was they who occupied the upper moral ground.

To a great extent, the advocates of change succeeded in their aims. This was helped, in large part, by three factors. In the first instance, there was a weak political class seemingly preoccupied with staying in power (now intimidated by the media as they were once intimidated by the hierarchy). Secondly, there was an insecure clergy unsettled by the revolution that was Vatican II, weakened by scandals, and unsure of their role in a modern secular State that emerged almost as an alternative to the 'sectarian violence' in the North. Finally, we have, as discussed above in detail, a rather long tradition of social conformity in this country, for which the Catholic Church must accept some blame. Like their counterparts in England in the 1930s, when first confronted with the 'new morality' that in time developed into the libertarianism adopted by modern Ireland, people in general, including many clerics and politicians, also found themselves in a predicament. They could not give reasons for what they knew to be right and wrong, remained mostly silent, and so lost the public debate to the self-confident and articulate sophists arguing for change.[9] More precisely, good decent people, including politicians and clergy, who in their heart of hearts opposed much of the 'liberal agenda', did not feel they could convincingly defend their position in the public forum and kept their counsel to themselves. Here, again, the Church must say *mea culpa*. The crisis in moral theology within the Church, to put it mildly, did not help matters. In reaction to the former rigorism that prevailed in moral theology, a more laxist position was, understandably, adopted by many Irish moral theologians and clerics.

But the triumph of the so-called, liberal agenda was aided in particular by a celebrated thesis about the separation of public and private morality that gained a certain currency among Irish theologians in recent decades.[10] It is instructive to take a brief look at this thesis, though a more exhaustive treatment must be left aside for the moment. Here I will examine the thesis against the broader background of a cluster of related questions, such as those concerning the nature of politics, the nature of morality within politics, and the tangled question of the Church's role in society. It is, unfortunately, necessary in the Anglo-Saxon context of which we are part to add immediately that the term 'morality' is to be understood in its original broad or full sense, namely every type of free human behaviour, and is not simply confined to the sexual sphere.

The morality of political life

Compromise is of the essence of politics. It is what distinguishes politics from religion. Religion, dealing as it does with ultimate and transcendent realities, is concerned with the Absolute, and so too those basic moral principles that have their source in Him. Our own country has seen the devastation caused by the transformation of politics and political goals into some absolute, quasi-religious 'cause', which demands human sacrifice (including suicide) or is marked by 'no surrender'. Such a perversion of politics is the seedbed of violence and despair. (Its most horrific manifestation was the recent attack on the World Trade Centre in New York and the Pentagon in Washington.) On the other hand, peace in the North has become a real possibility thanks to the acceptance by most politicians of some kind of political compromise. But democracy, which is built on the notion of the personal responsibility of all citizens for the well-being of the State, is in a sense based on a *refusal* to compromise on *moral* principles. Moral principles provide the framework within which practical compromises are worked out on a day-to-day basis. They – and they only – should at least be non-negotiable.

This is no longer self-evident. The present crisis in moral theology echoes a much deeper crisis in contemporary culture, caused by the prevalence of a denial that there is any such thing as a common moral imperative written into our being as humans which constitutes the measure of our free actions. Instead, there are various forms of what is called moral relativism, philosophical theories which became culturally dominant due to the historical circumstances of the past century. Partly in reaction to the various ideologies, which in the twentieth century caused such havoc and suffering to millions of people throughout the world, there is an understandable tendency today to shun anything that might smack of ideology, intransigence, or the 'imposition' of any particular value system.[11] The only option worth considering, it is claimed, is a pluralism not only of various cultural traditions but even a pluralism of what are misleadingly called 'moral values'.[12] Other cultural influences include the widespread philosophical denial, based on the reduction of reason to scientific or instrumental reason, that there is any such thing as an objective morality, binding on all.[13] Morality, in the final analysis, it is claimed, is something subjective, even irrational, and thus can be reduced to personal preference or sincere 'feelings', which must be consigned to the private sphere (provided they cause others no harm). Such subjective 'feelings', obviously, cannot be 'imposed' on society as a whole. But moral relativism, as even secular commentators are coming to recognise more and more, is a serious threat to democracy and the moral health of the political community.[14]

These tendencies are echoed by introducing the term 'moral beliefs' in analogy with religious beliefs, and calling on the authority of the Second Vatican Council's *Declaration on Religious Liberty* to propose extending the right of religious freedom to include 'moral beliefs'. In doing so, it is assumed that there is a legitimate plurality of moral systems, though such an assumption is in contradiction with the classical teaching on the natural law as articulated most clearly in that same declaration (art. 3).[15] In a word, it is the universal moral law that demands freedom of religious worship irrespective of the cultural and historical circumstances. As the moral law, it is objective, universal, and non-negotiable. It may be difficult at times to identify precisely what that objective moral order entails in a particular historical situation or faced with new moral dilemmas – and so debate among philosophers and theologians is demanded, as is the bringing of that debate to some kind of closure by the authoritative intervention of the Magisterium. But, a certain current of thought in modern moral theology has rendered such debate irrelevant by interpreting 'objective' to mean 'objective to the person in a particular situation', which is but another, more subtle, way of denying the objective morality of certain human acts irrespective of the situation.

In addition, influenced by the British legal debate in the 1960s about the 'enforcement of morals' by the State,[16] a distinction is made between the private (or personal) moral beliefs/values and those pertaining to the public realm. Accordingly, a Catholic may 'privately' hold that a particular practice (such as abortion) is wrong or forbidden or sinful. But, it is claimed, one ought not to 'impose' one's private views or morality on those who hold other views, in particular if one is a public representative. This was the stance advocated by Geraldine Fererro in her bid for candidacy for the highest political goal in America, the Presidency. Along the same lines, the thesis was advocated during the last divorce referendum that a citizen or legislator can as a Catholic vote 'in good conscience' for a measure that he or she personally (privately) holds to be immoral.

All of these views find a clear resonance in contemporary Western culture, though they cannot be reconciled with the logic of morality, the nature of positive law, or the traditional wisdom of all peoples, not to mention the Church's teaching outlined above. Little reflection is needed to recognise that the distinction between what one personally holds to be right or wrong in private and one's responsibility as a public representative is a false one.[17] Such a distinction undermines personal integrity, the bedrock of communal life and the source of trust in society. As Sir Thomas More, Lord Chancellor of England and now patron saint of politicians, once said: 'I believe, when statesmen forsake their own private conscience for the sake of their public duties... they lead their country by a short route to chaos.'[18]

In a word, the thesis we have just examined must in the final analysis undermine liberal democracy itself.

The Church, morality, and democratic pluralism

Plurality of opinions about practical solutions to solve the exigencies of the economy and social welfare is an essential component of any genuine pluralist democracy, giving rise to the party system. This encourages people with similar approaches to solving such questions to form manageable units (political parties) that can take collective action. Since there is no one solution to practical problems, various possibilities need to be debated and are usually resolved with some kind of compromise. The function of the party whip is precisely to keep the party united, once the debate within the party has achieved some kind of closure acceptable to the majority; those dissatisfied must submit; this is morally acceptable in matters where compromise is the most one can ever expect, namely in contingent matters when the issue at stake is not a matter of moral principle. Here, the Church through her leaders can, and should, also contribute to public debate, as in the case of various questions relating to education, health care, and social justice. Catholic bishops, priests, and lay leaders bring a unique perspective, including the wisdom of two millennia to bear on practical problems of living together and building a better society. But, as the Second Vatican Council teaches, 'Pastors do not have ready answers for all problems' (*Gaudium et spes*, 43).

Finding practical solutions to economic and social dilemmas is, however, ultimately the responsibility of the laity, politicians and citizens, who enjoy a real autonomy, into which the Church may not encroach.[19] The Council however adds, as though self-evident, that the laity must be guided by Christian wisdom, and pay 'eager attention to the teaching authority of the Church'. After condemning the Christian who 'shirks his temporal duty', the Council teaches that it is the task of the laity 'to cultivate a properly informed conscience and to impress the divine law on the affairs of the earthly city' (*Gaudium et spes*, 43). In other words, the moral order (the divine law) is the non-negotiable guide for Catholic citizens and politicians in finding practical solutions within the economic, social, and other fields of political endeavour.

This divine moral order transcends all positive laws.[20] It is their measure. This objective and universal moral order, knowable in principle by human reason, has been confirmed and clarified by revelation as articulated in the tradition of the Church and her living teaching authority. C.S. Lewis, an Anglican lay theologian, uses the Chinese term *Tao* (or *Dao*, literally 'the way') to describe this moral imperative written into our being and recognised to some degree by all peoples in every era as necessary for our personal and communal well-being.[21] It is the way for us to achieve full human flourishing, the denial of which in practice leads to the manipulation of the many by the few, what Lewis calls the abolition of man. Accordingly, the Council teaches that 'economic activity is to be carried out in accordance with techniques and methods belonging to the moral order, so that God's design for man may be fulfilled' (*Gaudium et spes*, 64). More generally, it points out that political authority 'must be exercised within the limits of the moral order and directed towards the common good' (*Gaudium et spes*, 74).[22] And quite specifically with regard to the population question (and thus family planning methods), the Council, addressing governments, 'exhorts all men to beware of all solutions, whether uttered in public or in private or imposed at any time, which transgress the natural law' (*Gaudium et spes*, 87).[23] The Church's indispensable role in the State, then, is to bear witness to the transcendent law of God, to teach in season and out of season the demands of the moral law, which are the indispensable parameters within which concrete solutions are to be found for the various practical problems that the State has to solve. The denial of 'moral absolutes' in moral theology undermines this role and, unintentionally – indeed contrary to the protests of these same theologians – promotes ethical relativism.

The indispensable role of the Church in society
As I have stressed over and over in the course of this book, the primary role of the Church in society is spiritual, to witness to the transcendent, pointing to God, the absolute point of reference, as

our ultimate goal, to His teaching as the way to that goal, and to His sacraments as the source of grace and help to achieve that goal. 'The Church is entrusted with the task of opening up man to the mystery of God' (*Gaudium et spes*, 41). Secularism is often seen as a liberation from the religious domination of politics in the past. But, despite certain immediate benefits, in the long run secularism is a real threat to communal well-being, not least because it leaves a vacuum in people's lives that leads them to seek escapism in drugs, extreme sports, and suicide, or transfers their longing for the absolute onto political goals. 'The alternative to religion is nothing.'[24] It is nihilism.

'Today, when many countries have seen the fall of ideologies which bound politics to a totalitarian conception of the world ... there is no less grave a danger that the fundamental rights of the human person will be denied and that the religious yearnings which arise in the heart of every human being will be absorbed once again into politics' (*Veritatis splendor*, 101). The kamikaze attacks on New York and Washington have sadly confirmed this. Human beings are acutely aware that their existence is precious and unique, that they are destined for greatness. If the religious yearnings of the human heart are denied, then substitutes are instinctively sought. If their personal or communal pride is offended, then they will seek to redress this humiliation that offends their own God-given sense of eternal worth. Grave injustice in society can lead to political movements that offer radical solutions of a quasi-religious, indeed violent nature, as we in Ireland sadly know from experience. More pertinently for our situation, the Pope adds: 'There is *the risk of an alliance between democracy and ethical relativism*, which would remove any sure moral reference point from political and social life, and on a deeper level make the acknowledgement of truth impossible.' Indeed, 'if there is no ultimate truth to guide and direct political activity, then ideas and convictions can be easily manipulated for reasons of power. As history demonstrates, a democracy without values easily turns into open or thinly disguised totalitarianism' (*Veritatis splendor*, 101).[25]

Democracy lives off moral resources beyond its own grasp and which it cannot itself reproduce, though it depends on them for its proper functioning.[26] In Ireland, as in the rest of Western Europe, these are the product of the Christian tradition with its roots in the fusion of Hebrew prophecy and Greek philosophy that formed Christianity. When these moral, philosophical, and theological resources dry up within the body politic, then all that is left is a naked power game. Recourse to human rights, one of the most promising signs in contemporary politics, is itself undermined by the absence of a vision of the human person made in the image of God, redeemed by Christ, and so the subject of rights and obligations, some of which are absolute and so transcend political activity.[27] In other words, some fundamental rights are absolute because of the constitutive relationship between the human person and the Absolute, which relationship constitutes the human person as such. It is an essential part of the Church's mission to keep this vision alive.[28]

And central to that mission is the obligation to clarify and (by a combination of persuasion and authoritative witness) to form the conscience of the faithful with regard to our moral obligations. In this way, we the faithful are empowered to bear witness before the world as to what is the divine, universal, and immutable moral law. As St Peter proclaimed: 'We must obey God rather than any human authority' (Acts 5:29, NRSV, cf. 4:19). This programmatic sentence, which strongly echoes that uttered by Socrates in his *Apologia* (29d),[29] became the singular most distinguishing mark of the early Christian martyrs, whose role in establishing freedom of conscience in Western civilisation, it has been argued, is more significant than the entire corpus of the Enlightenment.[30]

The growing disillusionment with politics and politicians (not only in modern Ireland) is intimately linked with the effective abolition of conscience from public life. (Conscience here is to be understood as that primordial consciousness of the basic moral imperatives shared by all human beings, as well as its application in particular circumstances.)[31] It is not unusual in contemporary democracies for the individual politician, increasingly subservient to the 'party-whip', to become faceless, a rubberstamp to approve or oppose any measure proposed by the government and, more often, its anonymous (un-elected) civil servants. Modern politics is dominated by 'pragmatism'[32] and so becomes a power-game carried out within the parameters of what the shifting sands of 'public opinion' (as dictated by the media) will tolerate at any particular moment. Debate, the life-blood of politics, loses its centrality, increasingly to be replaced by the attempted manipulation of public opinion. An upright conscience – or, more loosely, personal integrity – is the only effective bulwark against the ruthless power of the mighty, as well as against graft and corruption, which vices foster injustice and undermine confidence in the political process.

The plethora of tribunals set up by the Irish government to investigate allegations of corruption may for a time frighten prospective public servants and politicians from engaging in such actions. They can certainly help to sensitise the public moral sense, but they cannot make people virtuous. Neither can the frantic drawing up of ever more detailed 'ethical guidelines' and 'ethical committees', induce good behaviour. Such committees, though they can have an important role in hospitals engaging in research, can also constitute the abandonment of personal responsibility. This applies especially to those committees and commissions created by government to 'advise' on legislation concerning new moral dilemmas caused, for example, by developments in biology and embryology. The most infamous case is the Warnock Commission set up by the British Government to enable parliament introduce legislation to allow for experimentation on human embryos up to fourteen days. As a sop to morality, it is claimed that such committees must be independent. But the appointment of the members of such committees usually ensures that the majority of chosen 'experts' can be expected to give the decision favoured by the political establishment *and* big business (especially the pharmaceutical multinationals that mean so much to the Irish economy). And there are huge financial issues involved. Ireland at present seems to be intent on going the same way as the United Kingdom, even inviting Mary Warnock as an expert for a public consultation, which from the outset seemed to be little more than window dressing to give the impression of widespread consultation. There is only one alternative to easily manipulated bioethical committees: the Catholic conscience, moral integrity and moral courage of the honest citizen and politician.

Written ethical guidelines, no matter how useful, cannot replace personal integrity (which, of course, is not the same thing as being morally perfect). The restoration of confidence in politics, as Václav Havel has repeatedly affirmed,[33] depends in large measure on the recovery of the primacy of conscience and the abolition of the false distinction between 'private' and 'public' morality. It depends, in other words, on men and women of principle who are courageous enough to stand up for their principles in public, even risking a certain initial unpopularity in the media. This applies in particular to controversial issues involving clear moral principles.

Catholic legislators or citizens evidently cannot in good conscience vote for any measure that would approve actions that are of their very nature morally wrong and so can never be chosen under any circumstances or, indeed, for the best of motives. Such actions include racial discrimination, direct abortion, the freezing of, or experimentation on, human embryos, embryonic stem-cell research, or various methods of 'artificial reproduction', euthanasia.[34]

The Catholic Church in Ireland, despite its own embarrassment due to recent scandals, which are themselves condemned by the same Church's moral teaching, understands itself to be commissioned by Christ to catechise and proclaim what accords with God's will. It cannot remain silent on moral issues, be they related to social justice or to personal behaviour, when these issues are debated in the public forum. The Church, of course, cannot dictate the precise form legislation should take, but it must judge the basic thrust of the legislation. The precise formulation of legislation is entirely at the discretion of the legislators, though various lobbying groups tend to exercise considerable influence on legislators in modern democracies. The task of bishops and clergy in any political society is to measure any proposed legislation against the objective moral order and make its judgement public. Likewise, legislators and citizens who are Catholics are obliged to be equally attentive to the morality of any legislation being proposed and, if necessary, vote against what they recognise to be wrong or morally illicit. They cannot act in public against their personal conscience or 'private conviction'.

Constitutional amendments
In the recent past, most major public controversies concerning moral issues related to proposed changes in the Constitution.[35] Few disputants on either side of the debate seemed to pay any attention to the specific nature of amendments as such, namely the fact that a proposed change to the Constitution ought *not* to be treated simply as the equivalent of *legislation* by parliament. The Constitution by its very definition determines the *limits* to parliamentary legislation; it establishes the *principles* that should guide the lawmakers. This essential difference has significant implications. They deserve closer attention than they usually get, especially due to the tendency of late to fudge the distinction between legislation and constitutional amendment, as in the case of the last abortion referendum. Failure to attend to this essential difference by actually wedding criminal law legislation to a constitutional amendment might well have been one of the main reasons why some 58 per cent of the electorate failed to vote in the 2002 constitutional amendment on abortion. Apart from the mixed messages the public was getting from all sides of the campaign, the proposal – in effect a piece of legislation – was too complex: many understandably felt incompetent to judge its

merits or demerits. One of the reasons why we elect
representatives is, precisely, to legislate and attend to such detail,
which the rest of us have neither the time nor the experience to
assess. The citizen can say yes or no to clear principles, not to
complex legislation. The Maastricht and Nice referenda, requiring
citizens to master almost impenetrable international treaties, has
reduced the notion of an amendment *ad absurdum*.

When it comes to any proposed amendment to the
Constitution, it seems to me that everyone – including the
individual legislators or public representatives themselves – is
thereby reduced to the status of a 'mere' citizen. This, in turn,
means that for each legislation they must be free to act according
to their personal conscience – and so cannot be subject to the
party whip. But the question arises: does such freedom of
conscience and freedom of expression extend to the process of
legislation needed to hold a referendum (which is required for
constitutional change in Ireland)? The answer would seem to be in
the affirmative, in particular with regard to disputed moral issues,
which are strictly speaking 'matters of conscience', and in other
parliaments are generally left to a free vote. Freedom from the
imposition of the party whip would seem to follow from the
primacy and so the continuing validity of the existing
Constitution. It is the task of the government to *persuade* the
legislators (including their own party members) that such an
amendment is necessary for the common good – not to *impose* it
by means of the party whip, which of its nature tends to be, well,
partial. As our national parliament, the Dáil is, or should be, the
major forum for public debate leading to a definitive decision or
vote. That is its central purpose. Unfortunately, the immediate
imposition of the party whip (at best after some short discussion
within the parliamentary party behind closed doors, *after* the
Government had made up its mind!) seems to have been the
practice common to all Irish political parties in the recent past
when it came to constitutional amendments. As mentioned above,
the imposition of the party whip is demanded by the need for

compromise in matters that by nature involve no serious principle, otherwise parliamentary business would come to a halt. But it should not apply to matters of principle, be they moral or political (as in changes to the Constitution). The indiscriminate imposition of the party whip in ethical issues in the recent constitutional amendments meant that the person of integrity who challenged the party leadership was expelled from his or her own political party for giving public expression to their deepest convictions, and for doing so in the public forum to which they were elected to debate such issues! The result is the much applauded but highly questionable 'consensus' among political parties, not unlike that once found in communist parties, a consensus cemented by the fear of taking sides – and so possibly taking the losing side, thereby endangering one's prospects at the next general election. With regard to any proposed amendment to the Constitution, each citizen, it seems to me, including the individual legislators themselves, cannot be coerced by any party, even their own. Those whose vote is decisive must be *persuaded* by those advocating change, and each one must act – and be allowed to act – freely according to their principles, according to their personal conscience. To forbid this, it seems to me, is to undermine the very nature of democracy itself.

It is surprising that the constitutionality of the use of the party whip on voting in the Dáil to amend the Constitution has never been questioned. Even more disturbing, it seems to this writer, is the silencing of the individual public representative who, if free, might publicly oppose a party-approved amendment during the campaign leading up to the actual referendum. This resulted in one Minister of State campaigning publicly *in favour* of the Government's proposal to amend the Constitution (Nice I), which he personally opposed, and in fact voted *No* on the day of the referendum itself. Apart from anything else, this can only bring politics into disrepute.[36]

One implication of the various controversies surrounding amendments to the Constitution on 'social issues' has rarely been mentioned. It is the way such controversies can unwittingly undermine an existing moral consensus in the country. Take abortion. Before the first amendment was introduced with the object of preventing legislators going the way of the rest of the world and introducing laws to allow direct abortion,[37] the majority of citizens held it to be simply wrong, indeed gravely sinful, even in those tragic situations when people might be tempted to opt for such a drastic solution. Abortions were recognised as shameful deeds and so were sought under the cloak of anonymity (mostly in Britain). But the various debates on proposed amendments to the Constitution gave the (originally insignificant) pro-abortion lobby a platform they would not have had otherwise. In addition, advocacy of abortion 'in exceptional circumstances' (under the euphemism of 'choice') by respected figures, such as doctors, politicians, other professionals, and even theologians from difference Church traditions, undermined the real moral consensus about its wrongness. Abortion was reduced to a 'choice', something a woman could and should decide for herself – and so the numbers seeking abortion in Britain have increased dramatically, despite the great majority who said 'no' to abortion whenever the issue seemed to be clear-cut. Commenting on the defeat of the 2002 amendment on abortion, Fintan O'Toole noted that, before the first abortion amendment, the great majority of citizens considered abortion wrong in all circumstances, whereas now, it would seem, there is a body of opinion in Ireland that is more concerned with asking under what circumstances abortion is to be permitted. In other words, for them the absolute principle has been abandoned. The very campaigns to protect the unborn may have, unwittingly, placed the unborn child in greater danger than ever in a consumerist culture whose only 'moral' criterion is 'choice'. The so-called 'right to choose' is the political expression of moral relativism.

So too, *mutatis mutandis*, with regard to divorce, which was promoted by a small but well-organised pro-divorce lobby. The first campaign to introduce divorce may have failed in its immediate object, but it succeeded in shattering the moral consensus about the wrongness of divorce. The pro-divorce lobby was convinced that it would win eventually. And it did. The amazing thing was that the decisive divorce amendment was passed by the slimmest of majorities, which points to the unalloyed moral substance of the electorate that could not be shaken. That is a source of hope.

Another implication of the various attempts over the past twenty years to protect the unborn by anchoring its rights in the Constitution – something I supported – needs to be confronted. The movement to inscribe the rights of the unborn into the Constitution was not initiated by the Church, but by a group of concerned laity who, with good reason, feared that we might easily go the way of the USA and Britain and introduce legislation to allow abortion. To forestall such an eventuality, they argued, the rights of the unborn ought to be guaranteed by the Irish Constitution and so prevent a future generation of Irish legislators from introducing abortion. Once this proposal came into the public realm and so became a political issue, the official Church could not remain silent. Bishops and some clerics took a public stance, at times somewhat reluctanty, in support of the pro-life movement, which had always maintained its own autonomy vis-à-vis the bishops, and which sometimes adopted tactics that the hierarchy could not condone. Nonetheless, the disputes leading up to the referenda were perceived to be Church-State conflicts, a perception which was used by the opposition (in particular the media) to great advantage in their fight to create a 'modern, secular, pluralist' Ireland. Be that as it may, in effect the referenda on abortion had as their subtext: the elected representatives cannot be trusted. And this must have serious implications for democracy.

Democracy is always a fragile process. It is based on trust. In recent times, various scandals and accusations of corruption being investigated by the tribunals have tended further to undermine that trust and have added to the general scepticism of the public about politicians. This is not unique to Ireland but seems to be rather widespread in most modern democracies. But Ireland is a small country. And in Ireland, the long memory of centuries of unjust government under a foreign power has not entirely faded. That memory alone would suffice to put us on our guard concerning the decisions of those who hold the reins of power, even if now the power-brokers are 'our own'. Trust in elected representatives cannot be taken for granted in Ireland. It needs to be fostered. But it is at least arguable that the various campaigns to protect the unborn through constitutional amendment may have, unintentionally, further undermined the trust of the public in our legislators. If this is so, then the Church urgently needs to act publicly in ways that will counteract this unintended effect of the various campaigns to which it was party, whatever the initial reluctance. The Church must work to replenish the reserves of public trust in its representatives, including acknowledgment of the positive achievements of the State. Paradoxically, perhaps the greatest service the Church can render to the State is to encourage all citizens, but above all, legislators and other public representatives, to act according to their Catholic consciences, to think and judge for themselves in all political decision-making, to act with integrity and courage.

Towards a mature relationship between Church and State
Church-State relations cover far more than public tussles over moral and legal issues, which in any case will continue to engage both sides. It includes education and health, to mention but two vast areas where co-operation between Church and State is essential to our well-being as a nation. Prudent trust and respect – not mutual suspicion and scepticism – must mark all these relations. If she is to be true to her mission, the Church will continue to speak, in season and out of season, about public decisions and laws that touch on moral issues, but will do so respecting the autonomy of the legislators within the non-negotiable limits of the moral law. The State for its part must be

mature enough to take the Church's concern seriously and not simply reject the Church's position on the basis of 'political correctness'. Thus, for example, the shameful situation of the State's effective prohibition of advertising on radio and television by the Churches or any expressly Christian group needs to be rectified, a prohibition that seems to be based on nothing more than 'political correctness'. The absurdity of the situation is highlighted by the fact that no such ban applies to blatant superstition, such as advertisements for tarot cards and the like.

Apart from the contentious moral issues mentioned above, there are other issues affecting the common good, which call for a more broadly based debate between the Church and public representatives. These evidently include education and health, but must also embrace the growing violence in society, the abuse of drugs and alcohol, and, more recently, the positive integration of immigrants into Irish society, so that we as a country will be enriched by their contributions and their very presence. Many disturbing developments in Irish society, such as the increase in suicide, senseless violence (especially among the young), substance abuse, criminal behaviour, marriage breakdown, racialism, etc., can only be countered by mutual co-operation between all sectors of civil society and State agencies. The Churches are an essential component of civil society and must be an integral part of the solutions to society's problems. Civil servants, rightfully jealous of the State's autonomy (but also true to their origins and traditions as executors of the British administration in Ireland), generally tend to want to keep the Church at bay and so, I gather, can be negative to Church representatives in the areas of health and education. This might have been necessary in the youth and adolescence of the State, when the Church was perhaps a threat to the autonomy of the State. But perhaps a change of attitude is called for today in line with communitarian thinking in other countries, which see civil society (including Churches and other religions) as the necessary medium between the State and the individual citizen and not in terms of a struggle for power. Such a change of heart could only be for the good of the whole country.

With regard to the Church, it is becoming increasingly obvious that there is a need for some permanent offices in Dublin and Belfast to liaise between the Church and various State institutions.[38] Perhaps, also, the time has come, in the wake of the Good Friday Agreement, to consider working towards a concordat between the Catholic Church and the Republic of Ireland that would define more clearly, and anchor in international law, the relationship (and so the authentic separation) between Church and State. Be that as it may, there is an urgent need for some kind of permanent forum of a public nature for dialogue between the Church and various sectors of society, political, economic, cultural, and artistic. Here the Church might examine the possibility of setting up something like the Catholic academies to be found in the main German cities. These are full-time institutions run by competent lay people for the purpose of promoting dialogue and debate between the Church and various aspects of civil society and the State itself on issues of the day.[39]

This is not to imply that there was no such dialogue previously. This was surely the aim of the Jesuit periodical *Studies*, which is still of invaluable service in this area. In the heady, post-Conciliar days through the seventies and up to the beginning of the eighties, a number of initiatives, apart from personal contacts between theologians and other professionals, were taken to engage in dialogue with representatives from various areas of public life – law, literature, medicine, art – such as the day-long seminars organised by Professors Enda McDonagh and Matthew O'Donnell in Maynooth. The Dominican journal, *Doctrine and Life*, also aired issues of more general interest than in-house Church matters, as did the Divine Word Missionaries' monthly, *The Word*, admittedly at a more popular level. The monthly pastoral-theology periodical, *The Furrow*, played its own part not least through the weekend seminars it organised, which in time led to the headline grabbing *Pobal* conferences.[40] These initiatives, more or less tolerated by the hierarchy, were piecemeal and transitory. One of the most significant encounters between politics and theology, in my experience, was the colloquium 'Ireland and Europe: Rediscovering a Hidden Vision', organised by Professor Patrick Hannon and Dr Hugh Connolly (for the Pontifical University, Maynooth) in association with the Dublin Office of the European Parliament on 27 November 1998. It was a model for the kind of dialogue between Church representatives and politicians that could be fostered in a more permanent institution, such as the Catholic Academy.

Prompted by the Vatican, the Irish Bishops' Conference founded the Irish Centre for Faith and Culture in December 1997. The Centre organised several public conferences and supported others. It is a move in the right direction, and indeed, to judge alone from its list of publications, has achieved much over a short period with limited resources.[41] But it is far from ideal. In addition, basing such a centre in Maynooth makes little sense.[42] Somewhat closer to what I envisage is the type of public conference organised by Fr Harry Bohan at the Céifin Centre in Clare.[43] Nonetheless, I am convinced that at least one permanent forum, based in the capital, is needed for a fruitful and permanent exchange of ideas and concerns affecting the worlds of religion and politics, of culture and society at large.[44]

Finally, it should be pointed out in this context that the State also has obligations towards the Churches arising from the significance of these communities for civil society and the common good. Thus it is not just insulting to the religious sensibilities of the great majority of citizens to claim, as the Minister for Justice did recently, that he would accord the Church's canon law the same status as the rules governing a golf club. This fails to recognise the real nature of the contribution the Church offers to society, which unlike golf, is more than simply recreational (no matter how important recreation is, as mentioned above). I have already outlined the indispensable role of Christianity in modern democracy, but there is another aspect to that role that can only be touched on here very superficially.

According to contemporary communitarian philosophers, in particular in the United States, local communities and voluntary organisations that create bonds among particular neighbourhood communities are the *conditio sine qua non* in order to restore some sense of cohesion to society and reduce the sense of anonymity created by modern life. Under the influence of the Enlightenment, modern politics up to recently tended to reduce society to two poles, the individual versus the State, and ignore the intermediate communities between both (including the family, the Churches, and neighbourhood communities) that provide people with a local identity and a place in society, and so are indispensable for human flourishing.[45] Despite recent ideological and demographic changes in Ireland, there is still a strong residue of that *muintearas* (familiarity or community mindedness) that 'is integral to the culture and repeatedly addressed in the religious and poetical tradition'.[46] The Churches, Protestant and Catholic, and the other religions, are major components of civil society, creating local communities within the larger community of the State; their significance needs to be recognised and actively supported by the State as indispensable to the common good.[47] The present situation of the Catholic Church should also be of concern to civic leaders. As Joe Lee points out: 'The Church is a bulwark, perhaps now the main bulwark, of the civic culture... If religion were to no longer fulfil its historic civilising mission as a substitute for internalised values of civic responsibility, the consequences for the country no less than for the church could be lethal.'[48]

Well-spring of hope

But the Church's mission extends beyond the issues of social and economic welfare. In an increasingly merciless world, the Church's primary mission is to witness to God's grace in our midst and to the primacy of his transcendent mercy. There is an urgent need to recover that awareness of the early Irish Church that '[e]very human activity or state of being is an invitation to recognise the presence of God'.[49] In the sacrament of reconciliation, the Church offers God's infinite mercy to those who fail, and gives then the courage to make amends and begin again. It provides encouragement and support to those who struggle to live according to their conscience, and, by means of her spiritual traditions and communal worship, gives them access to the inner strength that God provides in the sacraments and prayer. An essential part of its task is to defend the defenceless and come to the aid of the poor, who are generally the real victims in the power game of an economics without principles and a politics devoid of conscience. A vibrant Church living out of the wellsprings of faith in God becomes the fundamental source of hope in society. It enables us to live according to conscience, to persevere in doing good, to experience and foster joy, and to tackle what often appear to be insurmountable obstacles in politics, economics, and cultural life, while accepting the imperfections of the human condition – and yet to persevere, confident of the ultimate victory of good over evil. The Church engenders hope.

The State – indeed, society at large – needs the Church more than the Church needs the State. That is the main point of what I have just discussed. But the State needs a dynamic, self-confident Church ready to give a reason for its hope, one that can persuade and not seek to impose its blind *fiat*. To become such a Church there has to be, first of all, a renewal of the faith, and that must embrace a certain public recognition of theology. And theology, for its part, must learn again, as in the days of yore, to speak to the heart and mind of our contemporaries from the mind and heart of God's self-revelation: Jesus Christ.

APPENDIX II: THE MORAL REVOLUTION: IRELAND SINCE THE SIXTIES[50]

The sixties. Revolution was in the air. New-found affluence after the austerities of the post World War II era coupled with the sudden, unprecedented burst of scientific and technological creativity in the 1960s (including space exploration) created the impression that human ingenuity could, given the political will, eliminate all pain and create paradise on earth. Many of the young, disillusioned with the values of their parents, would provide that political will and bring utopia into being. They rejected the narrow, restrictive moral values of former generations, and opted for a freer, more spontaneous, ultimately unrestricted lifestyle, in particular in the area of sex. The sexual revolution was unleashed – one of many.

In May 1968, students took to the barricades in Paris for a better world. Civil rights protests erupted in other major cities across the globe, including Belfast. The utopian dream of Marxism was given a human face in the Prague Spring. The Cultural Revolution in China had caught the imagination of the young. The cry 'make love not war' echoed to the sound of the Beatles from one university campus to another throughout the world, but especially in the USA, embroiled at the time in the Vietnam War.

In the Church, the theological and liturgical renewal inaugurated by the Second Vatican Council shattered old certainties. Suddenly everything was, in principle, considered capable of being changed, including the teaching of the Church. The issue of the moment was birth control. Technology had, through television, brought people in Europe and America literally face to face with the ravages of famine. Propagandists had convinced the world that humanity was threatened by humanity itself: the 'population explosion'. Technology, it seemed, had also provided us with the means of controlling population and eliminating famine in future: 'the pill'. The contraceptive pill was also the symbol of the sexual revolution, especially for feminists who saw it as giving women, for the first time since the dawn of history, a truly effective means to liberate themselves from their hated 'bondage to their bodies' (Simone de Beauvoir).

But the pill also seemed to offer an ideal solution to the various, excruciatingly difficult moral dilemmas faced by couples who for one reason or another should not have any (further) children. It is at this level that moral theology first debated 'the pill'. Did it offer a morally acceptable means to a morally good end? Did it offer to Christian couples a way to live the new theology of marriage with its emphasis on conjugal love, and the intrinsic value of its sexual expression, as recently proclaimed by the Second Vatican Council? Many theologians were coming around to an affirmative answer to both questions. Others were encouraged by the news leaked to the press that the majority on the special Commission originally set up to examine the question by Pope John XXIII approved of a change. Their hopes were dashed when, on 25 July 1968, Pope Paul VI issued *Humanae vitae* to a stunned (Western) world. Within a few days, Charles Curran had organised the collection of hundreds of signatures of theologians who dissented from the teaching. Revolution had erupted within the Church. Dissent was born.

Whereas the press conference in Rome announcing *Humanae vitae* was not exactly exemplary, the one held in Dublin is generally judged to have been a public relations disaster. That summer I had just completed Second Divinity, that section of the course in Maynooth, which included the tract on conjugal morality. I too was hoping for a change, as indeed, many of my professors seemed to be. Though their arguments were not always convincing, in the end compassion for the hard cases won out. The news came as a blow. But already during my studies in Donamon,

I had picked up the notion that one should 'read the text' before
forming a judgement based on second-hand information.

I remember vividly the afternoon I read *Humanae vitae* in the
Divine Word Missionaries' house in Booterstown overlooking the
sea. On my first reading two things struck me forcefully: this is
the truth and the Pope is the successor of St Peter, the Vicar of
Christ.

How many read the document at the time, I do not know. I
only know that, at the time, or indeed since, I met few who did.
The 'no change' at the press conference deadened sensibilities. It
was like a death knell that marked the end of an era, which it did.
In the world at large, the dream of utopia gave way to the
nightmare of terrorism, to the tanks in Prague, the killing fields of
Cambodia, the intensification of the Cold War, the worldwide
massacre of the innocents in the womb, the making of babies in
laboratories, the spread of divorce, the trivialisation of sex, the
horrors of AIDS. In the Church, it marked the beginning of an
intense battle between the so-called liberals and conservatives,
where moral theology provided the battlefield.

The core issue, in fact, was not birth control but the nature of
morality itself – more precisely, whether or not morality could change.
Could what was considered moral by former generations be moral for
this or any future generation? To take one example. Is the wrongness
of the direct killing of the innocent some culturally conditioned norm
of the past? Should we not say that the norm, generally speaking,
should be followed, while allowing for exceptions when the individual
alone, each person, weighing up the positive and negative
consequences, would judge 'according to his or her conscience'? The
majority of theologians, rejecting *Humanae vitae*, said yes to these
questions. The Magisterium said no: there are some absolute norms
which allow of no exception. There are some (few) actions that are
'intrinsically wrong', that, whatever the circumstances or external
consequences, cannot be chosen by anyone who wants to do the good,
to please God. The ability of the theologians who supported the
Magisterium to persuade others often left much to be desired.

Over thirty years later, a whole new generation of (mostly lay) thinkers, male and female, has emerged. They have succeeded in providing the philosophical and theological analysis needed to understand (and reject) the dissenting position and to articulate the truth not only of *Humanae vitae*, but of the Church's whole moral tradition, which at root is that of the wisdom of humanity. Here the contribution of the present Pope, both in his authoritative teachings and in his theological writings, has been immense. The insight of the Anglican lay theologian, C.S. Lewis, has been vindicated: 'There never has been, and never will be, a radically new judgement of value in the history of the world.' History changes, humanity does not.

How can one characterise *Humanae vitae*? Max Horkheimer, the only thinker of stature in Germany at the time who had a positive word to say about the encyclical, sums it up: contraception is the death of eros. Love and fertility are inseparable. When man, on his own initiative, separates what God has joined, the result can only spell disaster. But to experience the gift of married love while respecting its creative potential is to acknowledge 'that one is not the master of the sources of life but rather the minister of the design established by God'.[50] Periodic abstinence, however painful, can fuel love. Numerous couples have experienced the truth of this. They know too that God is at work in the conjugal act. In the words of Paul VI, 'In love there is more than love'. To protect that truth, among others, the successor of St Peter promulgated *Humanae vitae* thirty years ago. It was, and is, prophetic.

'No prophet is acceptable in his own country' (Lk 4:24; cf. Jn 4:44). One could add, or in his own time. Like Elijah, the Pope had in fact taken on the world single-handedly. He also warned of the dire consequences of rejecting his teaching. They have all, sadly, come true.[51] Why?

Underlining modernity is atheism, and its attendant rejection of anything we might call human nature. Jean Paul Sartre, the French philosopher, who stood behind the students at the

barricades in the sixties and stands behind their successors, the
terrorists and the liberal reformers, who want to change the world
to suit their respective ideologies, said: 'There is no such thing as
human nature because there exists no God to think it creatively.'
Instead man is condemned to be free, to choose his own values, to
make the world in his own image and likeness. Free choice is the
only absolute and 'conscience' alone decides what is right or
wrong. This is the ultimate justification for all the 'pro-choice'
movements (feminists, gay rights activists, pro-abortionists,
advocates of divorce, IVF, etc.). Since there is no human act
intrinsically wrong, morality is reduced to a calculus of
consequences. Since there is no objective moral truth, relativism
rules supreme, the law has no foundation. And the result is the
rule of the strong over the weak – the poor and oppressed, those
in the womb or on the edge of the tomb.

Pope Paul VI had touched the nerve ends of a whole spectrum
of fundamental questions concerning human life and behaviour,
as well as the nature of the Church and theology. This is not
surprising, considering the fact that the subject of the encyclical
was 'the transmission of human life', that unique act whereby a
new human being, body and soul, comes into existence. A new
human being is a new universe, one that will last for ever. There is
nothing greater in the created order. The act whereby this creation
may occur is one designed by God Himself. To ignore his design
written into that act is to reject God, whether one is aware of this
or not. When man, of his own initiative, separates the unitive
significance of this act from its procreative significance, he is
usurping the place of God. Is it any wonder that our Churches are
emptying and vocations falling?

6

VOCATIONS
AND THEOLOGY

I would like to find, a pleasant cheerful priest,
full of faith, charitable and kindly,
who would have sympathy for the poor and be gentle with his flock,
but I would not like a good-for-nothing in the fair livery of the Only Son.
(IRISH, ANON.)[1]

After a period in which quite extraordinary numbers joined the priesthood and the religious life, male and female, a period which reached its peak in the 1960s, a decline began that only recently has been fully registered by the Church at large with the quite dramatic decline in vocations to the diocesan priesthood. Religious engaged in the teaching and nursing ministries were the first to notice a change, as the number of novices dropped and soon almost vanished, as did the once ubiquitous convents in every town and city. They were soon to be followed by the missionary congregations, which had sent out record numbers of nuns, brothers, and priests to all parts of the world. Today they receive but a handful of vocations between them. Closing down their houses and moving to smaller communities has become almost a trend among religious. The main exceptions to this trend seem to be the more contemplative orders.

Initially, the decline was not particularly noticeable among the secular clergy. But then, within the past two decades, the numbers signing up for the diocesan priesthood began to drop, slowly at first and recently more dramatically. In the autumn of 1997, the country woke up one morning to the sensational news that no one had entered the seminary in Dublin that year – an archdiocese with a Catholic population of over a million.[2] Soon after, shortage of numbers forced the diocesan seminary, Holy Cross College, Clonliffe, Dublin, to close its doors. It was not the first. The older colleges at Kilkenny, Wexford, and Waterford had already closed their doors within the previous decade, after almost two centuries of supplying priests for the home mission and abroad. Thurles soon followed. More worrying, perhaps, is the fact that three years ago, not even one seminarian from the entire western seaboard, once a source of innumerable vocations, entered the seminary.

At the National Seminary in Maynooth, the fall in vocations could be observed at the beginning of each year when the seminary community gathered for sung Mass in the magnificent neo-gothic College Chapel, affectionately known as 'the Gunne', one of the undiscovered glories of Irish architecture and one of the most sublime sacral buildings in the land. Built to seat some five hundred seminarians – which was the number in the 1960s, when I studied at Maynooth – the sublime edifice soared over the continually decreasing numbers of seminarians clad in white surplices and black soutanes in the oak-timbered stalls – down to some sixty-six at present (2003) – their fading numerical presence reminiscent of Matthew Arnold's ebbing tide of faith. That was, until Autumn 2002. Since then, the College community no longer holds its Sunday Mass in the Gunne, but in the smaller chapel of St Joseph's. Soutanes and surplices are 'out' (lest they offend the laity, I was informed on enquiry). The great sacred edifice built to worship God in glory is now used for the occasional concert of sacred music, the annual Christmas Carol Service, and the Pontifical University's conferring ceremonies – while Solemn Mass is only celebrated on such occasions as the ordination to the diaconate, when space is needed to accommodate the guests. Otherwise, 'private Masses' are celebrated early each morning in the side altars that cluster around the main altar. And, of course, the Blessed Sacrament is reserved, at least on most days. The beauty of the church still reflects the Real Presence it was built to celebrate.

Quite obviously, recent widely publicised clerical scandals contributed to this development. But the fall in vocations had already begun long before the many cases of child and other abuse surfaced to shame us – and to make it difficult at times to be seen in public wearing a Roman collar, not to mention soutane and surplice in church. These scandals exacerbated the underlying crisis in the Church discussed above. The more disturbing question is: could what in public discourse, especially among clerics, is called a crisis of vocations be something more profound and disturbing, namely a crisis of faith? A closer look at the general reaction to the 'crisis' by religious and clerics alike is quite revealing about the state of the Church in Ireland today.

Different responses to the drop in vocations

Reaction to the fall of vocation among the female and male religious was, initially, unbelief, a sense of bewilderment, especially since religious were to the forefront in implementing the changes of Vatican II. Indeed, one must in all honesty ask to what extent that enthusiasm may itself, perhaps, have been a contributory factor to the fall of vocations. Members of religious orders (male and, especially, female) flocked to all kinds of courses in theology – anything from occasional lectures to a one-year diploma – to learn about the new changes and to repair the previous deficit in theology. There was a veritable thirst for theology, in particular among women religious in 'active' congregations, most of whom seem to have been denied any substantial theological nourishment for decades before the Council. Alas, theology, no less than any serious discipline, cannot be acquired by attending a few lectures or reading a few books and articles, or even completing full-time diploma courses lasting a year. Many, it is true, benefited from these courses. Scripture was opened up to religious (and to the laity) in a way that was previously unknown, and this, of course, is an important 'plus'. But due to the effective absence of any real theology before the Council, many others came away from the (at best superficial) immersion into this new arcane 'discipline' of theology either puffed up with their new knowledge or simply confused. Exposure to critical theology can quite unintentionally have the effect of creating the seeds not of faith but of doubt,[3] and this is all the more so for more mature people, when all that had given meaning to their lives was either implicitly questioned or indeed explicitly ridiculed.

More senior clerics who had undergone serious training in disciplines other than theology tended to preserve their critical spirit,[4] and so remained sceptical of what was being offered as 'modern theology', even while acknowledging that they were not theologians themselves. Such critical voices often had to suffer the opprobrium of being called 'conservative'. But most other clerics and religious tended to be intoxicated with a 'little knowledge', especially that which gave them cause to jettison the past (anything preconciliar) as antediluvian if not positively harmful. Soon priests, nuns, and brothers were seeking other avenues of 'self-fulfilment'. Fewer and fewer of those in training, often sensing a lack of direction or consistency, stayed the course. And since the bugle was sounding a very uncertain call, few were prepared even to get ready for battle (cf. 1 Cor 14:8).

The decline itself often gave those advocating change in the various orders the excuse to push through small but far-reaching transformations. These included changes to, and then the dropping of, traditional liturgical and devotional practices, withdrawal from traditional ministries in hospitals, schools, or indeed, in some cases, a contemplative life of perpetual adoration of the Blessed Sacrament, generally coupled with the option for more 'pastoral' activities in parishes and specialised ministries.

This in turn led to abandonment of the convent for smaller communities – sometimes demanded by the decrease in numbers, sometimes for more ideological reasons (insertion into deprived communities), and sometimes less exalted but very human reasons, such as comfort. Traditional pieties, such as the former intense devotion to Mary, were abandoned. These were replaced by anything from reflexology and counselling to courses in psychology and feminist ideology. Yet, few young people 'heard the call'. Of those who did hear the call, few stayed the course.

And so, it was argued, even more radical changes must be undertaken to 'renew' one's own religious congregation, to bring it in line with 'the spirit of Vatican II' and, even more so, 'the signs of the times'.[5] These were often undertaken under the imperative of the need to return to the 'charism' of the founder, usually selected to suit the perceived needs of the day. 'Facilitators' were brought in from outside the order to 'manage' these changes and even control the expected tensions within communities between the 'progressives' and the 'conservatives'. The basic skills of such well-paid 'facilitators' were honed in the world of business (manipulating employees to adjust to the needs of management, though few would admit to this) and so not exactly suited to the specific needs (or indeed spiritual tradition) of a particular congregation. Skills in community dynamics were employed to more or less 'move' communities towards the changes desired by those 'in administration' but which, it could be reasonably feared, might meet with some resistance, a resistance that had to be broken with the use of 'group dynamics'.[6] In any case, more radical changes were made. Yet, fewer still 'heard the call'. Others left. Communities aged.

Mission-sending congregations, devoid of a coherent theological vision,[7] took up with considerable zeal the causes of justice (especially gender equality), peace, and social *engagement*, for which no specific religious commitment was really needed. More recently, 'the integrity of creation' has been added to this list of priorities for missionaries.[8] Slowly these commitments were eventually taken over by Non-Governmental Organisations, often supported by professional bodies such as the Government agency APSO and other independent agencies such as Concern and the Bishop's agency, Trócaire. Generous young Irish people went in considerable numbers (mostly for a limited period of time) to feed the hungry, assist the poor in their plight, fight for justice, and help the downtrodden in innumerable ways. But few were inspired to become missionaries in the original sense of the term, as evangelisers sent to proclaim the *Good News* to those who did not know Christ. Vocations to the missionary congregations, men and women, very quickly dried up. Now, even the number of volunteers for the NGOs is apparently in decline.

There were other currents within the Church in the wake of the Council, which could have served to renew the congregations from within. One thinks immediately of the charismatic renewal. It helped restore a sense of personal communion with Christ, which, after all, is the bedrock of religious life, and engendered a new sense of mission and evangelisation. To say that the Church at large, which tends (not without good reason) to be rather sceptical of what Ronald Knox described as 'enthusiasm', did not wholeheartedly embrace the charismatic movement with its strong emotional component, is an understatement. Some religious, especially female, found it spiritually invigorating, others saw it as a distraction from their commitment to bring justice and peace to the world. Out of the charismatic movement[9] emerged at least two vibrant lay movements and a certain number of fine vocations to the priesthood and the religious life. Rome was wiser; from the outset, it gave the charismatic movement, as well as the various other similar, primarily lay, movements, the space they needed to flourish, while at the same time binding them to the more traditional structures of the Church. Other missed opportunities include the Post-Synodal Apostolic Exhortation on Consecrated Life (*Vita Consecrata*, 1996), which was practically ignored in Ireland. It expresses a genuine theological vision for religious life in the coming centuries. A serious attempt to understand its spirit would seem to be a *sine qua non* for the renewal of religious life here.

Reaction to the drop in vocations

It wasn't long before some began to think that perhaps the era of religious life was over, or at least religious life as we knew it, in particular that of the congregations founded in the eighteenth, nineteenth and early twentieth centuries (and that included most Irish orders). Many religious lost their sense of identity and, seeing the direction their congregation was heading, began to have doubts about inviting new members to join them. One popular theory (perhaps echoing Toynbee's theory of civilisations) was that all orders had a limited life-span: an enthusiastic beginning followed by growth and then its inevitable demise. The term 'inevitable' is the key term. This pattern of growth and decline was a kind of 'law' of nature, a form of historical determinism that marks the modern notion of progress, not unlike that found in Marxism (itself quite popular among religious at the time). One had simply to accept the inevitable with good grace. Such an hypothesis was somehow or other comforting – after all it was a 'law', something that could not be reversed, and could even be interpreted as God's will, the 'spirit of the times'. In the meantime, life for the survivors had to be made as bearable and comfortable as possible; any attempt at recruitment was abandoned, while the members waited for the inevitable disappearance of the tradition that had inspired them to leave everything and follow Christ. And so, some communities simply began the final phase of 'phased obsolescence'.

It should be added that these developments did not issue in any kind of perceptible angst or undue introspection. Most religious simply got on with their highly responsible and personally fulfilling jobs as teachers, nurses, and administrators, which they carried out with characteristic selflessness. Others found new apostolates and ministries, which promised great things – and sometimes delivered them quite spectacularly. In this context mention should be made

of the extraordinary work of Sr Consilio Fitzgerald in founding
Cuan Mhuire, five residential centres providing treatment for
alcohol, drug and other addictions, or the social work of Sr
Stanislaus Kennedy. Most communities were, understandably, not
particularly sorry to see the former restrictions lifted and a certain
amount of care and comfort to ease their daily lot. All these, it
could be argued, were welcome developments. What was, and still
is, missing, is an overarching vision of religious life and its
indispensable place in the Church's mission. The older vision, more
an assumption than anything reflective or conscious, simply faded
more and more into the background and was not replaced by a
new one. It was only when members of religious congregations
came together for assemblies or chapters that members became
aware of the absence of such a vision. An ersatz had to be found,
and was eventually found under the banner of justice and peace,
the integrity of creation, and feminism.

When the members declined from fifty to fifteen and less, big
convents had to be sold – almost one a week at one stage, or so it
seemed from the property section of the newspapers. Some were
given over to housing projects for the poor, the sick, and the aged.
Others were turned into retirement homes for old and infirm
religious, while a sizeable number of the remaining active
members moved into suburban houses, some on their own, others
in twos or threes, though there are also communities of six and
more. There is an interesting study yet to be carried out with
regard to the latter. How did members of religious orders,
accustomed all their lives to spacious buildings custom-built for
the observances of religious life (the Divine Office, Mass, the
silence, study) adapt to the tight living conditions of houses with
flimsy walls, built for the modern 'nuclear family' whose members
spend most of the day outside the house? How do these new
conditions impinge on what was traditionally understood as
religious life as distinct from domestic life?

It would be wrong to place the blame for the gradual
evaporation of religious life in Ireland on the Second Vatican

Council. The real trouble was that we were even less prepared for the council than most countries, as I pointed out above, primarily because of the absence of any genuine theological tradition. I do not deny that many of the changes made were needed and, indeed, have been beneficial. The former restrictive lifestyle is gone, as are many practices that were long past their 'best before' date, while the old legalism and external religious conformity are no more. Those in authority are now more sensitive to the implications of that responsibility for those in their charge. New initiatives were taken, such as the entry of (mostly women) religious into more direct pastoral life, such as parish work as well as chaplaincy to schools and hospitals, where they are providing an invaluable and much appreciated service. Neither did the turmoil destroy all the good done by religious in their traditional roles. Though their presence may not be as visible as it previously was, much great work is still being done by sisters, brothers, and religious orders in new and old ministries. Their work, oftentimes heroic, goes unnoticed by the general public. And this may be the way it should be for those called to live in a radical way that life 'hidden with Christ in God' (Col. 3:3; cf. Mt 6:4, 6, 8, 18).

Despite the fact that the Irish Church still has the highest proportion of clergy to laity in the world, the secular clergy are suddenly beginning to feel the pinch. What has been the reaction of the diocesan clergy to the drop in vocations? An issue of the diocesan magazine for the Diocese of Cork and Ross, *The Fold* (Spring 2001), is instructive in this regard. The cover article is devoted to the 'critical shortage of priests' in the diocese. 'Who will be your last parish priest?' was the not very encouraging title of the lead article. The article itself, complete with graph (age profile) and 'facts and figures' detailing the decline in active clergy and in vocations, was primarily concerned with statistics and with a dismal projection for the future. It ends: 'If present trends continue up to the year 2010, there will then be just six diocesan priests aged 45 or less.' The article gives no hope that present trends can be reversed.[10] The only change foreseen is more work for an already overburdened clergy, which seems to be obvious, but which in fact fails to take into account the falling number of those who regularly take part in the celebration of the sacraments. Fewer practising Catholics may mean less work.

This approach to clerical shortage, it will be noticed, is purely sociological. On its own, such an approach stifles the spirit. Another article in the same issue is entitled: 'Is ours the last generation to value priesthood?'[11] The title catches the tone of the magazine, namely that the present state may be bad, but worse is yet to come. It is not exactly an encouraging message for the readers of the diocesan monthly, who tend to be the more committed Catholics, whose faith in God and the Church has been severely tested in recent years – and not just by the 'scandals'. Neither is such a message likely to encourage vocations. What young man, contemplating a possible vocation to the priesthood, would join a sinking ship? Yet, when they touch on this subject in their sermons, this seems to be the only message priests convey. Such an exclusively sociological approach to the decline in vocations fosters unbelief, even despair.[12] It is basically fatalistic.

Fatalism v. faith?

Let us look more closely at the phenomenon of fatalism. Long before vocations to the diocesan clergy began to dry up, fatalism manifested itself in the theory already mentioned above, namely a kind of law of inevitable growth and decline governing religious life. It claimed that, after orders had reached their peak and fulfilled their time-conditioned purpose, they gradually faded away. Is this so? While it is true that, in the course of its history, the Church has seen the appearance and disappearance of various orders and congregations, the historical circumstances surrounding each are so diverse that it is hard to see how anyone could detect an overall pattern, not to mention a 'law'. Monastic life in Ireland went through various stages of decay and renewal. Sometimes the renewal came from within the Irish monastic tradition, as in the case of the emergence of the Culdees in the eight century, or from without, with the advent of the Cistercians and Augustinians in the twelfth century and the mendicant orders in the thirteenth. They too eventually went into decay, until in the fifteenth century the Observant reform from within the religious orders, especially the mendicants, renewed their spiritual life. This pattern of decay and renewal would have continued, if most of the ancient abbeys and monasteries of Ireland were not emptied and literally ruined by external force at the time of the final conquest of Ireland that unfortunately coincided with the Reformation. It is difficult to detect any internal 'law' of decline and eventual extinction. Indeed, it is simply banal to say that every human institution has its beginning, its peak of flourishing and then a gradual decline. Such a contention is probably as false as it is simplistic. In fact, religious institutions, like most other human institutions, more often display an up-and-down curve of expansion followed by contraction, followed by a renewal and a new expansion, again depending on the historical circumstances in different countries. And, of course, some have become extinct, though not all.

What is most remarkable is the fact that so many religious orders and congregations have *survived* internal upheavals and external assaults. One immediately thinks of the Benedictines and the various reform congregations they produced, or the great mendicant orders of the Middle Ages that are still flourishing. Thanks to its unique geographical situation and a unique set of historical circumstances, for example, the Augustinian Abbey of St Maurice in Switzerland founded at the beginning of the sixth century, though with even more ancient religious roots,[13] has survived intact down to today. The Irish Augustinians, Franciscans and Dominicans also survived, thanks primarily to their houses in Continental Europe, though their mediaeval monasteries in Ireland are mostly but ruins.[14] Never entirely eradicated, the mendicants re-emerged in Ireland in the eighteenth and nineteenth centuries together with native-born congregations of nuns and brothers, who, apart from the religious revival they instigated, also built-up the educational, health, and social-welfare infrastructure of modern Ireland.

It is also worth recalling that, for the greater part of the history of the Irish Church, there has been a shortage of priests. Reading Professor Corish's historical overview, it is striking how often he notes how inadequate the clergy were in coping with the basic pastoral demands of the day, and this over a period dating from the early Irish Church[15] up to the early nineteenth century.[16] Not only were the diocesan clergy low in numbers, but in the first half of the nineteenth century members of the traditional religious congregations who had been in Ireland since the middle ages (such as the Franciscans) were reduced to a handful.[17] And yet by the end of the century their monasteries were filling up, new houses were opened, and more recently founded congregations from the continent came into Ireland to reap a rich harvest of vocations. The huge numbers of vocations during the first half of the twentieth century were more the exception than the rule, perhaps for reasons outlined above by Desmond Fennell.

But none of this explains the emergence of the fatalism that seems to have overcome religious life in contemporary Ireland. This, it seems to me, has to do in the first place with the psychological impact of Vatican II and, secondly, with the all-pervasive cultural influence of a certain quasi-Hegelian interpretation of history as inexorably moving toward its own perfection, history understood as inevitable progress. Even in countries where there was greater preparation than in Ireland, the Council was so traumatic that it became fashionable to speak of the time 'before' and 'after' the Council, as though Vatican II was the inauguration of a new era, a new dispensation in Salvation History. The period before the Council was seen as the time of the strict law, whereas after the Council we now live in the time of freedom and grace. This, of course, is nothing less than an appropriation of the distinction between the Old and the New Testaments and the real discontinuity caused by the life, death and resurrection of Jesus Christ, and the emergence of the Church, the new People of God. And even then, the discontinuity was not radical, as the continuity with the Old Testament was preserved though transformed.

But that feeling of disjunction with what was pre-Vatican II was even greater in Ireland than in most other countries. The rock-like security on which religious life had been founded was no more. Further, the past form of religious life, it was thought, has really nothing to teach the present, apart from whatever in the lives of the respective founders could be detected as models for making a new start. What was stressed was the way such heroic men and women broke with the traditions of their day and stood up to opposition (even by bishops and clergy). The founder's preconciliar devotions and piety were quietly ignored, though these were, it could be argued, the real source of their extraordinary achievements – and of their courage – as in the case of Pope John XXIII recently beatified.[18]

Connected with this experience of radical discontinuity with the past was the emergence in the late 1960s and early 1970s of a secular progressivism associated with our new prosperity, technological advances, and the various revolutions of the sixties, which overwhelmed Ireland. 'Being up-to-date', being modern, was the imperative of the moment. In industry and agriculture, adopting the newest technologies and methods was *de rigueur*. In the Church, it involved the transformation of such theological notions as the Kingdom of God *beyond time* into inner worldly expectations of justice, peace, and prosperity for all *in this world*: 'the kingdom'. This new paradise on earth, it was felt, could be achieved in the not-too-distant future, if the political will could be mustered. To this end, protest marches were organised, which for many 'modern' religious tended to replace the old devotional processions. This was given a theoretical foundation in a philosophy of history as inexorably moving towards a better future, a better world. It found its most extreme expression in some Latin American theologies of liberation, but it was all-pervasive, especially in Ireland with our inbuilt, felt need to 'catch up' with the rest of the modern world. Change became the order the day, often change for the sake of change.

When all the changes introduced into religious life failed to rejuvenate the various religious congregations, then the underlying theory of historical determinism emerged as an explanation of the feared demise of the various congregations. They were, it was felt, being pushed aside by the onward march of history. They had perhaps outlived their historical usefulness – in effect, creating modern Ireland – and so would inevitably become extinct. This fatalism, for that is what it amounts to, betrays however a lack of faith, but it also prevents the exercise of any genuine self-criticism leading to *metanoia*, a change of heart.

The dominant progressivism does not allow for self-criticism. It is anathema even to suggest that some of the changes ushered in – at times imposed on reluctant, but basically obedient, communities – might not have been for the best. We seem incapable of even posing honest questions to ourselves, such as: were the many changes really true to the letter and the spirit of the Council documents? Is it time to take another look at the documents of Vatican II? Have we understood them properly? Is there anything in religious life that was thrown out in good faith but perhaps should be recovered – communal prayer, silence, and an otherwise distinctive way of life?[19]

Further, why is it that so many past pupils of schools run by priests and religious are not only disinterested in religion but are also often quite hostile? What went wrong with our religious education and catechetical programmes? Why is it that so few of our Irish youth, many of them attending Catholic schools, participated in the World Youth Days organised by the Pope in recent years – Santiago de Compostela, Denver, Paris and Rome during the Great Jubilee, and more recently Toronto? Why did the Catholic schools make little effort to promote these Youth Days? Indeed, why did so few of the younger diocesan clergy promote them? Why were there practically no Irish Mass servers in Rome for the meeting of some 20,000 with the Holy Father in August 2001? Why is it that there are almost no new religious foundations[20] or so few lay movements in Ireland, compared to

France, Spain, or Italy, for example, or rather why are they practically unknown to the Church at large?[21] Is it because our attachment to anything new or progressive prevents us from looking at the rich history of the Church for inspiration, though it is precisely there that so many new orders and Catholic youth movements in continental Europe have their source? Why is it that the hope which Pope John Paul II exudes, his tireless call not to be afraid, his rich theology, finds so little echo among most Irish clergy or religious? Is it because we have forgotten that the task of priest or religious is to become a witness in the modern world to man's openness to the mystery of God (cf. *Gaudium et spes*, 41)?

The crisis in vocations, I am convinced, is but a symptom of a much deeper and more serious crisis, that of faith. Faith implies a theological vision, namely the attempt to interpret life from God's perspective. As Paul, quoting Isaiah, reminds us: 'we teach what scripture calls: the things that no eye has seen and no ear has heard, things beyond the mind of man, all that God has prepared for those who love him' (1 Cor 2:9). This is the antithesis (and the antidote) to fatalism or resignation in the face of what seems to be 'the inevitable'.

Are present trends irreversible?

There are sufficient examples of how 'downward trends' can be reversed. In the first place, it should be remembered that, as a matter of fact, the present worldwide trend is that vocations are on the increase. Over thirty years ago, for example, the Churches in almost all the Latin American countries suffered a critical shortage of priests. Vocations had almost dried up. Seminaries closed down. Today, there is a renaissance of faith among the youth, leading to greater commitment to justice in society and more regular attendance to religious duties. The result is a resurgence of vocations to the priesthood and the religious life, including the missionary life. This renewal has various roots, but it seems to be not unrelated to the development within the Latin American theology of liberation that in recent years moved beyond a materialist notion of liberation to a more spiritual one, without giving up their 'option for the poor'. In a word, the theological ferment caused by the debate on liberation theology, as well as a very real option for the poor, it could be argued, created a new openness to the message of the Gospel.

The Church in France – the eldest daughter of the Church – is perhaps closer to home and closer to the Irish experience of a once predominantly (but not exclusively) Catholic country turned secular. After over a century of radical secularisation, the metropolitan diocese of Paris with over two million souls has a steady number of candidates for the priesthood. (The latest figure is 107.) This is due in no small part to the standing of the Archbishop of Paris in public life. Cardinal Lustiger's erudition, coupled with his courage in tackling the major questions affecting society and debating them in public, has helped to endow the Church in Paris with a new credibility. He also made vocations a priority, and set up a new training programme for his candidates to the priesthood, combining genuine scholarship with systematic pastoral training in parishes. A controversial figure in many ways, he has earned respect even from his enemies on the national stage as a thinker able and willing to speak coherently and convincingly about the issues of the day. When he enters the fray of public debate, he does so from an unapologetically theological perspective, and yet without any trace of dogmatism.

Indeed, the Church in France as a whole, which is beset with her own major problems, seems to be undergoing a springtime in vocations. It has in recent decades witnessed the emergence of several new religious orders and many vibrant youth movements – both phenomena are interrelated. No matter how difficult the situation was in France, the Church there continued to think, and to think theologically. It continued to foster scholarly theological research – symbolised by the publication of the patristic series *Sources chrétiennes* – and to address the burning issues of the age, which, of course, are intellectual, spiritual issues. It has a number of Catholic newspapers and periodicals of a high theological standard

addressed to educated Catholics. The situation is the same among
the Protestant Churches in France, who run no less than five
theological faculties, though they number but one million faithful.
The real materialism of the Church in Ireland is not manifest in the
excesses of the *nouveaux riches*, but in her singular disinterest in
serious thought of any metaphysical or theological nature.

Perhaps the most blatant manifestation of the basically
pragmatic and materialistic tenor of modern Irish Catholicism is
the way Latin and Greek were dropped from the curriculum by
practically all Church-run schools, including the diocesan colleges,
once these subjects were no longer needed for matriculation
purposes to the university! Latin (and possibly Greek)[22] were
taught in the early Irish monastic schools side-by-side with the
native language, making Ireland the 'harbinger of the middle
ages'.[23] After the destruction of the monasteries, the hedge schools
of Munster (especially Kerry), under circumstances which were
not exactly propitious, 'were renowned for their classical teaching
and attracted students from Connaught and Ulster'.[24] Their
influence was felt as late as the latter part of the nineteenth
century.[25] The diocesan colleges took up the torch and fed into the
Classics department in Maynooth, which was described by one
external examiner at the beginning of the twentieth century as the
best Greek school in 'the British Isles, if not in Europe'.[26] But at the
dawn of our new prosperity, Latin and Greek were simply
dropped, though they are still prized educational attainments in
much of the rest of Europe and are widely taught in the secondary
schools there. Within the space of a generation, Irish youth was
deprived of direct access to the main sources of Western thought
and civilization – and also deprived of that privileged access to
reason's capacity for knowing Truth (and thus God) first
discovered by the tragedians and philosophers of ancient Greece.
This encounter of reason with the truth of the ultimate depth of
the human condition – metaphysics – is one of the prerequisites
for theology, which endeavours to probe 'the Desired of all
nations',[27] the Word who became flesh.[28]

An educational system of a purely pragmatic and utilitarian nature – and devoid of any encounter with the ultimate truths of the human condition – must in time affect the study of literature and history as well as religion in the schools. Education then provides students with sophisticated skills and the means to earn a living, but deprives them of a reason for living or the resources to cope with the disappointments and struggles life inevitably brings in its course. The usual escape outlets – drink, drugs, sex, and now suicide – are embraced with abandon. It also means that fewer and fewer young people even entertain the thought of possibly devoting their lives to that which gives meaning to their own life and enriches the community at large. Trained to pursue careers that promise financial rewards and the 'good life' in abundance, it is hardly surprising that a life dedicated to God and the poor does not appear exactly attractive.

There are young men and women who do find such a commitment attractive – but few find the existing religious communities or the diocesan priesthood either inspiring or attractive. Some have gone overseas in search of a religious community, where worship and contemplation are given priority and where care for the poor, including the spiritually impoverished, is not reduced to a 'mission statement'.

When all is said and done, a vocation is not simply a human phenomenon. It is the working of divine grace in the heart and mind of a believer. There is a sense of intrinsic greatness about any calling to the religious life and to priesthood, since one is called to sacrifice what is so humanly appealing and good: marriage and a family, personal autonomy and career opportunities that would enable one to enjoy the 'good life'. Some are called by God to dedicate themselves to serving His people in various ministries, others to spend their lives spreading the Gospel overseas, others to devote their lives to the care of the old, the infirm, the retarded and dispossessed of this world, others to promote justice and peace. Perhaps we have not sufficiently stressed this call to humble daily heroism, or appealed to that 'spirit of generosity to the point of prodigality' that characterised the Irish people's initial response to the Christian message and accounted 'in large measure for the strikingly high numbers following the monastic calling in the new Irish Church'.[29] This spirit of generosity has never quite vanished in our long tradition. There is no reason to assume that the youth of today are devoid of it. Indeed, *Youth 2000* proves the point dramatically.[30] And even with regard to those who seem to be indifferent to the imperatives of faith, the opposite would seem to be case to judge by some of the lyrics of U2[31] or the phenomenal success of *Sacred Space*, the prayer website created by a small team at the Jesuit Communications Centre in Dublin, which has clocked up five million visits from around the world, with not a few from Ireland.[32] But to sound the bugle (1 Cor 14:8), we must once again learn the tune. Theologians are supposed to help compose that tune.

Irish theology

There are fine Irish scholars on the various faculties, and others working in parishes or attached to various religious orders, who studied at the best theology faculties at home and abroad. However, for most members of the few theological faculties remaining in the country, which should be the main source of theological research, serious scholarly research and regular publications generally tend to take second place to teaching. In recent years, considerable attention has been given to improving methods of teaching and keeping academic standards in line with the best university practice. But little time for sustained research is left after the average lecturer has completed his duties as teacher, examiner, supervision of postgraduate students, and after contributing to various administrative duties on the faculty. Lecturers have no research assistants and no secretarial staff. Only recently in Maynooth were postgraduate students engaged as tutors. I remember one semester when, for a number of weeks, I had an average of eighteen 'student-contact hours', eight being the maximum demanded of university lecturers. More recently, teaching has been subordinated to 'formation', once the provenance of the deans (of discipline), now called directors of formation. This trend has since been incorporated into new seminary statutes, which, following a somewhat literal interpretation of the Apostolic Letter on priestly formation, *Pastores dabo vobis*, now conceives lecturers primarily as part of the formation team, and so subordinated to some vague process called 'formation' rather than seeing the disciplined study of theology as itself *the* primary source of formation.[33]

One of the main reasons for an impoverished Irish theology is, apart from all the factors mentioned above (such as the language question and the pragmatism which the Irish Catholic Church has in common with secular 'modern Ireland' and which is reflected in the educational system), the simple fact that students who come to university to study theology generally have little foundation in terms of general religious knowledge. Many blame the catechisms approved by the hierarchy for both primary and secondary levels. And by all accounts, the situation is not exactly encouraging.[34] But it is hardly fair to put the blame on the shoulders of those who drew up the programmes or try to put them into practice. The real reason, it seems to me, is the lack of a rich, critical theological tradition in Ireland, which could provide both inspiration and content. I am not sufficiently familiar with the educational theories behind these programmes to comment on them, but I have heard much criticism, a criticism that is seemingly applicable to modern teaching methods in general. It would seem that the role of memory is greatly down-played, objective information tends to be somewhat neglected in favour of aimless discussions, and great stress is placed on one's feelings. In any case, those who register to study theology often come to university with little actual religious knowledge about the basics of the faith. They could be compared with students registering to study French literature with little or no knowledge of the French language. What is astonishing is that, because they are generally highly motivated, they gradually make up for so much they should have been able to take for granted and after three years acquire a remarkable grasp of the subject. A few have gone on to study at postgraduate level and are already established theologians in their own right. Many are now teaching at secondary level, and the improvement in the knowledge-level of their students when they sign up to study theology is noticeable. Religion as an examination subject for junior and leaving certificates should help improve the situations – provided the new examination subject overcomes its own distressingly non-denominational aspirations (for reasons which I discuss below in Appendix III), aspirations, I gather, that have received the Episcopal *placet*. But it will take at least another generation before theologically literate school leavers become the rule rather than the exception. All in all, from the point of view of preparing students adequately for theology as an academic subject, there are solid reasons for hope.

More serious is the fact that there is practically no open, public debate on the little theology that is published, no frank contentiousness between theologians fired by the passion for truth. Even in the realms of more measured scholarship, lack of public scrutiny by one's peers dulls the critical spirit and ensures that standards inevitably slip.[35] But that is not the main problem. The critical issue is the lack of appreciation, either by the public at large or by those in positions of responsibility in the Church, that theological research as such really *matters* and that open debate is essential to the health of the life of the Church. Indeed, how can one expect the public at large – as represented by the media – to take theology seriously, if the Church herself does not do so? The Church's lack of appreciation of the intellectual penetration of the faith and the need for serious engagement with contemporary currents of thought is demonstrated by three simple facts.

In the first place, there is an understandable but ultimately short-sighted reluctance when making appointments after ordination to give theological studies precedence over immediate needs (such as filling vacancies at the pastoral level or administration within the orders).[36]

Secondly, the fact that theological performance – or lack of it – in no way seems to affect the question of suitability of candidates for the priesthood. But that is a complex issue, as indeed many of the finest pastors were not scholastic high-flyers in the seminary but had shown other (indispensable) leadership qualities on the playing pitch or in the extracurricular activities in the seminary.

Thirdly, there is the lack of public recognition for the services of theologians *qua* theologians.[37] Of course, one is reminded of the hen and the egg. It could also be argued that Irish theology to date has not earned such public recognition. Irish theologians, I argued above, have yet to find their voice, to transform our acquired mother tongue into a suitable medium to express the divine and human mysteries. But for this to happen, there is one *conditio sine qua non*, namely that the Irish Church provide appropriate academic institutions and such back-up services as are required for the promotion of scholarly theological investigation. This calls for a radical change of mind and a new attitude to theology by *all* those who hold authority in the Church, an attitude that must find expression in a substantial investment of personnel and financial resources in theological scholarship. (These topics will be discussed in Appendix III.) Without a network of institutes devoted primarily to such scholarship – as distinct from seminaries and training centres for teachers of religion – the Irish Church is unlikely ever to produce an original thinker of the stature of a Rahner or a de Lubac. Without this change of mind and the creation of corresponding institutions, the long-term future of the Irish Church looks bleak indeed.

APPENDIX III:
THEOLOGY AS AN
ACADEMIC DISCIPLINE
IN IRELAND

It is true that recent decades have shown a remarkable increase in the number of courses in theology offered to the public, usually leading to a diploma of some kind. This is to be welcomed, as is the steady increase in the number of university-level students taking full-time degrees in Catholic theology at the Pontifical University, Maynooth, the Milltown Institute, Mater Dei Institute of Education, All Hallows College, and the Missionary Institute, Kimmage. But the significance of these degrees is seen primarily in pragmatic terms as providing teachers for secondary schools and offering careers in pastoral work, counselling, and the like. Nonetheless, it is noteworthy that, once they get a taste for theology, trained lay theologians are often more enthusiastic about theology than clerics – and more committed to it as a scholarly discipline. But what are the future prospects for full-time professional lay theologians in Ireland?

The recent Universities Act has opened the way for setting up faculties of theology in the State universities, and there are promising developments in that direction, in particular the incorporation of the Mater Dei Institute of Education into Dublin City University and that of Mary Immaculate College of Education into the University of Limerick. In Galway, the Western Institute of Theology has links to the university and the Institute of Technology there. But, apart altogether from the non-availability of sufficient suitably qualified theologians at present, few Irish universities have the extensive library facilities needed for research in the multiple sub-disciplines or specialisations that make up theology.[38] In addition, it must be said that, if theology in the State universities were to be conceived as being necessarily

non-denominational[39] (in fact, a contradiction in terms), then the
future for Irish theology looks even bleaker. As David Tracy put it,
'Indeed, on inner-theological terms all Christian theology is, in
some meaningful sense, church theology.'[40] The proposal to set up
'non-denominational' university faculties carries with it not only
the danger of a separation of theology from its matrix, the
Church, but also turning theology into something esoteric or
academic in the negative sense, thus furthering the impression
that theology does not really matter. Even at present, the absence
of a serious theological intellectual tradition in Ireland means that
almost anything can be labelled 'theology', including such things
a 'sacred dance' and 'eco-spirituality', to quote from a 'diploma in
theology' course I once saw on offer.

Even though theology is by nature denominational – Catholic,
Protestant, Anglican, Orthodox – yet every theologian by the very
nature of his or her discipline concerns himself or herself with the
findings of theologians from the other traditions, enters into dialogue
with them, is enriched by them, or refutes what is perceived to be
wrong in them. In fact, theological reflections cannot be simply
limited to theology but must include philosophy and literature, the
classics and history, as well as a number of other more specific
disciplines, depending on the area of theology. Thus fundamental
theology must be aware of developments in science, and the same
applies to moral theology, which must also examine such disciplines
as economics or politics as a science, while scripture scholars must
pay attention to such specialised disciplines as archaeology, linguistics,
and so on. After all, the object of theology as a scholarly discipline is
truth. No theologian, irrespective of the tradition within which he
operates has a monopoly on truth, even though each adheres to his
own tradition in the understanding that it is the most complete
expression of revelation, one that alone has remained faithful to
Scripture.[41] Every theologian worth his or her salt is in constant
dialogue with other thinkers, irrespective of their provenance.

In my own area of moral theology, the texts I have prescribed
over the years to the students for tutorial discussions and the

reading lists for further studies include writers and thinkers, both theological and non-theological, from every persuasion and none: Catholic writers are in the forefront, naturally, but Jewish and Protestant theologians, atheist and secular philosophers, are also to be found there. Their insights and objections must be taken seriously in the search for truth, just as the opposing opinions of exegetes and theologians within the Catholic tradition are an inevitable part of the indispensable struggle to make sense not only of the Church's doctrine, but of the human condition illuminated by the light of Christ that seeps through all human minds and hearts that are open to His mystery. The Church's teaching authority – the precise nature of its teaching being itself the object of scholarly study – is part of Christ's gift to humanity as a light in the darkness, and as an assurance that the human effort to understand is not doomed to the fate of Sisyphus, that reason will, in the final analysis, not go astray in its search for the Truth that alone can make us free.[42]

For all that, theology remains a scholarly discipline and thus needs institutions to foster the various specialisations, without which it cannot flourish. It is quite extraordinary that in the Republic of Ireland there are as yet practically no full-time, scholarly centres with the requisite human, financial, and textual resources devoted to professional, scholarly research in such highly specialised disciplines as Scripture,[43] the Fathers of the Church, or the great theologians of the Middle Ages. (The closest is the School of Celtic Studies, a department of the government-funded Dublin Institute for Advanced Studies, which over the years has produced critical editions of mediaeval Irish texts of the monastic period in the *Scriptores Latini Hiberniae* series.[44]) Despite the extraordinary Irish missionary tradition, there is as yet no full-time research institute devoted to the study of missiology and related subjects (such as anthropology and comparative religion).[45] The transformation of the Spiritan formation house into the Kimmage Institute run by the combined missionary congregations for the theological training of their candidates might in time develop such related institutes. With regard to more pressing ethical issues, while the Jesuit Faith and Justice Centre promotes the study of related issues, other pressing, highly specialised issues, such as bioethics have been ignored. Thus there is no institute in Ireland comparable to the Linacre Centre for Bioethics in England and the many similar centres in the United States.[46] By way of contrast, the Institute of Byzantine Studies in the Queen's University, Belfast, continues to flourish and its research programme has recently been approved by the British Academy. Exceptions to this general trend include the National Centre for the Liturgy, formerly in Carlow, now located in Maynooth, with affiliation to the Pontifical University, and the Irish School of Ecumenics founded by Fr Michael Hurley SJ, and now affiliated to Trinity College. In this context the initiative of the remarkable Fr Harry Bohan, Shannon, County Clare, should be mentioned. He proposes to build a 'IR£20 million research and retreat centre in Clare', the Céifin Centre.[47]

In the absence of any chair of patristic studies, despite an impressive number of scholars, both Catholic and Protestant, who did their research on the Church Fathers but ended up teaching other subjects (dogma, morals, history, philosophy), a few colleagues at Maynooth founded The Patristic Symposium in 1986 to foster the study of the Fathers of the Church. It was this field of specialised research that was responsible for many of the changes inaugurated by the Second Vatican Council. Patristic studies have taken on a new significance since then in the light of the new situation the Church finds itself in at present, namely one similar to that of the early Church: a minority in an alien environment. More importantly, to study the early Fathers is to be initiated into the original way of doing theology as well as becoming acquainted with a theology that is as spiritually as it is intellectually challenging. To date, there is no centre for such research in Ireland. Thanks primarily to funds from overseas,[48] the Patristic Symposium was able to organise four conferences (with papers given by members of various denominations and invited international scholars). The proceedings of the first three conferences were published and were well received internationally, though practically ignored at home. This is no substitute for a full-time chair or institute, where younger scholars can be trained in the required skills and continuity be assured. This, of course, would demand considerable financial investment – and the readiness to release suitable personnel for training. Maynooth, with its tradition of ancient classics, history, and patrology, would seem to be the ideal situation for such an institute. It possesses many of the resources needed and has a tradition of post-graduate research in related disciplines.

It is perhaps one of the most hopeful signs of today, that, thanks to either prayer groups or short courses in theology, so many young people have discovered the excitement and the enrichment that the study of theology entails, irrespective of the shortness or inadequacy of the course. More mature laity from all walks of life have discovered new hope and a sense of purpose on these courses. Young university students can now compare theology with their arts course, see how mutually enriching they both are, and know that, after an immersion in theology, they have something special to offer, once they graduate. Despite falling numbers of seminarians, the quality has not been affected. Indeed, I get the impression that the *proportion* of gifted seminarians has increased, and that even those who have little natural appetite for scholarship find theology more rewarding than was the case thirty years ago or more. This is one of the more positive gains from the present predicament of the Irish Church: a genuine openness, a search for answers, a humility or poverty of spirit that alone enables us to see God (cf. Mt 5:8).

Finally, the increase of centres of theological studies, even if they start out (as it were, on the wrong foot) by advocating 'non-denominational' theology, are still better than no centres at all. Once people begin to think about their faith, they will in time search for, and find the truth. This is part of our doctrinal tradition as Catholics, namely that human reason cannot be totally corrupted by sin, that human reason can reach God.

INSTEAD OF AN EPILOGUE

An tAthair Peadar Ó Laoghaire in his biography *Mo Scéal Féin* (p. 25) tells of his own experience in bringing the Viaticum:

> *Nuair a chuirinn an Ola Dhéanch ar sheanduine acu, agus nuair a thugainn an Corp Naofa dhó, agus nuair a deireadh sé ansan ó chroí amach, 'Mo ghrá mo Thiarna Íosa Críost! Mo ghrá go daingean É!' stadadh m'anáil orm agua thagadh luas croí orm agus scinneadh deoracha óm shúile i dtreo go n-iompainn i leataobh beagán.*

> When I anointed one of the old people and gave him the Sacred Body and then when he would say, 'My Lord Jesus Christ is my Love! My lasting love is He!' my breath would catch, my heart beat faster and tears pour down from my eyes, so that I would have to turn aside a little.[1]

This is the 'soul' of the Irish Catholic tradition, the spark that kept the embers glowing in the centuries that saw the destruction of its cultural richness. May it be rekindled among us!

Come, Holy Spirit…

NOTES

Introduction

1. 'Of the Cloth' in William Trevor, *The Hill Bachelors*, London: Penguin, 2001, 21.
2. This is the revealing title of a book that has been a major source of information and inspiration for my own reflections: Patrick Corish, *The Irish Catholic Experience: A Historical Survey*, Dublin: Gill and Macmillan, 1985. I should also like to acknowledge an enormous debt I owe to Mgr Corish for his stimulating conversations on many of the topics raised here, as well as for a fund of details that would be too tiresome to acknowledge in detail. It goes without saying that he is not to be held accountable for the use, or possible misuse, I made of his erudition and balanced judgement. He himself has often expressed the need for a theological analysis of the Irish Catholic experience as it was and as it continues to unfold. I don't think that I have done that, but perhaps in what follows the first tentative steps have been taken in that direction.
3. Cf., for example, John Gray, *Enlightenment's Wake*, London: Routledge, 2000.
4. Patrick Corish, *The Irish Catholic Experience*, 231.
5. With regard to the contribution of other theologians and scholars such as M. P Gallagher, Liam Ryan, P.R. Connolly, A. Falconer, E. McDonagh and S. Mac Réamoin, see the bibliography in J. J. Lee, *Ireland 1912-1985. Politics and Society*, Cambridge: University Press, 1989, 657, note 479. See also Denis Carroll (ed.), *Religion in Ireland. Past, Present and Future*, Dublin: The Columba Press, 1999, in

particular the contributions of Michael Drumm and Seán Mac Réamoinn; Dermot A. Lane (ed.), *New Century – New Society. Christian Perspectives,* Dublin, The Columba Press, 1999.

Chapter 1: The Irish Catholic Identity

1. *The Irish Catholic Experience,* 238, speaking about Irish missionaries of the nineteenth and twentieth centuries.
2. Cf. Mary Kenny, *Goodbye to Catholic Ireland.* Revised and updated edition, Dublin: New Island, 244-68.
3. Cf. Jonathan Sacks, *The Politics of Hope,* London: Jonathan Cape, 1997, especially 109-122.
4. See J. H. Whyte, *Church and State in Modern Ireland, 1923-1979,* second edn, Dublin: Gill and Macmillan, 1980, 196-238; Ruth Barrington, *Health, Medicine & Politics in Ireland 1900-1970,* Dublin: Institute of Public Administration, 1987, 201-21; Lee, *Ireland 1912-1985,* 313-22; 578-9; John Horgan, *Noël Browne. Passionate Outsider,* Dublin: Gill & Macmillan, 2000, 91-156, in particular 143-6, re Horgan's assessment of the role of Archbishop McQuaid of Dublin.
5. Cf. M. K. Flynn, *Ideology, Mobilization and the Nation. The Rise of Irish, Basque and Carlist Nationalist Movements in the Nineteenth and Early Twentieth Centuries,* New York: St Martin's Press, and Basingstoke: Macmillan Press, 2000, Ch. II, especially 58-64. See also Donald Harman Akenson, *Small Differences. Irish Catholics and Irish Protestants 1815-1922,* Dublin: Gill and Macmillan, 1991, 133-135. (The title probably alludes to what Freud called the 'narcissism of small differences'.) Akenson draws attention to the larger cultural background (nineteenth-century British colonial expansion and social Darwinism) out of which the modern concept of 'race' emerged. It also gave rise to 'Celticism', which A. J. Curtis, Jr, argues, was 'an ethnocentric form of nationalism with a strong measure of race consciousness' (ibid., 133).
6. See Brendan P. Devlin's critique of the bestseller, John O'Donoghue, *Anam čara,* London: Bantam Press, 1997, in *ITQ,* 64/4 (1999), 425-6.
7. Seán de Fréine, *The Great Silence, A study of a relationship between language and nationality,* Dublin & Cork: Mercier Press, 1978, 104-7, graphically describes the extent of our cultural dependence on

England. At the level of popular culture things have not exactly improved since he wrote in the 1960s, except that now we tend to be more dependent on North America. However, in the arts – music in particular – a new cultural confidence and independence can be observed, enabling artists to be open to the influence of other cultures and integrating the best of other cultures into our native traditions, thereby enriching them. This has been the pattern of creativity in Ireland since the earlier times. Only in the past two centuries did we become insular. Re Fennell, see below, chapter 2, n. 23.

8. Akenson, *Small Differences*, 134.

9. Cf. Corish, *The Irish Catholic Experience*, Chapter 3, 63-95; also the chapter entitled 'Irish and Catholic' in John J. Ó Ríordáin, *Irish Catholic Spirituality, Celtic and Roman*, Dublin: The Columba Press, 1998, 74-100. 'Although lacking a single political rallying point for centuries, the sense of national solidarity was so strong that Irish nationality survived despite disruption and oppression. Had some such national essence not already existed, it is unlikely that political nationalism could have created a sense of nationality in nineteenth-century Ireland, having regard to the inertia then so evident in Irish life, and to the weakening effects of emigration' (Seán de Fréine, *The Great Silence*, 51, who highlights the role of the Irish language in forging that national solidarity).

10. This was later given international legal articulation in the principle of *cuius regio, eius religio* of the Peace of Westphalia (1643).

11. Seán de Fréine, *The Great Silence*, 28, quoting Fr Canice Mooney; see also ibid., 58.

12. Thomas O'Connor, 'Towards the Invention of the Irish Catholic *Natio*: Thomas Messingham's *Florilegium*', ITQ, 64/2 (1999), 157-77, here 175.

13. Ibid., 175.

14. Ibid., 176.

15. O'Connor concludes: 'A *Natio* at home, a state on the map of Europe and an assured place in heaven: these were the ambitious aspirations which early seventeenth-century Irish intellectuals could entertain in their continental refuges as they reimagined Ireland for the Iron Century' (177).

16. Thomas O'Connor, 'Custom, Authority, and Tolerance in Irish Political Thought: David Rothe's *Analecta Sacra et Mira* (1616)' in ITQ, 65/2 (2000), 133-56, here 154.

17. Ibid. 155.
18. Edward Anwyl, *Celtic Religion in Pre-Christian Times*, London: Archibald Constable & Co Ltd, 1906, 65.
19. Cf. Thomas O'Loughlin, '"Celtic Spirituality", Ecumenism, and the Contemporary Religious Landscape' in *ITQ*, 67 (2002), 167. According to O'Loughlin, Muirchú and his fellow-cleric and writer, Adomnán, were engaged in creating a perception of Ireland that they hoped would help overcome endemic tribal warfare.
20. Cf. Thomas O'Loughlin, *Celtic Theology. Humanity, World and God in Early Irish Writings*, London and New York: Continuum, 2000, 93-4.
21. Kim McCone, *Pagan Past and Christian Present in Early Irish Literature*, Maynooth: An Sagart, 1990, 73. See, in particular, Chapter Four, 'The Law and the Prophets' (84-106), which describes how the early medieval monastic *literati* drew parallels between the Old Testament and their native traditions, seeing in the latter the inspiration of the Holy Spirit at work in their law-givers and poets, thus preparing the Gaels for the reception of the New Law from St Patrick.
22. Cf. Paul Johnson, 'The Almost-Chosen People: Why America Is Different' in Richard John Neuhaus (ed.), *Unsecular America* (Encounter Series: 2), Grand Rapids, Mich.: Wm. B. Eerdmans, 1986, 1-13. The title is a phrase used by Abraham Lincoln. (I am grateful to Fr John Donaghey SVD, for drawing my attention to this article.) Cf. also the comprehensive and stimulating discussion by Conor Cruise O'Brien, *God Land. Reflections on Religion and Nationalism*, Cambridge, Mass.: Harvard University Press, 1988. The ever-present actuality of this notion (the chosen people) may be seen in an article by Siobhan Nash-Marshall, 'On the Fate of Nations' in *Logos*, 4/2 (2001), 32-65.
23. As an example of this view, cf. the seventeenth-century poem by Seán Ó Connaill, 'Tuireamh na hÉireann', quoted by Diarmuid Ó Laoghaire, SJ, 'Irish Spirituality in Modern Times' in Michael Maher (ed.), *Irish Spirituality*, Dublin: Veritas, 1981, 125. Ó Laoghaire comments: 'No doubt Ireland was in a bad way in that dark century of fierce repression. Yet, as always, the Irish regarded the English as the instrument of God to punish them for their sins.' With regard to the Great Famine in the nineteenth century, 'Studies of the Irish folk tradition have shown that the commonplace reaction was to interpret the Famine as some form of divine punishment by the

Christian God for the people's sins. Alternatively, it was commonplace to explain events by invoking the action of non-Christian spirits who, in some way, had been vexed and therefore attacked the Irish people' (Akenson, *Small Differences*, 145).

24. Ó Laoghaire, op. cit., 126, theologically more perceptive, speaks about the 'purifying fire of the Penal Times'.

25. Corish, *The Irish Catholic Experience*, 214. See also Donald Harman Akenson, *Small Differences*, 139-40.

26. Corish, ibid., 215; note the context, 214-6. Nineteenth-century Irish Catholicism became in turn increasingly clerical and the clergy became increasingly political, as they stepped into the vacuum created by the absence of educated and articulate lay leaders (cf. ibid., 216; 229; see also Corish's generally positive evaluation of the controversial Paul Cullen, 222-3). With regard to the heavily politicised clergy of the early twentieth century, see Patrick Murray, *Oracles of God, The Roman Catholic Church and Irish Politics, 1922-37*, Dublin: University College Dublin Press, 2000. Murray questions the explanation for the recurring political assertiveness throughout the period simply as an impulse to power: 'Clerical power was an essential means to a greater end: to ensure that Irish society functioned in conformity with Catholic moral and social principles, which churchmen could not but regard as fundamental to individual and communal well-being' (419).

27. Corish, ibid., 195.

28. See Edmund M. Hogan, *The Irish Missionary Movement. A Historical Survey 1830-1980*, Dublin: Gill and Macmillan/Washington D.C.: C.U.A. Press, 1990.

29. 'Here then', Corish comments on the early 1900s, 'was a cultural "nation" in great need of something to hold for pride. The Catholic religion was the clear response to this search for identity and inspiration. One consequence of the drain of emigration was that the Irish Catholics could see themselves as the mother country of many millions in "Ireland's spiritual empire", especially in the United States and Australia' (ibid., 237-8).

30. Ibid., 244. Commenting on the fact that life in the newly born Irish Free State took on a certain conservative Catholic ethos, Corish writes: 'It should be noted that this did not happen because the clergy brought pressure on the government. The government was as anxious as the clergy to preserve what were regarded as

traditional values.' Murray, op. cit., 420, comes to a similar
conclusion.

31. In *The Irish World*, 15 June 1945, as quoted by Paul Blanchard, *The
    Church and Catholic Power. An American Interpretation*, Boston:
    Beacon Press, 1953, 3.

32. A. Fitzgerald, 'Reservation No. 2', *Reports of the Commission on
    Emigration and other problems*, Dublin, 1956, 222, as quoted in J.J. Lee,
    Ireland 1912-1985, 380. The rest of the quotation deserves closer
    study also by theologians. Lee comments (382-3) that the
    questionable thought process that led to the 'casual op-option of
    "Providence" in support of a particular social analysis' in fact
    'enjoys a respectable ancestry in what historically passed for social
    thought in Ireland.' He also perceptively notes that the concept of
    'Providence' is rather elastic. According to Lee, Fitzgerald 'was in
    practice rationalizing a viewpoint that was widespread among a
    defeatist political and professional elite, spiritual collaborators in the
    mass eviction process that drove more than half a million out [of
    the country] between 1945 and 1960' (383-4).

33. Indeed, the term 'diaspora', originally coined to designate the exiled
    Jews scattered throughout the world, is still used in public discourse
    to describe the Irish abroad. In this context, one might note the
    comparison made by Professor Myles Dillon with reference to the
    heirs of the Celtic tradition in Brittany, Wales, Scotland, and Ireland:
    'Like the Jews, it has been their destiny, for many centuries, to suffer
    wrongs rather than to inflict them. This is not an ignoble history,
    and the Celtic heritage is no mean tradition.' Myles Dillon, 'Celtic
    Religion and Celtic Society' in Joseph Raftery (ed.), *The Celts* [The
    Thomas Davis Lectures], Cork: The Mercier Press, 1964, 70.

34. The statistics reveal a more sober picture. 'It would now appear that
    the descendents of Irish Catholics, leaving aside entirely the vexed
    question of "leakage" among the emigrants themselves, have lapsed
    on a mass scale, with only 7.5 million of the 44 million Americans
    who acknowledged at least partial Irish descent in 1979, claiming to
    be Catholics' (Lee, op. cit., 383).

35. Cf. Mary Douglas, *Natural Symbols, Exploration in Cosmology*,
    London: Barrie and Jenkins, 1973 (second edn), 59-64; see also the
    comments by Mary Kenny, *Goodbye to Catholic Ireland*, 182f.

36. Seán de Fréine, *The Great Silence*, 94. One may ask in passing, does
    any other people refer to itself as we do, namely as strangers, as is

implied with the use of the definite article, 'the Irish'? In the mouths of foreigners it may be excused, though one suspects that English people use it in a derogatory sense, but when used by ourselves it indicates an alienation from our own self-identity.

37. See Mary Douglas, *Natural Symbols*, 59-64.

38. *Letter to Diognetus*, translation from the Greek by Henry Melvill Gwatkin, *Selections from the Early Writers Illustrative of Church History to the Time of Constantine*, London: James Clarke & Co. Ltd, 1958 edition, 15.

39. This tradition had its origin in the Greek translation (the *Septuagent*, completed around 132 BC in Alexandria, Egypt) of the late scripture text, Deuteronomy 32:8-9; see Peterson in the following note, 43.

40. Cf. the study by Erik Peterson, 'Das Problem des Nationalismus im Alten Christentum' in his collection entitled *Frühkirche, Judetum und Gnosis. Studien und Untersuchungen*, Rome-Friburg-Vienna: Herder, 1959, 51-63, for a detailed account.

41. See Vincent Twomey, *Apostolikos Thronos*, Münster, Westf.: Aschendorff, 1982, 138-229.

42. In the East, that idea filtered down through the Byzantine Empire to the Russia of the Czars, when Orthodoxy became the soul of the Russian nation; nationalism and faith became identical. The Russians were a chosen people with a mission. For an exposition of this complex tradition, cf. Eric Voegelin, *The New Science of Politics. An Introduction*, Chicago & London, The University of Chicago Press, 1952, 97-104; 114-7.

43. See ibid., 105-11; Christopher Dawson, *The Making of Europe. An Introduction to the History of European Unity, 400-1000 A.D.*, London: Sheed & Ward, 1939. See also in this context Cruise O'Brien, *God Land*, op. cit., 1-42.

44. Nobel Prize Lecture, 1970. I regret to say that I am unable to identify the translator; for a less satisfactory translation (by Nicholas Bethell), cf. Alexander Solzhenitzyn, *Nobel Prize Lecture*, London: Stenvally Press, 1973, 33.

45. 'The great arc along which all possible human behaviours are distributed is far too immense for any one culture to utilise even a considerable portion of it' (Ruth Benedict, as quoted by Seán de Fréine, *The Great Silence*, 112), for which reason, it has been argued, a diversity of nations is a requirement of our humanity as designed by the Creator. On the notion of nation, philosophically considered,

cf. Jacques Maritain, *Man & The State*, edited by Richard O'Sullivan, Q.C., London: Hollis & Carter, 1954, Chapters I and II. In this context, see the critique of Desmond Fennell, *Beyond Nationalism: The Struggle against Provinciality in the Modern World*, Swords, Co. Dublin: Ward River Press, 1985. -

46. For the Church's attitude to culture, see *Gaudium et spes*, 54-62, in particular 58-9. Since the Council, two interrelated debates have taken place within theology, one concerning the dynamics and limits of so-called interculturation, and the other on the relationship between the local Churches and the Church universal represented in a unique way by the See of Peter, itself also a local Church.

47. Conformity for many was primarily external, a survival strategy. Even if Blanchard was not exactly an impartial observer, he found sufficient confirmation for his prejudices in what he saw and observed in Dublin to justify not mentioning his sources by name, as Ireland 'is not a place where men can express frank and unorthodox opinions on church and state without penalty' (Blanchard, *The Church and Catholic Power*, vi). That has the ring of truth.

48. 'Down through the penal times the nation as a whole stood firm, and commentators record an air of cheerfulness and hope among the poorest' (Seán de Fréine, *The Great Silence*, 76).

49. Mary Kenny, *Goodbye to Catholic Ireland*, 185.

50. Corish, *The Irish Catholic Experience*, 224. Compassion with the sufferings of Christ and Mary is a marked aspect of traditional spirituality, and can be traced back at least as far as the long poem on 'Mary and her Son' by Blathmac, son of Cú Brettan, composed around AD 700 (cf. John J. Ó Ríordáin, *Irish Catholic Spirituality*, 28-30 for excerpts; cf. ibid. 63-6 re the bardic poets of the late Middle Ages). Note the observations by W. M. Thackeray on the devotion displayed by Catholics in Waterford Cathedral around the mid-nineteenth century (cf. Corish, 174). The Passion is, unsurprisingly, central to the traditional prayers associated with the Mass, cf. Diarmud Ó Laoghaire, *Our Mass, Our Life. Some Irish Traditions and Prayers*, Dublin: Irish Messenger Publications, 1968, 19-22; 26-28.

51. Cf. Murray, op. cit. According to Corish, we should speak of two Church establishments around 1880, one Catholic and the other Protestant, despite the fact that there was no longer a legally

established Church, a development which foreshadowed the existence of two political communities four decades later (cf. ibid., 226f.).

52. Corish, *The Irish Catholic Experience*, 245.

53. This is but an impression, and needs further investigation.

54. Brian Fallon, *Age of Innocence. Irish Culture 1930-1960*, Dublin: Gill & Macmillan, 1998, 190.

55. See Hans Urs von Balthasar, *Schleifung der Bastionen. Von der Kirche in dieser Zeit*, Einsiedeln-Trier: Johannes Verlag, 1989, fifth edition with an epilogue by Christoph Schönborn OP.

56. It is significant that a collection of essays entitled *The Irish Mind: Exploring Intellectual Traditions*, edited by Richard Kearney, Dublin: Wolfhound Press, 1985, should contain sections covering mythopoeic, philosophical, political, literary, and scientific thought – but nothing on theological thought! This is so, even though the editor in his introduction (30) draws attention to the profound impact of the emergence of an Irish Christian culture as a crucial factor in shaping Irish cultural history.

57. The textbooks (or manuals) of moral theology in use in Maynooth for most of the nineteenth century came from the pen of the rather balanced and moderate Jean Pierre Gury SJ, which 'had come to be widely adopted in seminaries because of their real virtues of moderation in judgement and careful clarity' (Patrick J. Corish, *Maynooth College 1795-1995*, Dublin: Gill and Macmillan, 1995, 209). But, like most Jesuit moral theology at the time, it was basically legalistic and casuistic in method.

58. The reasons for this will be discussed in Chapter 6 and Appendix II.

59. Cf. Declan Kiberd, *Inventing Ireland. The Literature of the Modern Nation*, London: Vintage, 1996, 645. Kiberd's positive appreciation of this modernity is of note.

60. St Augustine, *De Praedestinatione Sanctorum*, 2,5 (PL 44, 96) as quoted by Pope John Paul II in *Fides et Ratio*, 79.

61. Cf. Joseph Cardinal Ratzinger, *The Nature and Mission of Theology. Essays to Orient Theology in Today's Debates*, translated by Adrian Walker, San Francisco: Ignatius Press, 1995, esp. 13-16.

62. John Henry Newman, *The Via Media of the Anglican Church*, London: Basil Montagu Pickering, 1877, I, xlvii, as quoted by Sr Consilio Rock RSM, *John Henry Newman's Prophetic Office of the Church: An Investigation* (STL Dissertation, Maynooth 2001), 91.

Chapter 2: How Catholic is Irish Catholicism?

1. *The Great Silence*, 53.
2. According to the mediaeval *Vita*, Blessed Albert, on returning from a pilgrimage to the Holy Land, came to Regensbug to visit his friend, Bishop Erhard, who in fact had just died. Albert himself died soon after, from sorrow, it is said, and was buried next to his old friend. Both were venerated as saints since *c*. 700. I am grateful to Dr Katharina M. Bommes, Regensburg, for this information.
3. The northeast corner of Temple Ciáran in Clonmacnoise is said to be the 'reputed buried place' of the saint. Two crosiers of the Abbots of Clonmacnoise, now in the National Museum, were found there during excavations, which certainly would support such a claim. There is no report of any relics found (cf. Peter Harbison, *Guide to National and Historic Monuments of Ireland*, Dublin: Gill & Macmillan, 1992, 108-9). It was only after the Norman invasion that the relics of St Patrick, St Brigid, and St Columba were reportedly found in Downpartick, thus enabling John de Courcy to transfer the See of Bangor to Down. What happened the relics later is unknown. The large granite slab in the graveyard of the Church of Ireland Cathedral was placed there in 1900 (cf. Harbison, 277).
4. The Irish monastery in the centre of Vienna still functions as a Benedictine monastery. It is also a boarding school, perhaps the most prestigious in Austria.
5. It is now generally accepted that the architect of the much smaller Romanesque Cormac's Chapel on the Rock of Cashel was probably a monk from Regensburg, an opinion I first heard proposed by the late Liam de Paor at a lecture he gave on the University of Regensburg.
6. G. K. Chesterton remarked in his 1932 pamphlet, *Christendom in Dublin*, that the iconoclasm of the Puritan conquerors had brought about an impoverishment of the visual arts in Dublin. (Cf. John McCarthy, 'The Irish in America' in *Crisis*, March 1999, 16). However, this iconoclasm resulted in more than an impoverished aesthetic sense, however unfortunate that may be. It effectively broke one of the most important cultural links between the present and our rich Catholic mediaeval past.
7. See Corish, *The Irish Catholic Experience*, 43, for a brief description of the little mediaeval architecture that survived the ravages of Irish

history. As Corish comments, 'the bulk of the population must have had their religion impressed on them in the first instance by such tangible things'.

8. *Hughie O'Donoghue: Episodes from the Passion.* Exhibition at the RHA Gallagher Gallery, Dublin 8 January-21 February 1999. Italian culture – Catholic in all its wholeness, embracing flesh and spirit – also left its mark on Seán Ó Faoláin and on his work, cf. Daniel Murphy, *Imagination & Religion in Anglo-Irish literature, 1930-80,* Dublin: Irish Academic Press, 1987, 55-57: 'In *A Summer in Italy* he describes his rediscovery of the mystery of the Incarnation, and his enthusiasm for the simple affirmations amongst the Italians of a truth which had been distorted in his own [Irish Catholic] experience: "In those seconds I knew that I was caught, and caught forever... People approached the altar. The Light of the World became flesh of their flesh"' (57). To judge by the many impressive neo-Classical and even the occasional neo-Romanesque churches (such as the Cathedral in Thurles with its Northern Italian façade), the higher forms of Italian culture evidently left their mark on many a nineteenth-century cleric who had studied in Rome. Today, there is perhaps less appreciation for the other great Italian influence on the Irish Church in the nineteenth century, namely the various novenas, confraternities, and other devotions that became so popular, in particular in the cities.

9. I remember a trip I made one summer in the late 1970s to the Great. Skellig, Sceilig Mhichil. Apart from the captain of the converted fishing boat, my parents and I were the only Irish visitors to the island. The other tourists on the hastily converted fishing boat were German, French, and Dutch.

10. Cf. Jeremy Williams, *A Companion Guide to Architecture in Ireland 1837-1921,* with an introduction by Mark Girouard, Dublin: The Academic Press, 1994.

11. One of the new Bank Holidays, now accepted by the public at large without demur, is, paradoxically, May Day, introduced by the Labour Party, when the socialist feast was on its last legs in the rest of the world as international socialism crumbled with the fall of the Berlin Wall.

12. During my noviciate in Donamon, I already tasted something of the 'flavour' of Advent, thanks to the German influence on my own congregation, Divine Word Missionaries, but it was overlaid

with the usual post-Christian preparations typical of Ireland, which owe more to secular Britain and America than to Christian tradition.

13. This is not to deny that German Catholics also had reservations about some of the excesses of Carnival. Up to recently, there was a tradition of holding public prayers and penitential services at the same time for the sins committed during Carnival. This did not prevent either clerics or faithful from entering into more innocent fun and games.

14. Ó Faoláin identifies 'Gallican Catholicism' – itself condemned by the Church's magisterium – as the source of the world-negating religion he grew up in and so abhorred: 'I do not think that any western church revels so perfervidly as the Irish Catholic Church does... in the liquefaction of common life, the vapourisation of the mortal into the mystical, the veiling of the natural in the fumes of the supernatural' (as quoted in Murphy, *Imagination & Religion*, op. cit., 59). Perhaps a bit extreme, but the author has a point, which I will take up later. The 'Puritanism' of the Irish Church, especially its priests, is one of the motifs of his fiction, as is its suffocation of the intellect; both are related and lead to the death of the spirit. For a description of Irish attitudes to morality in the first half of the twentieth century, in particular 'the virtual equation of immorality with sexual immorality', see Lee, *Ireland 1912-1985*, 644-8 (quotation from 645).

15. In predominantly Catholic States (*Länder*), the Faculty of Theology is Catholic, while in predominantly Protestant States, it is Lutheran. On some universities, such as Tübingen, there are both Catholic and Protestant faculties.

16. By way of example, one could point to the page-long interview with Cardinal Ratzinger in the *Frankfurter Allegmeine Zeitung*, 22 September 2000, on the reaction of the Protestant Churches to *Dominus Iesus*. There was nothing even faintly resembling this in the Irish media at the time.

17. Fallon, op. cit., 190-1.

18. Ibid., 191.

19. Cf. Frank O'Connor, *The Collar. Stories of Irish Priests,* with an introduction by Harriet O'Donovan Sheehy, Belfast: Blackstaff Press, 1993.

20. Ibid., v.

21. Cf. Andrew M. Greeley and Conor Ward, 'How "Secularised" Is the Ireland We Live In?' in *Doctrine and Life*, 50 (2000), 581-617; see the critical analysis of this survey by Liam Walsh OP, Anne Thurston, and Donal Harrington in the same issue; see also Noel Barber, SJ, 'Religion in Ireland: Its state and prospects' in Brendan Bradshaw and Dáire Keogh (eds), *Christianity in Ireland. Revisiting the Story*, Dublin: The Columba Press, 2002, 290-1.

22. Fallon, *Age of Innocence*, 196.

23. The articles were, together with another paper, published by Dominican Publications as a short book in 1984 under the title: *Irish Catholics and Freedom since 1916*. Quotations are taken from this version. For a critical appraisal of his writings, see Toner Quinn (ed.), *Desmond Fennell: his life and work*, Dublin: Veritas 2001. As the contributors point out, Fennell is an original thinker who rarely fails to stimulate and, in almost equal measure, rarely finds agreement.

24. Seán de Fréine (*The Great Silence*, 100-1) explains the appearance of modern Irish nationalists as one of those 'prophetic pioneering minorities' described by Maritain, who are 'the dynamic leaven or energy which fosters political movement… [as] needed in the normal functioning of the democratic society.' But de Fréine does not mention Maritain's critique of such figures and the ambiguous nature of their endeavours (cf. Jacques Maritain, *Man & The State*, 126-130, especially 128). Later, Fennell was to modify his original enthusiasm for nationalism, cf. Risteárd Ó Glaisne, 'A Protestant Response' in Toner Quinn (ed.), *Desmond Fennell*, 83-99, espec. 86-9.

25. Quoted by Desmond Fennell, *Beyond Nationalism. The Struggle against Provinciality in the Modern World*, Swords, Co. Dublin: Ward River Press, 1985, 299. According to Fennell, provinciality is a characteristic condition of contemporary humanity, not just in Ireland. Solzhenitzyn evidently agrees, and quotes as an antidote the old Russian saying: 'Do not trust your own brother. Rather trust your own eye, even if it is a crooked eye.' He adds: 'And this is the most healthy basis of all for understanding our surroundings and our behaviour inside them' (*Nobel Prize Lecture*, London: Stenvally Press, 1973, 21).

26. For a discussion of the various reasons given for this 'language cataclysm' (Seán de Fréine), see J. J. Lee, *Ireland 1912-1985*, 662-6; see also Akenson, *Small Differences*, 135-9. With regard to the implications of this language shift, see Lee, 666-70; 674. Lee is

particularly illuminating in the way he shows how, paradoxically, our adoption of a world-language helped create a provincial mentality that still dominates much public discourse and determines patterns of behaviour. For a criticism of Lee's approach to history, see Declan Kiberd, *Inventing Ireland*, 644-6.

27. Cf. Declan Kiberd, *Inventing Ireland*, 2 (echoing Benedict Anderson). According to Seán de Fréine's penetrating analysis, the first consequences of the loss of Irish were a radical break with tradition, the loss of an enormous amount of knowledge and wisdom, and a sense of uprootedness (*The Great Silence*, 75-85); the secondary consequences amounted to a distortion of history resulting in an extraordinary 'amount of bitterness which the telling of Irish history engenders' (cf. 86-98, here 94).

28. Lee, *Ireland 1912-1885*, 668.

29. Fennell, *Irish Catholics and Freedom*, 18.

30. Ibid., 15. Writing in 1892, 'Tim Healy complained that the result of [the courses in the National Schools] in "English philistinism" was that folk around the fireside, who had once held conversations in Irish about knightly chivalry, were now reduced to talking in English about the price of a cow' (Declan Kiberd, *Synge and the Irish Language*, Second Edition, Dublin: Gill & Macmillan, 1993, 225). On the transformation of the newly adopted language by Irish writers, cf. Sean O'Faolain, *The Irish*, London: Pelican Book, 1969 (revised edition), 122-44.

31. Cf. de Fréine, *The Great Silence*, 68-9.

32. Corish, *The Irish Catholic Experience*, 194.

33. Cf. ibid., 254-5. See also Seán de Fréine, op. cit., 66-74; Donal Kerr SM, 'The Early Nineteenth Century: Patterns of Change' in Michael Maher (ed.) *Irish Spirituality*, Dublin: Veritas, 1981, 137-144. Emmet Larkin observed that 'the Irish before the Famine had nearly all become cultural emigrants, that they had in fact moved in their minds before a good many of them had actually to move in space'. This also 'accounts for their becoming pious and practising Catholics in the generation after the Famine' (what he famously entitled the 'devotional revolution'), thereby resisting absorption into the greater English culture' (Emmet Larkin 'The Parish Mission Movement, 1850-1880' in Brendan Bradshaw and Dáire Keogh (eds), *Christianity in Ireland. Revisiting the Story*, Dublin: The Columba Press, 2002, 204). The real question is, did they really succeed?

34. Tomás Uasal de Bhál, 'Patterns of Prayer and Devotion, 1750-1850' in Placid Murray, OSB (ed.), *Studies in Pastoral Liturgy*, vol. 3, Maynooth-Dublin: The Furrow Trust/Gill & Son, 1967, 213. With regard to the dilemma faced by the Church at the end of the eighteenth century, which led to meeting the demand for education appropriate to an English-speaking world, see in particular de Fréine, *The Great Silence*, 70-2. To what extent is the crisis of the contemporary Church due to the fact that, with the foundation of Maynooth College in 1795, 'continental cultural influence in Ireland would wane' (72)?

35. Corish, op. cit., 131. With regard to the (probably unfounded) charge of Jansenism brought against 'traditional Irish Catholicism' in the nineteenth century, and in particular the Maynooth Priest, see Corish, *The Irish Catholic Experience*, 117-8; 120; 162; see also his *Maynooth College*, 122; 153.

36. 'His *Garden of the Soul*, first published in 1740, was the ancestor of all our prayer books' (de Bhál, *Patterns of Prayer*, 212). John Carpenter, Archbishop of Dublin and an Irish scholar, who tried to emulate Challoner (and Archbishop George Hay of Scotland), faced a dilemma common to Irish clerics of the day. 'He had difficulty in making up his mind which language to use.' (ibid., 213).

37. Cf. Corish, *The Irish Catholic Experience*, 131. With regard to the European continent as an 'equally prominent source' for the Irish spirituality of the time, see John J. Ó Ríordáin, *Irish Catholic Spirituality*, 109-111.

38. Already in the mid-eighteenth century, the need to adjust, at least externally, to the prevalent Protestant ethos of the cities can be seen in the advice given in 1751 by Charles O'Connor to his son in Dublin: 'You live now in a busy, elbowing scene; if you have any sagacity, you will make reflections on every incident and reap instruction and, whatever it be, strive to adapt it to the rank you are to fill hereafter: that of a Roman Catholic in a Protestant country, that of one in a low way, obnoxious to the laws' (as quoted in Roy Foster, *Modern Ireland 1600-1972*, London: Penguin, 1989, 209).

39. The need to achieve social 'respectability' was also a decisive factor in the unparalleled phenomenon of the repudiation of Irish by most parents in the nineteenth century, and indeed has been documented as late as 1911 (cf. Seán de Fréine, op. cit., 66-74).

40. Cf. John J. Ó Ríordáin, *Irish Catholic Spirituality*, 103. Ó Ríordáin comments: 'There was more to the above-mentioned address than

the sonorous language of the obsequious memorialists. It was the voice of a new breed, a Catholic merchant and propertied class who felt that there was a future for them in Ireland if they would but accept the language and the tradition of their masters. ... The tradition was neither Irish nor Catholic, but an Anglo-Saxon puritanical culture which had come to pervade not only English society, but that of America and indeed of the entire English-speaking world' (103-4).

41. Cf. John J. Ó Ríordáin, ibid., 105.

42. Lee, *Ireland 1912-1985*, 645.

43. Ibid.

44. Fennell, *Irish Catholics and Freedom*, 15.

45. This is well illustrated in the difficulty of translating traditional Irish prayers, rich is terms of affection, into the banalities of the few terms of affection used in English, cf. Diarmud Ó Laoghaire, *Our Mass, Our Life*.

46. See Voegelin, *The New Science of Politics*, 152-62; 179-87.

47. Cf. John Henry Cardinal Newman, *An Essay in Aid of a Grammar of Assent*, London: Burns, Oates & Co., 1870, 54-5.

48. David Jones, *The Anathemata, fragments of an attempted writing*, London: Faber and Faber, 1990 (second reprinting of the second edition), 15-16.

49. Ibid., 16. Gertrud von le Fort analyses this phenomenon and its implications for understanding the significance of gender differences, cf. *The Eternal Woman. The Woman in Time. Timeless Woman*, translated by Placid Jordan OSB, Milwaukee: The Bruce Publishing Company, 1962.

50. Noting that few Irish contributors to the social thought of the English-speaking world can compare with the contribution of thinkers from other small countries who learned English as a foreign tongue, Lee asks rhetorically: 'Is it purely accidental that the sole European sovereign state in the twentieth century to have acquired the supreme gift of English as her vernacular in the nineteenth century should have made so insignificant a mark on international thought since independence?' (J. J. Lee, *Ireland 1912-1985*, 668). The same could be said of the absence of any major, internationally recognised, Irish contribution to philosophy or theology, despite impressive theological scholars such as William Crolly, Daniel Murray, Edward Kissane or Patrick A. Boylan (see

the respective entries in Corish, *Maynooth College*). The future for philosophy looks promising, to judge from the recognition accorded to the writings of the Cork-born philosopher, William Desmond, and the Dublin-born David Walsh; however, it is not without significance that neither has a chair on an Irish University. (Desmond is now in Louvain, while Walsh is in Washington.) Kiberd's *Inventing Ireland* seems to have broken the mould with regard to studies of modern literature. According to Edward W. Said, 'Declan Kiberd's book lifts Ireland out of ethnic studies and lore and places it in the post-colonial world. In doing so he situates its great cultural achievements where they jostle not only the major texts of English literature, but also those of writers like Salman Rushdie and García Márquez.' Kiberd's approach has been of inspiration to others, cf., for example, Peadar Kirby, Luke Gibbons, and Michael Cronin (eds), *Reinventing Ireland. Culture, Society and the Global Economy*, London-Sterling, Virginia: Pluto Press, 2002, an impressive attempt to explore the interaction between economy and culture in a modern Ireland conscious of having reinvented itself in the recent past. Unfortunately, by the time my attention was drawn to this book (by Toner Quinn), it was too late to incorporate it in the above discussion, something I hope to do on another occasion.

51. Cf. Kenneth Clarke, *Civilisation. A Personal View*, London, British Broadcasting Corporation and John Murray, 1969.

52. Ibid., 175.

53. 'The great religious art of the world is deeply involved with the female principle' (ibid., 177). Clarke takes up the distinction made by H. G. Wells between the communities of obedience (the comprehensive religions of the world, as in Egypt, India or China) which gave the female principle in creation as much importance as the male and communities of will (like Israel, Islam and the Protestant Northern Europe), which conceived their gods as male.

54. Cf. ibid., 177-8.

55. Ibid., 181.

56. Ibid. Later, Clarke (191-2) admits to certain 'misgivings' about the Baroque, 'summed up in the words "illusion" and "exploitation"…'.

57. This monastery on the banks of the Danube to the west of Regensburg was, some historians claim, founded in the seventh century by the Irish monks Eustasius and Agilius of Luxeuil,

though this is disputed (cf. *LThK*, second edition, 1938, vol. X, col. 816). In an even more dramatic setting, further downstream on the Danube is Melk in Austria, founded in 984, another striking baroque church and monastery with a strong Irish connection. Its fame and fortune owed much to the fact that in the main church is the shrine of St Colman, the reputed son of Brian Boru, who was murdered in Stockerau on 12 July 1012, and venerated as the patron saint of Austria for some six centuries (cf. Ingeborg Meyer-Sickendiek, *Gottes gelehrte Vaganten. Auf den Spuren der irischen Mission und Kultur in Europa*, Stuttgart: Seewald, 1980, 271-273).

58. Among the many churches and monasteries with an Irish connection, it must suffice her to single out two in particular, the Cathedral of St Kilian at Würzburg, and the great monastic, now cathedral, Church of Sankt Gallen, Switzerland, founded on the site of the hermitage of St Gaul in 613, a companion of St Columbanus (cf. Peter Ochsenbein (ed.), *Das Kloster St. Gallen im Mittelalter. Die kulturelle Blüte vom 8. bis zum 9. Jahrhundert*, Darmstadt: Wissenschaftliche Buchgesellschaft, 1999). Würzburg and St Gallen have preserved some of the most precious early Irish manuscripts to have survived the centuries, including rare glosses in Old Irish.

59. Clarke, *Civilisation*, 174.

60. Fennell, *Irish Catholics and Freedom*, 19.

61. Like Mr Duffy in 'A Painted Place', *Dubliners*, as quoted in Richard Ellmann, *James Joyce* (New York: Oxford University Press, 1965), 218.

62. This is what the great French spiritual writer, Jean Pierre de Caussade, SJ, called 'the sacrament of the present moment'.

63. More recently, Vincent Buckley could describe Ireland as 'a nothing – a no-thing – an interesting nothing, to be sure, composed of colourful parts, a nothing mosaic' (*Memory Ireland*, London, 1985, ix, as quoted in Lee, op. cit., 661). Lee comments: 'There is a good deal of truth, if not quite the whole truth, in Buckley's observations.'

64. Once, while hastily rushing through Pope Paul VI's new gallery of modern art in the Vatican to see the newly restored frescos of Raphael in the *Stanza della Segnatura* and those of Michelangelo in the Sistine Chapel, I caught sight of one of Bacon's tortured versions of Velasquez's *Pope Innocent X*, the only work of art by an Irish artist in the collection, as far as I could see. Catholic Rome never fails to surprise.

65. Fennell, *Irish Catholics and Freedom*, 26. Re Irish begrudgery, see the illuminating, though disturbing, analysis by Lee, *Ireland 1912-1984*, 645-8.

66. Fennell, *Irish Catholics and Freedom*, 27. 'Alcohol, for the Irish, is the emigration of the soul.' John Waters, *An Intelligent Person's Guide to Ireland*, London: Duckworth, 1997, 161. See also Lee, *Ireland 1912-1984*, 645. See also Murphy, *Imagination & Religion*, 60f., for a brief account of Ó Faoláin's critical perception of the complex character of the traditional Irish priest, a 'contradictory synthesis of the magical and the religious, and of the temporal and the spiritual'; the image of the priest in his fiction 'brings into focus dramatically the constrictions of an unsophisticated, authoritarian and intellectually stifling culture, and the condition of social uniformity which it endeavours to impose'.

67. Apart from Cardinal Newman, who soars among them as a giant, one thinks immediately of Ronald Knox, C. C. Martindale SJ, Christopher Dawson and Victor While OP, to name but a few.

68. Fennell, *Irish Catholics and Freedom*, 19, emphasis in the text. It should also be mentioned that in the seminaries, philosophy and theology were taught in Latin up to the early 1960s, effectively stifling any truly creative theological reflection.

69. John Waters, *An Intelligent Person's Guide*, 160.

70. That the need for this is universal is attested by George Steiner's remarkable essay *Real Presences, Is there anything in what we say?*, London-Boston: Faber and Faber, 1989; see also Roger Scruton, *An Intelligent Person's Guide to Modern Culture*, London: Duckworth, 1998. Of course, neither Steiner, despite his allusion to Catholic theology, nor Scruton believe that faith can any longer satisfy that need. It is the Christian's task to try to convince them that it does. (Scruton, I believe, has since become convinced.)

71. One could begin by studying again the Constitution on the Sacred Liturgy (*Sacrosanctum concilium*). For a modern, critical theology of liturgy inspired by this document, see especially Joseph Cardinal Ratzinger, *The Spirit of the Liturgy. An Introduction*, San Francisco: Ignatius Press, 2000.

72. Cf. in particular the pioneering work of the anthropologist Victor W. Turner, *The Ritual Process. Structure and Anti-Structure*, New York, 1969. The eminent American liturgist, Aidan Kavanagh, once said that, had Turner's insights into the nature of ('pagan') ritual been

known at the time of the reform of the liturgy after the Second Vatican Council, they would have produced quite a different rite for the Mass. These insights (coupled with the findings of patristic scholars) were used to good effect in devising the new *Rite of Initiation for Adults.*

73. While in Trieste, Joyce 'often went to the Greek Orthodox Church to compare its ritual, which he considered amateurish, with the Roman' (Richard Ellmann, *James Joyce*, 202). One wonders what Joyce would have thought of the present 'Roman Rite' as practised in most Irish parishes and religious houses.

74. Constitution on the Sacred Liturgy (*Sacrosanctum Concilium*) 7-8, Austin Flannery OP, *Vatican Council II*, vol. 1, New Revised Edition, New York/Dublin, 1996, 5.

75. While the concern of Rome to improve the translations of the various rites is understandable, it would be a pity if the new, apparently rather rigid, rules for translation resulted in a disregard for the particular syntax of the different vernacular languages – or, with regard to English translation in particular, a disregard for the differences found in countries, such as Ireland and USA, where in varying degrees English is gradually evolving almost into separate dialects. One may well question the wisdom of having only one standard English translation, as the experience with ICEL seems to confirm. One must expect the lowest common denominator to prevail in the final compromise. In ritual, which links our deepest human instincts with the Sublime, the lowest common denominator is the enemy.

76. Cf. the Dogmatic Constitution on the Church, *Lumen Gentium*, 2, 16; see also the Decrees on Ecumenism (*Unitatis redintegratio*) and on the Relation of the Church to Non-Christian Religions (*Nostra Aetate*), where the seminal ideas found in *Lumen Gentium* are further developed.

77. Akenson, *Small Differences*, 148.

78. Contrary to the impression given by the Irish media – including some Church publications – the Instruction *Dominus Iesus* issued by the Congregation for the Faith does not row back on the ecumenical vision of Vatican II. Quotations from Council documents make up much of the body of the text of the Instruction, which was primarily concerned with the Church's relationship to Non-Christian religions. The Instruction is mainly concerned with a growing

religious indifferentism. For a selection of the best contributions to both sides of the debate sparked off by the document, cf. Stephen J. Pope and Charles Hefling (eds), *Sic et Non. Encountering* Dominus Iesus, Maryknoll, NT: Orbis Books, 2002.

Chapter 3: Which Path to Follow?

1. *The Irish*, 119.

2. Newman once remarked that, to the Catholic populations of mediaeval Europe or modern Spain, unlike the majority in the England of his day, 'the Supreme Being, Our Lord, the Blessed Virgin, Angels and Saints, heaven and hell, are as present as if they were objects of sight; but such a faith does not suit the genius of modern England' (*Grammar of Assent*, 55-6).

3. For other recollections of growing up in Ireland around the same time, see the final chapter of Mary Kenny, *Goodbye to Catholic Ireland*, 338-54, which contains brief, mostly positive memoirs of prominent Irish men and women, who grew up in Ireland around the same period. A German confrere of mine who read Alice Taylor's book said that it also conveyed life as he remembered it in rural Emsland, the northern lowlands of Germany. At times, I get the impression that we in Ireland think our experience is unique, when in many respects it is shared by others in similar sociological circumstances. Cf. Declan Kiberd's criticism of earlier Irish nationalist writers, who failed 'to regard Irish experience as representative of human experience, and so... remained woefully innocent of the comparative method' (*Inventing Ireland*, 641), an innocence that, with few exceptions in the Irish academic scene would still seem to be widespread (646f.).

4. Translated from the German by Leila Vennewitz, London: Secker & Warburg, 1967, with an Epilogue, where the author casts a cold eye on the transformation that had taken place in Ireland during the thirteen years since he first penned his diary, especially the enthusiasm with which 'the Pill' was greeted!

5. Fallon, *Age of Innocence*, 194. See also Corish's concluding reflections, *The Irish Catholic Experience*, 254-8.

6. Maureen Dalzell, *Irish America: Coming into Clover, The Evolution of a People and a Culture*, New York, London, Toronto, Sydney, Auckland:

Doubleday, 2001, 76. With regard to the way Irish Catholics adapted so remarkably to the WASP culture, see Cruise O'Brien, *God Land*, op. cit., 22-39. 'Of the more successful cases of adaptation, one might almost say that an American Catholic is a Protestant who goes to Mass. The name of John F. Kennedy comes to mind' (33-4). One might also almost say the same for many traditional Irish Catholics in Ireland. The operative word, however, is 'almost'; here Dalzell hints at the truly significant difference, Fallon (cf. note 5) identifies it.

7. Cf. Andrew M. Greeley and Conor Ward, op. cit. above (cf. footnote 21, chapter 2). According to the 1999 European [Union] Values Study, Ireland still has the highest percentage in Europe in three of the five categories surveyed (belief in God: 90%; cultic practice: 43%; religious ceremonies: 95%). It has the second highest percentage of those who claim to belong to a religion (86%; Austria and Denmark register 90% each), but – what is most noteworthy – the fifth lowest percentage of those with confidence in the Church (29%; the lowest is Holland, 20%, followed by Spain, 23%, Sweden, 24%, and Austria, 27%). More significant is the general trend, which is undeniably downward. In 1981, 98% of those surveyed in Ireland claimed adhesion to some religion; in 1999 it was down to 86%. Whereas 'belief in God' only dropped 2% between 1981 and 1999, 'cultic practice' was almost halved, from 83% to 43%, while confidence in the Church dropped from 64% to 29% – the largest drop in all twelve countries, some of which, in fact, actually registered an increase (Portugal, 67%, up from 43% in 1990 [sic], followed by Italy, Denmark, Germany, and Sweden). Source: report in *Le Monde*, 24 July 2002. For a more detailed account (and critical interpretation) of recent sociological surveys from the 1960s to 1999, see Noel Barber SJ, 'Religion in Ireland: Its state and prospects' in Brendan Bradshaw and Dáire Keogh (eds), *Christianity in Ireland. Revisiting the Story*, Dublin: The Columba Press, 2002, 287-97. Barber's rather bleak conclusions about the possibility of evangelising mainstream secular culture are ones I do not entirely share.

8. According to Emmet Larkin, the perceptive French traveller and man of letters, Alexis de Tocqueville made up his mind about Ireland almost immediately on arrival. His subsequent notes are but variations on three themes. 'The first was the extraordinary poverty

of the Irish people. The second was their enduring and implacable hatred for the Irish aristocracy, and the third was their deep and touching attachment to the Church of their fathers' (*Alexis de Tocqueville's Journey in Ireland*, July-August, 1835, translated and edited by Emmet Larkin, Dublin: Wolfhound Press, 1990, 6-7). As the then Mgr Nolan, Bishop of Kildare and Leighlin, observed: 'There exists between the clergy and the people of this country an unbelievable union' (42, cf. 48). This is illustrated by de Tocqueville's account of his visit to a rural parish priest near Tuam, County Mayo, on 28 July 1835 (ibid., 111-27), a moving pen-picture of mutual love and respect between priest and people. The following day, the Frenchman also visited the Protestant minister in his house. The visitor described the totally different circumstances and attitude of the latter, for whom the natives were 'savages' needing to be civilised by the 'aristocracy'. De Tocqueville warned the minister not to repeat such sentiments in France, as he 'would be taken for a Catholic priest' (128)! Reflecting on the contrast between the secluded mansion of the minister and the humble home of the priest among the hovels of the village, he jots down: 'There wealth, knowledge, power; here strength. Difference in language according to position. Where to find the absolute truth' (129).

9.   Edward T. Oakes SJ, review in *Theological Studies*, 62/2 (2001) 386; the quotation is from *The Letters and Diaries of John Henry Newman*, ed. Charles Stephen Dessain et al. Vol. 30 (1977) 102; emphasis added.

10. The only significant – and dubious – initiative in connection with the celebration of feast days was the recent decision by the Irish Bishops to move the Feasts of the Ascension and of Corpus Christi from Thursday to Sunday, a decision which at the time caused dismay and incomprehension among faithful Catholics at the grass-root level, especially the older generation who had remained loyal despite the scandals. According to David Quinn, Editor of the *Irish Catholic*, the controversy drew one of the strongest ever reactions from his readers. They protested to no avail. The change did not even register with those who no longer practised; the whole notion of a feast day had become unintelligible to them.

11. 'The world will be saved by beauty', quoted by Solzhenitzyn, *Nobel Prize Lecture*, translated by Nicholas Bethell, London: Stenvally Press, 1973, 11.

12. Many former schools run by religious congregation have been handed over to dedicated Catholic laypeople anxious to preserve the ethos and tradition of the various orders. Similarly, Irish health care officials, oftentimes heroic in their dedication, still display the Christian charity and devotion to the sick that characterised the Catholic hospitals of the past. And yet, in the absence of the public witness of men and woman religious who represent the Church's radical call to *single-minded* service (this is what celibacy means), one cannot but wonder if the older Catholic ethos can indeed be sustained by youth raised in a predominantly secular society, whose image of what constitutes the Catholic ethos has been formed mostly by films such as *The Madgalen Sisters* and TV documentaries like *Cardinal Secrets*, that cleverly and, it would seem, systematically associate images of Catholic ritual with clerical sexual abuse, to the detriment of the former.

13. See John Henry Cardinal Newman. *Grammar of Assent*, Chapter VII.

14. Tom Inglis, *Moral Monopoly. The Rise and Fall of the Catholic Church in Modern Ireland,* Dublin: University College Press (second edition), 1998, 257.

15. Daily papers, such as the *Frankfurter Allegemeine Zeitung* or *Le Monde* regularly contain articles on theological subjects, reviews of theological books of an academic nature, and descriptions of exhibitions of religious art; they are of a quality and seriousness which one looks for in vain in an Irish paper.

16. See Václav Havel, 'Politics and Conscience' (transl. E. Kohék & R. Scruton) in *Living in Truth*, edited by Jan Vládislav, London-Boston: Faber and Faber, 1989, 136-52.

17. No one appreciates this more than politicians and journalists. I remember, during the early debates on legislation re contraception, abortion, and divorce, how the proponents of change tried to intimidate the Church into not using the pulpit, accusing the Church of 'unfair intervention in politics'.

18. Considering the actual involvement of Irish clergy in secular politics since the time of Daniel O'Connell, though apparently against his better judgment, up to the birth of the Irish Free State and after, it is not surprising that the Irish clergy seem to be politically astute to a most unusual degree. This trait is not always guaranteed to promote the Kingdom of God. Cf. Patrick Murray, *Oracles of God. The Roman Catholic Church and Irish Politics, 1922-37*, Dublin: University College Dublin Press, 2000.

19.   Newman, *Grammar of Assent*, 117.

20.   See, among the vast material now available, John J. Ó Ríordáin, *Irish Catholic Spirituality*, which also contains useful literature on the subject; also Michael Maher (ed.), *Irish Spirituality*, Dublin: Veritas, 1981; Thomas O'Loughlin, *Journey on the Edges. The Celtic Tradition* [Traditions of Christian Spirituality Series], London: Darton, Longman & Todd, 2000; likewise *Celtic Theology. Humanity, World and God in Early Irish Writings*, London and New York: Continuum, 2000. See also *Celtic Spirituality*, [The Classics of Western Spirituality], a useful collection of original sources (Latin, Irish and Welsh) translated and introduced by Oliver Davies, New York/Mahwah: Paulist Press, 1999. However, Irish Catholic experience is not limited to the 'Gaelic' or 'Celtic' current, deep and rich though it is, but also includes other currents, such as the Norman and Old English (cf. for example Angela M. Lucas, ed., *Anglo-Irish Poems of the Middle Ages*, Dublin: The Columba Press, 1995) and the English-speaking spirituality of the towns of the eighteenth century and later, already mentioned above.

21.   This is a term used by James Joyce (see Richard Ellmann, op. cit., 181), who possibly got it from Newman, though Ellmann does not mention this.

22.   'A fine talker, but devoid of the critical sense, vaunting and verbose... Full of physical courage, he is often deficient in moral courage; he lacks confidence in himself, initiative, and energy, and has lost the habit of looking things in the face. He quails before responsibilities, and has forgotten how to will, for his soul is still a serf.' L. Paul-Dubois, 1908, as quoted by Fennell, *Irish Catholics and Freedom*, 27. Cf. also the comments of Mgr William Kinsella, Bishop of Ossory, as reported by de Tocqueville, op. cit. 62: 'These people have all the divine virtues. They have the faith. No one is a better Christian than the Irishman. Their morals are pure. Their crimes are very rarely premeditated. But they lack essentially the civil virtues. They are without foresight, without prudence. Their courage is instinctive. They throw themselves at an obstacle with extraordinary violence and if they are not successful at the first attempt, they tire of it. They are changeable, love excitement, combat.'

23.   See Christopher Dawson, 'Christianity and Sex' in *Enquiries into Religion and Culture*, London and New York: Sheed & Ward, 1933, 259f.

24. Last year, the St Vincent de Paul Society had to advertise for volunteers, something unheard of a decade ago. Perhaps the most dramatic incidence of this phenomenon is the collapse of the Sick Poor Society in Cork's North Parish and the threat of a similar fate for that in the South Parish. The Sick Poor Society was founded over 250 years ago and must be one of the oldest charitable organisations in Ireland that survived famine, emigration, and economic depression – but not present-day prosperity.

25. Cf. Josef Pieper, *Justice and Fortitude*, London: Faber and Faber, 1957, 107-8, with reference to *S.Th.* II/II,114, 2 ad 1.

26. What Cotton Mather said in 1702 about 'Christ's great deeds in America' could, *mutatis mutandis*, be said about modern Ireland: '*religion* brought forth prosperity, and the *daughter* destroyed the *mother*.... There is danger lest the *enchantments* of this world make them forget their *errand into the wilderness*.' (The 'errand into the wilderness' was, of course, a reference to the Puritans and the early pioneers.) Quoted in Paul Johnson, 'The Almost-Chosen People: Why America is Different' in Richard John Neuhaus, *Unsecular America*, Encounter Series: 2 (Grand Rapids, Mich.: Wm. B. Eerdmans, 1986), 1.

27. Tom McGurk, 'Land of Brands and Consumers' in the *Sunday Business Post*, 3 September 2000, as reported in *Response*, 19/3 (2000), 29-30. It is interesting to compare his observation with that made by Father Andrew Farrell, Navan, December 1965: 'The real reason for the so-called rebellion of the young is under the surface; it is a blind, unconscious protest against a society which has not helped them to see that there is more to life than the material...', as quoted by Fennell, op. cit., 13.

28. Hauntingly evoked by the British poet, David Jones, *The Anathemata, fragments of an attempted writing*, London: Faber and Faber, 1990 (reprint of the second edition, 1955). 'The cult-man stands alone in Pellam's land: more precariously than he knows he guards the *signa*: the pontifex among his house treasures (the twin-*urbes* his house is) he can fetch things new and old: the tokens, the matrices, the institutes, the ancilia, the fertile ashes – the palladic foreshadowings: the things come down from heaven together with the kept memorials, the things lifted up and the venerated trinkets' (50). According to the notes, 'King Pellam in Malory's *Morte D'arthur* is lord of the Waste Lands and the lord of the Two Lands'.

29. As quoted in Corish, *The Irish Catholic Experience*, 183.

30. *The Wexford Carols*, Assembled and Edited by Diarmaid Ó Muirithe, Music transcribed with a commentary by Seoirse Bodley, Dublin: The Dolmen Press, 1982, 14. Ó Muirithe quotes from a letter to *The People*, a Wexford newspaper, in January 1872: 'I have stood within many of the grandest Cathedrals of Europe and under the dome of St. Peter's itself, but in none of them did I ever feel the soul-thrilling rapturous sensation that I did as a boy listening to six aged men on a frosty Christmas morning sing the carols beneath the low straw-thatched chapel of Rathangan' (15).

31. There are significant exceptions, such as Aidan Mathew's play, *Communion*, and, in art, Patrick Pye and Imogen Stuart. Moreover, in her book entitled *Theology and Modern Irish Art*, (Dublin: The Columba Press, 1999), Gesa Elsbeth Thiessen, a Lutheran theologian in Dublin, claims to be able to discern certain rather broadly defined 'theological aspects' in a number of modern Irish artists (believers and atheists alike).

32. Bloomsday (16 June) could be described as the principal 'feast-day' of secular Dublin and is enjoyed in a way that could teach the Church a lesson in celebration. Even children in primary schools dress up and join in the fun, as once girls dressed up during the month of May in their white Communion dresses to crown Our Lady 'Queen of the May'. At least in Dublin, the closest we have got to a Latin-American-style *carnival* is St Patrick's Day. The paradox is that it developed in recent years not in harmony with its character as a Christian feast day, but almost in opposition to it. Today, it has become a celebration of 'Irish identity', whatever that might be. As a result, our national apostle has become a caricature, a quasi-mythical figure of fun. The legendary serpents seem to be more appealing. Since its inception as a *national* feast day, St Patrick's Day has been shrouded in ambivalence, to put it mildly; the public holiday was an attempt to use the saint for political purposes (nationalism) rather than to celebrate his holiness. It was inevitable that it would deteriorate into its present form, namely as a tourist attraction and money spinner. The one-time national celebration of Easter commemorating the 1916 Rising is another instance of the way the Nation as god became fused with the Risen Lord, though such was Catholic Ireland that few thought much of it, even Churchmen. It only became problematical when the Troubles in the North worsened.

33. See Vincent Ryan OSB, *The Shaping of Sunday: Sunday and the Eucharist in the Irish Tradition*, Dublin: Veritas, 1997.

34. Joseph Cardinal Ratzinger, *Weggemeinschaft des Glaubens. Kirche als Communio. Festgabe zum 75. Geburtstag herausgegeben vom Schülerkreis*, edited by Stephan Otto Horn and Vincenz Pfnür, Augsburg: Sankt Ulrich Verlag, 2002, 258.

35. A liturgical renewal conceived primarily in aesthetic terms would be a perversion. The liturgy can be, and indeed must be, supremely beautiful, but the aesthetic dimension must remain secondary to what actually takes place in the sacraments, the transforming power of Christ. For this reason, a theology of liturgy is indispensable. In addition, at the core of the Christian liturgy is the service of the Word, including the sermon or homily, which must speak to the heart and the head. Theology, in other words, is the form and substance of the liturgy. As an aesthetic experience, the Holy Week Liturgy appealed to Joyce long after he turned his back on the Church, cf. Ellmann, *James Joyce*, 320.

36. The phenomenal success of 'Harry Potter' and even Tolkein's *Lord of the Rings* (though intended for adults) is a reminder to us that children are particularly sensitive to what is mysterious and magical. They do not expect to understand everything. But the rationalist approach to children's Masses (making everything understandable and, thus, banal) robs them of the true 'magic' of the Mass.

37. Ratzinger, *Weggemeinschaft*, 257 (my translation).

38. Cf. Ibid., 257-8.

39. Cf. Ó Ríordáin, *Irish Catholic Spirituality*, 87-92, drawing on the work of an tAthair Ó Laoghaire. See also Vincent Ryan OSB, *The Shaping of Sunday*.

40. Our own tradition provides prayers to be said in preparation for Mass, cf. Ó Laoghaire, *Our Mass Our Life*, 10-14; see also the appropriate prayers for the other parts of the Mass.

41. Cf. David Jones, *The Anathemata*. The mid-fifth century Bishop Diadikos of Photike well captures the attitude of soul a priest should have in his description of a priest-friend: 'He celebrates the liturgy as the law prescribes for priests but he is so intent on the love of God that he looses all awareness of his own dignity in the depths of his love for God' (*Office of Readings*, Friday of Week 2).

42. See below, Chapter 6, note 20.

43. Cf. M. K. Flynn, *Ideology, Mobilization and the Nation*, 36-37

44. Cf. Ibid., 76. On the significance of the GAA for the development of a distinct Irish nationalism, see Oliver MacDonagh, *Ireland*, New Jersey: Prentice Hall, 1968, 65-6.

45. Cf. Leon J. Poddles, *The Church Impotent. The Feminization of Christianity*, Dallas: Spence, 1999, 168.

46. Cf. Poddles, *The Church Impotent*, 168-174, for a discussion of the important but essentially ambiguous nature of sport – and thus its dangers – which are rooted in the phenomenon of masculinity. The main preoccupation of his study, however, is with the gradual feminisation of the Church resulting from developments in spirituality, theology, and philosophy in the Middle Ages and leading to the alienation of men from active participation in the Church. It is at least arguable that the GAA's close association with the Church was to a great extent responsible for preventing such a development in Ireland, particularly rural Ireland, in former generations.

47. H. Schürmann, as reported in Joseph Cardinal Ratzinger, *The Meaning of Christian Brotherhood*, San Francisco: Ignatius Press, 1993 (2nd English edition), 69.

48. Ibid. 69-70. Ratzinger adds: 'And the parishes ought to come to see one another as sisters, according to the words of John's second Epistle (5:13) – sisters who, in the fellowship of their faith and love, build up together the great unity of Mother Church, the body of the Lord.'

49. Those same car parks could be made less functional and desolate-looking by planting trees, which would also provide shade in the summer. The parish Church of Kinnegad, Co. Meath, has taken the lead in creating such a public space in front of the church.

50. In fact, the Harvest Festival has its roots in primeval religion and formed the basis of the Israelite Feasts of Pentecost (for the first fruits of the products of the field, cf. Ex 23:16) and Tabernacles.

51. In preconciliar times, the Marian processions on the Sundays of May were a source of joy and piety, especially for the parents and relatives of the children who had made their First Communion that year and made up the procession. These celebrations were an 'overflow' of the joy of First Communion. They have been revived in some parishes in the southern USA, thanks to the arrival of the Hispanics there, and have been received with great enthusiasm by all concerned. It is to be hoped that immigrant Catholics from other cultures, who are now coming to Ireland in considerable numbers, will likewise enrich our own parish communities, provided we give them the necessary

welcome and space. Unfortunately, the reception these African and other refugees received in Irish parishes when they first came was such that many have left and founded their own Churches. To the best of my knowledge, no programme for the pastoral care of immigrants has been put in place at national or diocesan level, which is astonishing considering the traditional care of Irish emigrants abroad. Has the Irish Church forgotten the Golden Rule?

52.   '[Hurling] was more than a game; it was a ceremonial, for even in places where hurling began to die out as a normal pastime, it was considered proper to play it at one time of the year – at Christmas'. David Greene, 'Michael Cusack and the Rise of the GAA' in Conor Cruise O'Brien (ed.), *The Shaping of Modern Ireland*, London, Routledge & Kegan Paul, 1960, 74-5. Greene mentions the Blasket Islands, Connemara, Donegal, and the Scottish Highlands. However, it seems that there was both summer and winter hurling, though the latter was not a spectator sport (see Seamus J. King, *A History of Hurling*, Dublin: Gill & Macmillan, 1996, 11). King claims that hurling was always an essential component of all festivities in pre-Christian times. This would have been taken up into the celebration of the Christian Sunday and feast-days (or Pattern Days), until 'under the new puritan dispensation, "Dicing, Dauncing, vaine players of Enterludes, with other idle Pastimes, etc. commonly used on the Sabbath-day" were to be forbidden' (ibid., 9).

53.   Cf. Corish, *The Irish Catholic Experience*, 108; 120.

54.   Ibid., 181.

55.   Cf. ibid., 135-6; 190; 213. See Donal Kerr SM, 'The Early Nineteenth Century', 135-7. For a description of the pilgrimage to Clonmacnoise in the middle of the nineteenth century by the antiquarian, W.F. Wakeman, see John J. Ó Ríordáin, *Irish Catholic Spirituality*, 116.

56.   Seán de Fréine, *The Great Silence*, 81

57.   We have ever been a people greatly influenced 'by places and their associations, the *dindsenchas*' (Corish, *The Irish Catholic Experience*, 5). For an illustration of this, see de Tocqueville, op. cit., 121-2.

58.   Cf. Kerr, 'The Early Nineteenth Century', 135.

59.   Cf. Elizabeth Healy, *In Search of Ireland's Holy Wells*. According to Máire MacNeill, *The Festival of Lughnasa*, Oxford: 1962 (as quoted by Healy), this is 'one of the three most strongly lasting survivals of Lughnasa' (the others being Garland Sunday on Croagh Patrick and

Puck Fair, Kilorgan, Co. Kerry). This may be so, but equally important is the way these pagan feasts were Christianised (Puck Fair may be the exception). But the fact of pre-Christian celebrations or places (such as holy wells) by no means accounts for all the pilgrimages and patterns that flourished in Ireland. In any case, most pre-Christian practices had been transformed by a Christian faith later purified by persecution. In addition, the dwelling place or grave of the local saint, or indeed a reliquary, inevitably gave rise to pilgrimages; cf. John J. Dunne, *Shrines of Ireland*, Dublin: Veritas, 1989.

60. Cf. Thierry Maertens, *Heidnisch-jüdische Wurzeln der christlichen Feste*, Mainz: Matthias-Grünewald, 1965, translated from the French by Sigrid Loersch; Joseph Ratzinger, *Die sakramentale Begründung christlicher Existenz*, Meitingen-Freising: Kyrios, 1966.

61. Cf. Benedict Kiely, *Poor Scholar. A Study of William Carleton (1794-1869)*, Dublin: Talbot Press, 1972 (first edition: 1942), 65-71.

62. Ibid., 72.

63. Cf. ibid. 73-8. Kiely perceptively comments: 'The one unpardonable, damnable thing is that puritanical tendency to judge the hearts of other men, to see their penance as something almost obscene and masochistic, dissociated utterly from all saving repentance' (76).

64. It should be noted that many of these ritual practices have their roots in primeval religious practices which are not simply 'Celtic' or even 'pre-Celtic' but, it seems, fairly universal, as Turner, *The Ritual Process*, has demonstrated. See also Victor Turner and Edith Turner, *Image and Pilgrimage in Christian Culture. Anthropological Perspectives*, Oxford: Basil Blackwell, 1978; the chapter on Lough Derg is particularly interesting. The ritual shape, for example, of 'doing the rounds', is probably rooted in our nature as embodied ritual beings and should not be treated as superstition, as the disembodied rationalists would claim. It is the basis for all religious processions.

65. Commenting on the decline of sport and recreation of all kinds in the middle of the nineteenth century, King observes: 'It would appear that the Catholic Church was joining the Protestant churches in the desire for orderliness and respectability' (*A History of Hurling*, 23). Their efforts could not wipe it out completely. Up to relatively recently, hurling was part of the celebration of the pattern on the 15 August (the feast of the Assumption) in different parts of the country, as I was informed by former hurlers, one from Galway, the other from Limerick.

66. Cf. John J. Ó Ríordáin, *Irish Catholic Spirituality*, 121
67. Elizabeth Healy, *In Search of Ireland's Holy Wells*, 37.
68. Patrick Kavanagh, *The Green Fool*, London, Martin Brian &
     O'Keeffe, 1971 (first edition 1938), 63-70.
69. Ibid., 68. The 'old Fianians' evidently refer to the Gaelic
     mythological warrior band the Fianna led by the hero Fionn mac
     Cumhaill (Finn Mac Coole). Brigid could be saint or goddess!
70. This sense of celebration was somehow or other retained in the
     more modern, popular pilgrimages to Lourdes, helped by the very
     fact that the great Marian shrine is situated in the South of France
     where the sun shines more than at home and where wine is a regular
     part of the main meal. The criticism I have heard over the years
     about such pilgrimages is that, very often, they lacked any genuine
     spiritual direction or theological substance. All that was expected of
     the priest (or bishop) was that he would say Mass for the pilgrims,
     visit the sick occasionally, and hear confessions. Even at times the
     last two expectations were not always fulfilled. What missed
     opportunities! My own experience of pilgrimages, when I was living
     in Germany, was that in the course of travelling to a shrine,
     preferably on foot, people experience true liminality, that is they
     become open to God and the things of God in a unique way. Such
     pilgrimages recall the experience of the two disciples on the road to
     Emmaus. Amidst all the camaraderie and fun, people also talk about
     the things that really matter to them. They expect that their spiritual
     and, yes, their intellectual or theological concerns will be addressed
     in a way that gives them reasons for their hope (cf. 1 Pet 3:15).
71. 'The road in the vicinity [of the holy well] was like a rowdy bazaar-
     ground. There was singing, not of hymns, but of comic songs that
     had nothing to do with piety. There were beggars of all breeds.'
     Kavanagh, *The Green Fool*, 66.
72. Ó Ríordáin, *Irish Catholic Spirituality*, 129, draws attention to Irish
     love of the ancient Christian practice of nightly vigils. We are, he
     reminds us, 'people of the night'. This might be remembered when
     planning pastoral strategies, especially for the youth. It was
     experienced again in the various vigils that accompanied the relics
     of St Thérèse of Lisieux on her triumphant 'march' through the
     country in 2001.
73. Quoted by Donal Kerr, 'The Early Nineteenth Century', 136. I doubt
     if Carleton's picture was too 'highly coloured', as Kerr suggests. I

experienced something similar in the 1960s on the smallest of the Aran Islands, Inisheer. At the Sunday morning Mass, I was greatly impressed by the deep devotion of the islanders – and almost equally amazed, by way of contrast, at the wild, almost Dionysian, Irish traditional dancing in the boathouse on the strand that evening. With regard to the Irish love of dancing in the nineteenth century, see the remarks made by the Englishman, Arthur Young, quoted in John J. Ó Ríordáin, *Irish Catholic Spirituality*, 122.

74. In the capital, the Franciscans in Adam and Eve's, the Carmelites in Whitefriars' Street and the Carmelites (Discalced) in Clarendon Street are already giving the lead. Of particular note is the liturgy of the Benedictines at Glenstal, Co. Limerick, the early pioneers of liturgy in Ireland, and that of the Cistercian Abbey of nuns, Glencairn, Co. Waterford. There are other examples throughout the country, especially in the cathedrals, which have well-trained choirs, such as the famous Palestrina Choir of the Pro-Cathedral, Dublin, which celebrates its centenary this year. In this context, it is worth mentioning the initiative by the Irish bishops in the area of sacred music, namely creating the Schola Cantorum, a boarding school specialising in training young talented musicians in Church music, at St Finian's, the Meath diocesan college, Mullingar. (Its immediate future, it seems, is uncertain.) Some dioceses have begun appointing diocesan directors of music. There is also an impressive body of modern liturgical music, such as that composed by Seán Ó Riada and, more recently, Fr Liam Lawton, John O'Keeffe and Ronan McDonagh (cf. the CD, *Feasts & Seasons. Music for the Church Year from St Patrick's College*, Maynooth, 2003). It would be a pity if modern composers of Church music should be seduced by the popularity of what claims to be 'Celtic' music (evoking mists and magic), which is basically self-centred, as it is more concerned with massaging subjective feelings than worship of the transcendent God.

75. See the chapter entitled 'Fasting like an Irishman' in Ó'Riordáin, *Irish Catholic Spirituality*, 120-135; see also 36-7. However, I beg to disagree on the author's evaluation of the more morally dubious Irish 'tradition' of hunger strikes.

76. Cf. Michael Haren & Yolande de Pontfarcy (eds), *The Medieval Pilgrimage to St. Patrick's Purgatory. Lough Derg and the European Tradition*, Enniskillen: Clogher Historical Society, 1988. See also Turner, *Image and Pilgrimage*, 104-39.

77. Ó Ríordáin, *Irish Catholic Spirituality*, 126.
78. Cf. 'Repentance and Self-Limitation in the Life of Nations' in Alexander Solzhenitsyn et al., *From under the Rubble*, translated under the direction of Michael Scammell, London: Fontana/Collins, 1976, 105-43.

Chapter 4: Structures for a New Millennium

1. *Sermon* 46,6 (*Office of Readings* for Wednesday, Week 24).
2. Corish, *The Irish Catholic Experience*, 35.
3. Cf. ibid. 32. For a fuller account of this 'revolution', see Kathleen Hughes, *The Church in Early Society*, London: Methuen, 1966, 266-74.
4. Cf. Corish, *The Irish Catholic Experience*, 194-225 for a critical but balanced assessment of the achievement of Paul Cullen (1803-78), Archbishop of Armagh (1849), Dublin (1852), and Ireland's first Cardinal (1866).
5. Cf. ibid., 210-2.
6. ODCC (second edition, 1974), 1405.
7. Corish, 201
8. See Emmet Larkin 'The Parish Mission Movement, 1850-1880' in Brendan Bradshaw and Dáire Keogh (eds), *Christianity in Ireland. Revisiting the Story*, Dublin: The Columba Press, 2002, 195-204.
9. John J. Ó'Riordáin, *Irish Catholic Spirituality*, 139.
10. Ibid., 140.
11. The term 'superior' is avoided today among religious sensitive to language and the issues of equality. Some women religious, if they acknowledge any such individual in authority at all, prefer to use the term 'leader' and so describe their various councils as 'leadership teams'. There is a strange paradox here, since they appear to be oblivious of the fact that the English for *Führer* or *Duce* is 'Leader'!
12. The title was changed to CORI, it would seem after the Taoiseach of the day, having being asked for his reaction to a stinging criticism of his government's budget by the Justice and Peace Desk of the Conference of Major Religious Superiors, as it then was, said that he found it hard to take any institution seriously that could manage to combine the words 'major' and 'superior' in its title.
13. Corish, *The Irish Catholic Experience*, 198.
14. Ibid., 199. Cullen was suspicious of the Royal Catholic College of Maynooth, and so tended not to promote its staff.

15. The statistics evidently include retired bishops as well as those in office. In Ireland, there are 36 bishops in office, while 11 are listed in the *Irish Catholic Directory 2000* as retired, not counting Cardinal Daly. The remaining figure is presumably made up of retired missionary bishops, some of whom help out at Confirmation time.

16. Taken from the *Statistical Yearbook of the Church, 1999*, Vatican City: Libreria Editrice Vaticana, 2001.

17. The seniority system, it seems to me, is basically unjust to all concerned, those who simply do not have what it takes in terms of ability and those whose justified ambitions are frustrated, as well as parish communities who have to suffer an incompetent parish priest or are deprived of the ministry of one who can really make a difference. This is an offence against distributive justice. Recently, some priests with the required seniority have asked not to be made parish priests, but to be allowed to continue as curates.

18. Dublin, of course, was the exception.

19. Cf. Seán Ó Faoláin, *The Irish*, 143-4.

20. Joseph Cardinal Ratzinger, *Salt of the Earth. The Church at the end of the Millennium*. An Interview with Peter Seewald, San Francisco: Ignatius Press, 173. It should be mentioned that Ratzinger is here criticising the extensive bureaucracy of the contemporary German Church, due in no small measure to the Church-tax system operated by the State, a situation quite the reverse of that which obtains in Ireland. But the principle is valid for any local Church. In this context, one should mention that, after Volkswagen, the German Church has the greatest number of employees in Germany, equal to that of the Lutheran Church. Cardinal Joachim Meisner, Archbishop of Cologne, in a homily to the German Episcopal Conference that unleashed a heated public debate, criticised the numerous structures, commissions, statutes and secretariats within the Church, which he said run the risk of 'obfuscating the faith'. He also expressed his concern about the weakness of the faith of lay collaborators in the Church (such as catechists and lay pastoral assistants). Source: *Zenit.org*, 10 October 2002. These observations should be kept in mind, when, in the following, I suggest that we could benefit from some more diocesan and national structures in our own Church, which are at present rather thin on the ground.

21. Six dioceses might suffice, the existing provinces plus Dublin and Armagh/Down & Connor as metropolitan sees (See next note).

Desmond Fennell, *Heresy. The Battle of Ideas in Modern Ireland*, 246, suggested calling a Church Assembly to redraw diocesan boundaries.

22. For the primatial See of Armagh, a solution such as that found in Hungary might be contemplated, where Esztergom (the historical centre of the Hungarian Church) and the capital Budapest form one archdiocese. A similar solution might be found for the other so-called 'metropolitan' sees now situated in small towns.

23. The difficulty is often more practical, namely that the amalgamated parishes expect the same services as heretofore and so put enormous pressure on an ageing clergy.

24. This is in contrast with a neighbouring diocese, where the shortage of priests is beginning to be felt in a serious way and where already a few parishes have been amalgamated not by choice but of necessity.

25. Information supplied by the Irish Missionary Union, 2001.

26. The visit of President Mary McAleese to missionaries in Kenya (2001) was a belated but much appreciated gesture of recognition on the part of the State.

27. Cf. Corish, *The Irish Catholic Experience*, 11.

28. Cf. ibid., 196.

29. The residual resentment among some (admittedly few) clergy to the relatively recent amalgamation of one particular diocese in the southwest with a neighbouring one demonstrates the very real difficulties arising from traditional loyalties to place.

30. See Hughes, *The Church in Early Irish Society*, op. cit.

31. 'The diocese of Meath grew out of seven dioceses that were linked to major monastic sites. ...At the Synod of Kells in 1152 the seven dioceses were reduced to three – Duleek, Clonard, and Kells – on the understanding that over time these three would become one. This happened towards the end of the twelfth century...' (*Irish Catholic Directory 2000*, 262).

32. *Irish Catholic Directory 2000*, 180.

33. Ibid., 154.

34. However, what one author said about Lord Stanley's formula for a National School system in Ireland (originally intended to be 'ecumenical' in character) should not be forgotten: '...as was often (actually, almost always) the case with outsiders' solutions to Irish problems, it ran headlong into the doleful realities of Irish life'

(Donald Harman Akenson, *Small Differences*, 120). The 'doleful realities' include those factors mentioned above which make change imperative. They should not be underestimated.

Chapter 5: Beyond *Church v. State*

1. *Non enim apud nos persona, sed ratio valet.* (*Sancti Columbani Opera*, transl. by G. S. W. Walker, Dublin: Institute of Advanced Studies, 1970, reprint of 1957, 49).
2. Cf. John Horgan, *Noël Browne*, 156; the quotation is from a letter to the Editor, the *Irish Times* (23 April 1951) by Mr Ernest P. Hare of Enniskillen in the aftermath of the Mother and Child affair.
3. For a comprehensive discussion of the main philosophical issues involved, see in particular Brendan Purcell, 'Church, State and Society: A Discussion of Professor Clarke's *Church and State: Essays in Political Philosophy*' in the *Irish Philosophical Journal*, 3 (1986) 58-79.
4. For details, see Appendix II.
5. Cf. Allan Bloom, *The Closing of the American Mind*, 296. Desmond Fennell coined the term 'fundamental individualism'. More recently, former Taoiseach, Mr John Bruton, when speaking about the ban on religious advertising, attacked what he called 'fundamentalist secularism'.
6. It is not just in Ireland that the real forum of public debate has shifted from parliament to the media. It is doubtful if this is a change for the better, as far as the nature of democracy and the quality of public debate are concerned. The modern media with its need for the sound bite, its transitory nature, and its tendency to reduce everything to entertainment is not exactly the best forum for serious and prolonged debate that would lead to some commonly accepted resolution to a particular social dilemma. Further, the more powerful and well-endowed political parties can afford to employ the most able spin-doctors to manipulate an increasingly passive citizenry. Should politicians and media agree on basic policies – as was the case in most 'social issues' debated in Ireland over the past two decades – then the possibility of a balanced debate where opposing views are given equal hearing is rather slim, as was the case with the RTÉ coverage of the 1995 divorce referendum. With regard to the latter, the Supreme Court ruled (26 January

2000) that RTÉ's coverage was unconstitutional and in breach of fair procedures (cf. *Media Report*, 18, 2000).

7.   Cf. Lee, *Ireland 1912-1985*, 658-70.

8.   Cf. Fennell, *Beyond Nationalism*.

9.   See above, p. 72f.

10.   Cf. Michele Dillon, *Debating Divorce. Moral Conflict in Ireland*, Lexington, Kentucky: University Press, 1993, 91-109, for a useful overview of the tensions within the ranks of hierarchy and the theologians that emerged in various referendum campaigns. See also Jeremiah Newman, Bishop of Limerick, *Ireland Must Choose: Religion, Politics and Law in Ireland Today*, Dublin: Four Courts Press, 1983.

11.   This is, understandably, the main preoccupation of the writings of Isaiah Berlin, whose reflections have had such a profound influence on British and American public discourse. For a useful introduction to Berlin's thought, see that of Roger Hausheer, *Against the Current. Essays in the History of Ideas*, edited by Henry Hardy, London: Pimlico, 1997, xiii-liii.

12.   On the way '*values* take the place of good and evil', see Allan Bloom, *The Closing of the American Mind*, New York et al.: Simon and Schuster, 1987, 194-216.

13.   See the encyclical of Pope John Paul II, *Fides et ratio*, 46-7, on the emergence of totalitarian ideologies, on the crisis of rationalism, including the latter's nihilistic implications, and on the danger of 'instrumental reason' and its utilitarian ethics, all products of the historical separation of faith from philosophical reason since the later 'Middle Ages'. Cf. also *Fides et ratio*, 88-89, on scientism and pragmatism.

14.   See Francis Fukyama, *The End of History and the Last Man*, London: Penguin, 1992, 332.

15.   Cf. Rodger Charles, *The Social Teaching of the Vatican II. Its Origins and Development*, Leominster: Fowler Wright Books Ltd, 1982, 9-71.

16.   If ever the title of a book was responsible for undermining the main arguments of that book, then it must be Lord Devlin's *The Enforcement of Morals*, Oxford-New York: Oxford University Press, 1965. The book had its origins in the second Maccabean lecture in Jurisprudence of the British Academy in 1958 as a critique of the principles informing the *Wolfenden Report* (1957) and the famous controversy the lecture aroused with his opponent, Professor Hart. It is of note how, in the discussion of so-called 'public morality' (namely what may be incorporated into positive law), the terms

'enforcement', 'imposition', etc., are used to emphasise the element of coercion, as it were, which, to put it mildly, goes against the grain of modern man's sense of freedom and autonomy. Arguing within that frame of reference for any kind of intrinsic connection between positive law and the broader moral order was doomed to failure from the very outset.

17. Thus, for example, a politician in Nazi Germany who knew that the policy to liquidate the Jews and Gypsies was wrong would not be excused for his or her continuing involvement with the Government, unless it were to do everything in his or her power to reduce the damage. Even then, a legislator could not vote in Parliament or otherwise in favour of laws to promote this policy, though the logic of the thesis we are discussing would imply that they could.

18. As quoted by George William Rutler, *Beyond Modernity: Reflections of a Post-Modern Catholic*, San Francisco: Ignatius Press, 1987, 90.

19. For a succinct summary of the Church's teaching on the rational principles which ought to regulate the relationship between civil law and moral law, see *Donum vitae*, III.

20. This truth was already recognised by the ancient Greeks, as in Sophocles' *Antigone*.

21. Cf. C.S. Lewis, *The Abolition of Man*, Oxford: University Press, 1943.

22. Cf also *Gaudium et spes*, 74, 87, 89.

23. 'It is part of the duty of the public authority to ensure that the civil law is regulated according to the fundamental norms of the moral law in matters concerning human rights, human life and the institution of the family. Politicians must commit themselves, through their interventions upon public opinion, to securing in society the widest possible consensus on such essential points and to consolidating this consensus wherever it risks being weakened or is in danger of collapse' (*Donum Vitae*, III).

24. Lee, *Ireland 1912-1985*, 659.

25. This is a quotation from the encyclical *Centesimus annus*, 46, emphasis given in text.

26. Cf. Justice E.-W. Böckenförde quoted by Joseph Ratzinger, *Church, Ecumenism and Politics*, Slough: St Paul's Publications, 1988, 206. This is a truth which de Tocqueville learned to appreciate in his examination of democracy in America and which has been developed by a whole school of new thinkers from both sides of the political spectrum (especially in the USA), from the 'conservative'

Gertrude Himmelfarb and Roger Scruton, on the one hand, to the 'communitarian liberals' John Gray and Amitei Etzioni on the other. 'If there is a common strand to their thought it is the conviction that the health of society depends not only on its political and economic structures but also on its moral resources and the institutions that give them vitality' (Jonathan Sacks, *The Politics of Hope*, 49; see also 236 re 'faith-based' initiatives).

27. See John Finnis, *Natural Law and Natural Rights*, Oxford: Clarendon Press, 1988, espec. 198-230, for a discussion on the complexity of the contemporary human-rights discourse; see also Mary Ann Gendon, *Rights Talk. The Impoverishment of Political Discourse*, New York et al.: The Free Press, 1991, espec. 18-46, re the 'illusion of absoluteness' in public discourse.

28. Cf. Enda McDonagh, *The Gracing of Society*, Dublin: Gill and Macmillan, 1989, 106-8

29. See Thomas Finan, 'The Desired of the Nations', 10.

30. Regarding the significance of Christianity for the emergence of the specifically Western concept of the separation of Church and State, see Ratzinger 'Theology and the Church's Political Stance' in his book *Church, Ecumenism and Politics. New Essays in Ecclesiology*, Slough: St Paul's Publications, 1988, 152-164, espec. 160-4.

31. This is quite other than the idea of conscience that has gained ground as a result of the dominance of emotivism both in moral philosophy and in our contemporary culture, which found an echo in the conception of morality in terms of 'moral beliefs'. Conscience is thus reduced to *the choice of one's own moral principles* (something is wrong simply because *I choose* to think so). It is no longer the moral imperative I hear in the depths of my heart, the echo of the voice of God to which I should submit, no matter how little it appeals to me. Conscience, properly understood, makes us aware of what we *ought* to do, not what we *would like* to do. Cf. Ratzinger, *Salt of the Earth*, 41, 67f., 131. For a full discussion of the nature of conscience, cf. Joseph Cardinal Ratizinger, 'Conscience and Truth' in John M. Haas, *Crisis of Conscience*, New York: Crossroad Herder, 1996, 1-20; see also Servais Pinckaers OP, Conscience, Truth, and Prudence', in the same volume, 79-92.

32. Cf. *Fides et Ratio*, 89.

33. See Václav Havel, op. cit., esp. 36-122 and 136-57.

34. In the case of legislation to change existing laws permitting acts that are 'intrinsically wrong', such as contraception or abortion,

legislators and citizens may, of course, vote for measures aimed at *reducing* the extent of existing laws.

35. See Enda McDonagh, 'Constitutional Jubilee' in his book, *The Gracing of Society*, Dublin: Gill and Macmillan, 1989, 101-12.

36. He campaigned and voted for the Second Nice Amendment.

37. For an account of that campaign, cf. Tom Hesketh, *The Second Partioning of Ireland. The Abortion Referendum of 1983*, Dún Laoghaire: Brandsma Books Ltd, 1990.

38. Addressing the ambassadors accredited to the Holy See on 13 January 2003, Pope John Paul II said: 'We believe it desirable that, in full respect of the secular state, three complementary elements should be recognized: religious freedom not only in its individual and ritual aspects, but also in its social and corporative dimensions; *the appropriateness of structures for dialogue and consultation between the Governing Bodies and communities of believers*; respect for the juridical status already enjoyed by Churches and religious institutions in the Member States of the Union' (*Zenith.org*, emphasis mine). A similar point was made by Cardinal-Elect Desmond Connell in a wide-ranging interview he gave to the *Sunday Business Post* (18 February 2001) '...there should be a formal relationship between the state and the Church', adding that the same should apply to the other Churches. This point, like many other significant points made in the course of the interview, were totally ignored in the wake of a typical Irish media pseudo-controversy about a somewhat imprudent remark he made in passing about his Church of Ireland counterpart's reputation as a theologian. In any other country, such a remark would hardly have raised an eyebrow.

39. It is significant that, when Berlin was once again made the capital of Germany, the Catholic Church in Germany immediately set about establishing a Catholic Academy there, a kind of conference centre (with an 800-seat lecture hall, restaurant, and 60 rooms en suite). It is designed to provide a permanent forum for dialogue with the political, scientific, philosophical, artistic, and economic worlds. There is also a permanent office in Berlin to establish contact with government institutions and politicians. There is, to the best of my knowledge, nothing like it in Ireland.

40. I am grateful to Enda McDonagh for much of this information.

41. Eoin G. Cassidy, *A Faith Response to the Street Drug Culture. A Report Commissioned by the Irish Catholic Bishops' Drugs Initiative*. Maynooth:

Irish Centre for Faith and Culture, 2000; Eoin G. Cassidy (ed.), *Prosperity with a Purpose: What Purpose?*, Dublin: Veritas, 1999; Eoin G. Cassidy, Donal McKeown, John Morrow (eds), *Belfast: Faith in the City*, Dublin: Veritas 2001; Eoin G Cassidy (ed.), *Measuring Ireland: Discerning Values and Beliefs*, Dublin: Veritas, 2002; James McEvoy (ed.), *The Challenge of Truth. Reflections on Fides et Rato*, Dublin: Veritas, 2002.

42. For various reasons, a refurbished Clonliffe College would seem to be the ideal location for a more permanent Catholic Academy incorporating a modern, fully equipped conference centre right in the heart of the capital.

43. The papers of these annual conferences have also been published, cf. Harry Bohan and Gerard Kennedy (eds), *Are We Forgetting Something?*, Dublin: Veritas, 1999; *Working Towards Balance* (2000), *Redefining Roles and Relationships* (2001), *Is the Future My Responsibility?* (2002), and *Values and Ethics* (2003).

44. Such a Catholic Academy would require a permanent, full-time director, preferably lay, appointed by the Archbishop but chosen by a panel of representatives from the relevant areas of public life and culture. The latter would constitute the 'academy' with the right to elect new members, subject only to the veto of the Archbishop.

45. Cf. Pope John Paul II's encyclical *Centesimus Annus*, 49.

46. John J. Ó Ríordáin, *Irish Catholic Spirituality*, 23. For some practical implication of this concept for social development, see Harry Bohan, *Ireland Green: Social Planning and Rural Development*, Dublin: Veritas, 1979.

47. See the comments by Chief Rabbi Jonathan Sacks, *The Persistence of Faith. Religion, Morality and Society in a Secular Age*, London: Wiedenfeld and Nicholson, 1991, espec. 95-8. What is said here about the Churches, also applies to the recognised communities of other faiths, such as the Jewish and Islamic communities.

48. Lee, *Ireland 1912-1985*, 657.

49. John J. Ó Ríordáin, *Irish Catholic Spirituality*, 24.

50. One version of this appendix originally appeared in the *Irish Catholic* on 23 July 1998, while another was published in the *Irish Independent* on 30 July 1998 to commemorate the thirtieth anniversary of the publication of *Humanae vitae* [=HV]. This is a slightly amended version of the latter.

51. See HV 13.

Chapter 6: Vocations and Theology

1. *B'áil liom sagart breá sultarach pléisiurtha,*
    lán de chreideamh is carthanach nádúrtha,
    a bheadh báidheach le bochtaibh is cneasta lena thréadaí,
    ach níorbh áil liom stollaire fé chulaith mhín an Aon-Mhic.
    (Cf. D. Ó Laoghaire, *Our Mass, Our Life*, 16-17).

2. At present, there are eleven candidates for the priesthood studying for Dublin. By way of comparison, the new capital of Germany, Berlin, with less than half-a-million Catholics – a minority in a largely atheistic environment (as in former East Germany) – had circa fifty seminarians studying for the priesthood in 2002, half of whom admittedly are non-German and members of the Neo-Cathechuminate.

3. While teaching at the Regional Seminary of Papua New Guinea and the Solomon Islands (1979-1981), I made a rather sobering discovery. At the time I was teaching Mariology, among other subjects. Part of the course addressed traditional objections to various Marian dogmas. It soon became clear that the seminarians were more affected by the questions, which up to then had never entered their heads, than the answers provided. Admittedly, this may have been due to deficiencies in the answers, but it still makes the point that it is easier to sow the seeds of doubt by raising questions than to resolve them, a task that may take a lifetime.

4. Characteristic of diocesan seminarians trained in Maynooth was (and still is, to a great extent) their first-class graduate training in arts and science. As well as giving them a broad education, arts in particular sharpened their critical thought. Most male religious congregations had similar training programmes.

5. To illustrate his contention that many religious congregations are in disarray, David Quinn gives the following example: '[F]ive years ago Ireland's biggest congregation, the Mercy Sisters, issued a new mission statement. God received no more than passing mention, Jesus none at all. What was highlighted were all sorts of politically correct "social concerns" of the type that would do the UN proud. Some of the more conservative members of the order had deep reservations, but said nothing in public because they are not represented at the decision-making level of the Mercy Sisters.' David Quinn, 'Muddling through: The Catholic Church in Ireland' in *Crisis* (March 2001), 25.

6   In the final analysis, however, those calling for change and progress
     rely on a very traditional practice to achieve their enlightened goals:
     namely obedience to one's superior or to the 'decision' of the
     community once the communal 'discernment process' has been
     completed. In my own experience, I should add, these 'discernment
     processes' have more recently matured into processes of genuine
     listening and learning, indeed often leading to collective judgments
     that are truly communitarian. But also, it must be added, that the
     expectations of most religious today who have more or less
     survived the constant re-cycling are now fairly limited. One is
     grateful for small mercies.

7.   By 'theological vision', I mean one based on God's self-revelation
     with the object of redeeming all humanity, and the Church's
     indispensable role in this. This is what makes the *missio ad gentes* (the
     mission to the nations) an imperative for the Church, to quote the
     apostle of the nations: 'Woe to me, if I do not preach Christ, and
     Him crucified'. This vision in no way conflicts with the axiomatic
     statement by the 1971 Synod of Bishops: 'Action on behalf of justice
     and participation in the transformation of the world appear to us as
     a *constitutive part* of the preaching of the gospel' (my emphasis).
     Justice is a constitutive part, it is not the entire gospel, nor a substitute
     for it. Neither is it the *unum necessarium* called for by the gospel.

8.   The newsletter issued by the Irish Missionary Union, *IMU Report*, is
     particularly instructive on the rather this-worldly orientation and
     self-consciousness of the leaders of the Irish missionary movement
     today. The September/November 2002 issue of the *IMU Report*
     gives us a taste of the new orientation. The cover article is on
     funding. It begins with a brief history of the IMU, highlighting the
     members' involvement in 'humanitarian development for over a
     century'. In pursuit of its five objectives (support for missionaries,
     promotion of ecumenical dialogue, cross-cultural dialogue,
     research into, and dissemination of relevant material on, justice and
     peace), the IMU, we are informed, have focused on two areas: (i) the
     reduction of poverty, and (ii) the empowerment of people. All very
     worthy aims, but not a word about God or evangelisation. The
     main article is on biotech agriculture. The only article in the issue,
     as far as I could see, that could be described as 'religious' is a
     description of the remarkable Franciscan Missionary sister, who
     spent 52 years working in Africa, Mother Kevin. She is described, in

sum, as a woman who pioneered the rights and dignity of women, who saw the importance of empowering people. A woman of faith, of love, of courage, who gave and received love. A prophetic woman. Was she not also – indeed, in the first place – a holy woman, a saint?

9. According to Louis Power (*Irish Catholic,* 20 September 2001), there are still 450 charismatic groups continuing on a regular basis throughout the country.

10. Neither does it attempt any analysis of the reasons for such a decline, which would have been helpful. The questions it could have raised include the following: why did the main source of vocations in Irish dioceses run dry, namely the diocesan colleges and schools (especially boarding schools) run by religious? Why (long before the present scandals) were so few priests actively involved in youth organisations, such as the Boy Scouts, another source of vocations in the past, especially to the missionary congregations? Why is being a Mass-server no longer the first step on the road to priesthood (or, with female servers, to the convent)? Why are priests themselves so shy about encouraging young people to embrace the priesthood or the religious life?

11. The author (at present working in the US), however, makes one important point, namely that the contemporary situation is such that the priesthood that will interest modern youth 'is a deeply spiritual one that shines out in charity and care and has a genuine ring about it'. But authenticity alone is not sufficient.

12. Another major article in the same issue of *The Fold* is entitled: 'Can the Station Mass be saved?' – another pessimistic title. It deals with the question (the last of a list of discussion topics): 'What other models can be used for these gatherings so that they can happen without Mass. Very soon, there will be places where a local priest will not be available …' (8).

13. Indeed, the monastery (founded in 515) was built on the site of an early fourth-century church erected over the tomb of St Maurice and his companions, Roman soldier/martyrs of the Theban Legion, who, according to tradition (whose authenticity has been questioned by Dr David Woods, UCC), were martyred nearby during the Diocletian persecution. The original fourth-century church itself was built on the ruins of a Roman temple, which in turn was built on the site of a Celtic sanctuary. In other words, the

monastery has been the site of religious worship for about three
thousand years.

14. Multyfarnham (Franciscan) is one of the few mediaeval monasteries
     to have survived relatively intact, that is, both the community and
     building itself, though after the Reformation the community was
     alienated from the building until around 1827, when they could
     return and restore the church. Others include the Dominican Black
     Abbey in Kilkenny and the Augustinian Abbey at Ballyhaunis, which
     the order has now decided to close (mostly for pragmatic reasons, it
     seems), despite local protests. Other mediaeval abbeys, such as
     Ballintubber, Co. Mayo, Holy Cross, Co. Tipperary, and
     Graiguenamanagh, Co. Kilkenny, have been restored in recent years
     and now serve as parish churches.

15. Cf. Corish, *The Irish Catholic Experience*, 17.

16. Cf. ibid., 159; 175.

17. 'In 1811 the Franciscans had only one priest in most of their houses
     and had been forced to drop the traditional practice of naming
     titular superiors to all the pre-Reformation foundations because
     they had not sufficient friars. In other places they had to abandon a
     physical presence: the last friar went' (ibid., 163). 'In 1849 the
     Franciscans were still complaining of shortages: forty-two friars
     were trying to staff fourteen friaries' (ibid., 164).

18. See, in particular, his *Journal of a Soul*. In a commentary on a recent
     survey of active apostolic religious in Ireland (as distinct from
     contemplatives and missionaries) by John A. Weafer, Tony Fahey
     perceptively comments: '… there may be limits to the degree to which
     founders can be lifted out of their context and looked at as a source of
     fresh impetus for the religious life today' ('Money, Spirituality and the
     Religious Congregation' in Michael J. Breen, *A Fire in the Forest.
     Religious Life in Ireland*, Dublin: Veritas, 2001, 98). Further, he say, 'It
     may be satisfying today to represent [religious founders of nineteenth
     century Ireland] as social activists who happened to be in the religious
     life but the reality was that they were religious ascetics who pursued
     the path of spiritual perfection through pastoral and social service
     work for the Church' (99). More significant, Fahey rightly points out,
     was the absence of any systematic reflection on the social issues of the
     day. As a result, the congregations' social engagement 'was
     characterised by a lack of intellectually grounded social awareness'
     (100). As I have pointed above, systematic reflection, which in turn

presupposes self-criticism, on any serious cultural or social – and thus by implication, theological – issue was, and still appears to be, lacking in the Irish Catholic Church.

19. It would seem that already a major shift in the self-awareness of leaders of religious congregations to a more hope-filled, and spiritual, perspective can be discerned. Weafer concluded his interpretation of his survey of apostolic religious life (the greater majority female) with the following comments: 'The majority (74%) of congregational leaders are either enthusiastic or hopeful towards religious life' and that 'more than nine in ten leaders believe religious life has a future in Ireland, even if, for many of them, the future is different from its present form' (Weafer, 'Trends in religious life' in Breen, ibid., 53-4). The fatalism of the 1980s and 1990s seems at last to have been overcome on the level of congregational leaders, and this is a most welcome development. For a critical appraisal of the survey as such (noting in particular the lack of comparative studies), see Dermot Keogh, 'Setting the Changes in Historical Context' (ibid., 83-93). Keogh speculates that the sense of Irish Catholic 'particularism may have lulled religious leaders in the 1960s into a false sense of security … After all, this was Ireland' (90-1), with the result that religious leaders, when vocations were still plentiful in the 1960s, were incapable of evaluating or planning for the new pastoral changes in the latter part of the last century. This 'particularism' – echoes of being the 'chosen people'? – would seem to be intrinsically related to the lack of 'systematic reflection' mentioned by Fahey (ibid., 98). As the commentaries on the survey indicate, the religious leaders are also refreshingly and clear-sightedly aware of the enormous task ahead. See especially the contribution of Elizabeth Maxwell, PBVM, Secretary General of CORI, 'Apostolic Religious Life in Ireland and Western Europe' (ibid., 57-72), which is indicative of a new, comparative and more spiritual approach to religious life. Both she and, especially, Christopher Dillon, 'Spirituality for Religious in Ireland today in the Light of Vita Consecrata (1996)' (ibid., 73-82), draw inspiration from a critical reading of the Pope's post-synodal exhortation, which, as already mentioned, has not otherwise featured much in the discussion, as far as I can tell.

20. Attempts are being made to found new communities in the Franciscan (Poor Clares) and Dominican traditions, which is a

hopeful sign. At Skreen in the diocese of Killala, a new Carmelite monastery (Holy Hill Hermitage) was founded recently; the founding members come from the USA, and have already attracted some Irish members. In the diocese of Dromore, French Benedictines monks are in the process of building a new monastery.

21. There are a number of vibrant lay movements, such as the *Nazareth Community* in Dublin and Belfast, and the *Family of God Community* in Dundalk (both native to the soil, with origins in the charismatic movement). Particularly noteworthy is the dynamic and flourishing *Youth 2000*, a movement centred on the Eucharist (Mass and Adoration), Rosary, and retreats. Evangelisation of their peers is a major concern, and they appear to have been quite effective. Some of the continental movements have followers in Ireland, such as *Cursilio, Communion and Liberation, Emmanuel Community, Focolare, Opus Dei,* and, from Mexico, the *Legionaries of Christ,* though with some exceptions, their numbers tend to be relatively low. Also noteworthy is the ecumenical *Emmaus Community,* not to mention the various local communities, such as those who gather in St Kevin's Oratory of the Pro-Cathedral in Dublin for evening Mass, or those who are part of *Muinntearas Íosa* in Limerick. (I am grateful to Fr Barry Horan CC for much of this information.) *The Legion of Mary* now has a team of enthusiastic young members, who are attracting new members. Also of note is the popular *Marian Movement for Priests.* What is common to most (but not all) of these groups is that they would be considered 'conservative' by most of the ruling Church establishment and so treated with some suspicion, not to say disdain.

22. Cf. John J. Ó Ríordáin, *Irish Catholic Spirituality*, 40. See W. B. Stanford, *Ireland and the Classical Tradition*, Dublin: Irish Academic Press, 1984 (second edition), 1-18. Stanford doubts, on the basis of the fragmentary evidence at our disposal, that there was much acquaintance with Greek up to the ninth century, when a remarkable group of Irish scholars, such as Sedulius and Eriugena, emerged in France at the court of the Emperor Charles the Bald (ibid., 8).

23. Cf. Ludwig Bieler, *Ireland: Harbinger of the Middle Ages*, London: Oxford University Press, 1966, 41-4, for an account of the place of study in the monastery; see also Ó Ríordáin, *Irish Catholic Spirituality*, 40-2.

24. Stanford, *Ireland and the Classical Tradition*, 25; on the hedge schools, cf. 25-8; 36-7. These schools 'in the early eighteenth century gave the basis of their education to many future priests' (Roy Foster, *Modern Ireland 1600-1972*, 208). For an appreciation of the achievements of the Hedge Schools, see Seán de Fréine, op. cit., 59. The Carmelites (OCarm) came to Knocktopher, Co. Kilkenny, in 1356, and remained in the locality after the monastery was dissolved in the seventeenth century. When they eventually returned to the village, they set up a classical school in a building next to their thatched chapel, the College of the Immaculate Conception. Students stayed with the surrounding farmers. It is claimed that some 400 priests received their basic education there (in the classics).

25. On the love of the classics and widespread colloquial use of Latin in rural Ireland from the sixteenth to the latter part of the nineteenth centuries, cf. Stanford, 25-7.

26. This is a remark attributed to Professor Harrower of Aberdeen by Christopher O'Neill of Kerry in praise of the brilliant and gifted teacher of Greek, Michael Sheehan, who became coadjutor Archbishop of Sydney on 28 May 1922 (cf. Corish, *Maynooth College*, 322).

27. See Thomas Finan, 'The Desired of All Nations' in Thomas Finan and Vincent Twomey (eds), *Studies in Patristic Christology* (Proceedings of the Third Maynooth Patristic Conference), Dublin: Four Courts Press, 1998, 1-22, who discusses the acute awareness the early Church had of the riches of the Greek tradition. As they put it, that tradition at its best contained 'seeds of the Word'. This is the case with *all* the wisdom traditions of humanity. As the Chinese scholar and convert, John Wu, once put it in his book *The Science of Love* on St Thérèse of Lisieux, the philosophy of a Confucius or Lao Tzu is like pure, crystal spring water, which, in Christ, is turned into wine.

28. Admittedly, the quality of the teaching of the classics, on indeed most other subjects, cannot always have been impressive, since the most the average student picked up was a few Latin tags to be used to 'show off'. Yet, others (always but a few) with a thirst for what these great thinkers alone could help to slake did become familiar with the location of the wellsprings.

29. John J. Ó Ríordáin, *Irish Catholic Spirituality*, 32.

30. See above, chapter 6, note 20.

31. Indeed, one could also mention Bono's spectacular promotion of
     what was initially the Pope's pet Jubilee project, namely the
     reduction of the international debts incurred by the poorest Third-
     World countries. It was no accident either that *Band Aid*, the media
     extravaganza to raise money for relief of famine in Ethiopia, was
     organised by Bob Geldof, who was reared in the womb of Irish
     Catholicism.

32. Cf. the report by Peter Scally, 'The web's sacred corner' in *The
     Tablet*, 18 January 2003, 14-5.

33. Under the influence of *Pastores dabo vobis*, the emphasis in
     seminaries has tilted in favour of 'pastoral training', 'spirituality',
     and 'human development'. Again, this kind of approach was
     perhaps long overdue. But, however good the intentions, the result
     is that little time is left for serious study or reflection, despite the fact
     that, paradoxically, contemporary seminarians tend to show a
     greater eagerness for theology than earlier generations.

34. Criticism of the new catechetical programmes is, understandably,
     usually met with indignation by those who drew them up. Rather
     than take the objections seriously, the main line of defence seems to
     be that the programmes had been approved by the 'appropriate
     authorities'. Thomas Deenihan's article 'Religious Education and
     Religious Instruction: An Alternative Viewpoint' in *The Furrow*, 53
     (2002), 75-83, raised the debate up to a higher level. Diocesan
     Advisior, Micheál de Barra, critiqued the article in *The Furrow*, 53
     (2002), 292-301, which also contains Fr Deenihan's reply to the
     criticisms. There is too little debate of this quality within the Church.

35. This is, to a great extent, conditioned by the smallness of Ireland:
     everybody knows everybody else. Very often theologians must live
     and work together with colleagues whose views are often
     diametrically opposed to theirs but which can rarely be discussed in
     the open for fear of creating division or causing other
     unpleasantness – or, indeed, creating tension among the
     undergraduates, who are not always able to judge between such
     diametrically opposed viewpoints.

36. It must be admitted that there were always exceptions to this,
     especially in some of the religious orders with a venerable tradition
     of scholarship. It is also of note that, within the diocesan
     priesthood, this trend seems to have changed within the very recent
     past, despite falling numbers. This is a hopeful sign.

37. Even the customary way for scholars to honour their peers, namely by publishing a *Festschrift* in honour of their achievement, is a rare occurrence in Irish theological circles. In 1989, Seán Ó Ríordáin, CSsR, and in 1996, Martin McNamara, MSC, were so honoured.

38. These include Dogma, Moral Theology, Scripture, Church History, Canon Law, Patrology, Liturgy, Missiology and Comparative Religion. In turn, each sub-discipline contains its own areas of specialisation such as Old Testament and New Testament exegesis (in Scripture), Trinitarian theology and Christology (in Dogma), Catholic social teaching and bioethics (in moral theology). The original texts for the study of Scripture and Patrology, for example, are in Hebrew, Greek, Latin and Syriac, which call for further highly specialised expertise. Since the great modern theologians wrote mostly in French, German, Spanish, or Italian, at least one of these languages has to be learned, if one is to be taken seriously as a theologian. Finally, it has to be admitted that there are few libraries in Ireland with the necessary resources for scholarly research, apart perhaps from Maynooth, Trinity College, and the Milltown Institute.

39. Such a thesis is defended by Fiacra Long, 'Theology in the Secular University' in *ITQ*, 62 (1996/97), 228-247, in an article that otherwise is a valuable attempt to argue the case for theology as an academic discipline before a sceptical Irish academic public.

40. David Tracy, *The Analogical Imagination. Christian Theology and the Culture of Pluralism*, New York: Crossroads, 1981, 21. Tracy comments that this is not only true for Karl Barth but is also the case for Friedrich Schleiermacher's own self-consciousness as a theologian (42, n.76). See the comments of one of the great literary critics, Frank Kermode, *The Genesis of Secrecy. On the Interpretation of Narrative*, Harvard: University Press, 1979, viii. See also Christopher Derrick, *Church Authority and Intellectual Freedom*, San Francisco: Ignatius Press, 1981.

41. It stands to reason that the theologian will also be judged by his or her own 'tradition' as to the status of one's own 'orthodoxy', namely the extent to which one's public utterances are in harmony with the truth upheld by the Church. Thus, for example, simply being a Catholic who teaches or writes theology does not automatically make one a 'Catholic theologian'.

42. On the reciprocal relationship between faith and reason, see the recent encyclical of Pope John Paul II, *Fides et ratio*.

43. The Irish Dominicans have just set up such a centre in Limerick. It is too early to say how it will develop, but it seems to have got off to a good start.

44. Over a period of forty years, fourteen volumes of critical texts have been produced, the last appearing in 1998.

45. On the joint initiative of the chair of ecclesiastical history, Pontifical University, Maynooth, and the NUIM Department of History, a project to promote the study of the Irish missionary movement has been undertaken. Maynooth was the origin of three foreign missionary movements in the nineteenth and early twentieth centuries, to India, China, and Africa, cf. Edmund M. Hogan, *The Irish Missionary Movement*.

46. A centre for bioethics of a secular orientation, it seems, has recently been established at NUIG, with a view to providing expertise on this and related ethical issues for the benefit of the nation. At one time, it looked as though a Catholic centre for the study of marriage and the family, that would include bioethics, was going to be established in the Newman Institute of Ireland, Kilalla, in affiliation with the John Paul II Institute in Rome.

47. Report in the *Irish Examiner*, 9 July 2001. It is a sign of the times in modern Ireland that the company set up by Fr Bohan to build the institute was named Céifin 'after the Celtic Goddess of Inspiration'.

48. Requests to the various religious orders for financial support for the first public conference brought in one cheque for £50! While the Maynooth Scholastic Trust contributed within its resources to the public conferences and publication, as did my own congregation, the main support had to be sought from a private foundation in Germany.

Instead of an Epilogue
1.   From Diarmuid Ó Laoghaire SJ, *One Life, One Mass*, 31-2.